German-Language Comedy
A Critical Anthology

Translated and with a Historical Introduction
by Bert Cardullo

SUP

Selinsgrove: Susquehanna University Press
London and Toronto: Associated University Presses

Associated University Presses
440 Forsgate Drive
Cranbury, NJ 08512

Associated University Presses
25 Sicilian Avenue
London WC1A 2QH, England

Associated University Presses
P.O. Box 39, Clarkson Pstl. Stn.
Mississauga, Ontario,
L5J 3X9 Canada

The paper used in this publication meets the requirements
of the American National Standard for Permanence of Paper
for Printed Library Materials Z39.48-1984.

Library of Congress Cataloging-in-Publication Data

German-language comedy : a critical anthology / translated and with a
historical introduction by Bert Cardullo.
    p.   cm.
  Includes bibliographical references and index.
  Contents: Minna von Barnhelm / by Gotthold Ephraim Lessing — The
broken pitcher / by Heinrich von Kleist — Woe to the liar! / by
Franz Grillparzer—The beaver coat / by Gerhart Hauptmann.
    ISBN 0-945636-24-5 (alk. paper)
  1. German drama (Comedy)—Translations into English. 2. English
drama (Comedy)—Translations from German.
PT127.E5   1992
832'.052308—dc20   91-50195
                                               CIP

PRINTED IN THE UNITED STATES OF AMERICA

German-Language Comedy

Contents

A Historical Introduction to German Comedy

[Comedy's] aim is no less than the highest to which man can aspire—to be free from passion, to survey the surrounding world with constant clarity, constant tranquillity, to find everywhere more evidence of caprice than of fate and rather to laugh at absurdity than to revile and bewail evil.

—Schiller

The earliest stages of a purely secular comedy in Germany are to be found in the rough *Fastnachtsspiele* that became popular in Nuremberg in the latter part of the fifteenth century. The *Fastnachtsspiel*, like the *Narren* (fools') literature of the age,[1] was an outcome of the amusements and masquerades of carnival. The wearing of a mask was in itself a step toward mimic representation, and in the *Schembartlauf* (rite of the false beard or bearded mask) organized every year by the butchers of Nuremberg from about the middle of the fourteenth century to the time of Hans Sachs (1494–1576), there were many dramatic features: among other things, the *Schembartläufer*, like the pagan rites from which they are descended, represented symbolically the conflict of spring and winter, one of those elemental conflicts that have left their traces on the primitive drama of all literatures. The biggest day for the presentation of the butchers' cultic pageantry and dances was Shrove Tuesday, carnival time (Shrovetide—the three days before Ash Wednesday—was a special period both for confession and festivity just before Lent). The next step, to accompany these representations with dialogue, or to perform comic scenes of everyday life, was all the more easy since such scenes lay readily at hand in the *Schwänke* (short and witty anecdotes, usually with a moral, that were very popular during the century of the Reformation). In this way arose the *Fastnachtsspiel*, or Shrovetide play, which in its earliest stages, as cultivated by Hans Folz (ca. 1450–1515), was little more than a comic conversation. The *Fastnachtsspiel* did not, it is true, become highly dramatic even in Hans Sachs's hands,[2] but this type of play was always essentially a dialogue rather than an

7

action; and, as Sachs conceived it, it is virtually only a *Schwank* in dialogue form.

The *Fastnachtsspiele* dealt with such everyday occurrences as family quarrels and courtroom trials, often in peasant settings. They began with processions introducing the characters and ended with a plea to the audience to enjoy the subsequent carnival dancing. The plays were usually in one act of about four hundred irregular four-beat verse lines (*Knittelvers*) spoken in declamatory fashion by three to six typed characters; changes of scene were announced rather than presented. The dominant theme was the exposure of human folly—especially the follies of the lower class—by good, moral burghers. Folz's best *Fastnachtsspiele* were *König Salomon und Markolf* (*King Salomon and Markolf*) and *Ein hübsch Vastnachtspil* (*A Pretty Carnival Play*). Among Sachs's eighty-five *Fastnachtsspiele* the following deserve mention: *Das Kälberbrüten* (*The Calf-Hatching*), *Der fahrende Schüler im Paradeis* (*The Traveling Scholar in Paradise*), *Der schwanger' Bauer* (*The Pregnant Farmer*), and *Das heiss Eisen* (*The Hot Iron*).

There was, indeed, at the start of this epoch some promise that Germany might produce a national drama not inferior to that of Spain or England;[3] but in the following century, when this promise should have been realized, the land was devastated by a catastrophe hardly less appalling and demoralizing than the migrations of early Germanic tribes: the Thirty Years' War (1618–48). The novel, the satire, the lyric—such literary forms were still possible amidst the political confusion of the seventeenth century, even if they could not flourish as they might otherwise have done; but drama cannot exist in an era of social disintegration, or it can exist only in the seclusion of courts and schools. Thus the dramatic beginnings of the sixteenth century, instead of being a prelude to greater achievement, received a check that hindered further development for nearly a century.

The sixteenth-century scholarly humanists provided later German dramatists with models by their revival of Latin comedy: Terence, whose works had lived a charmed life throughout the Middle Ages, became still more popular, the performance of his pieces being a favorite aid to instruction in Latin. Public performances were instituted by the schools, on which occasions prologues in German acquainted the audience with the subjects of the plays; and a complete translation of Terence into German was published in 1499. Plautus stood in almost as high favor, and from Plautus to original plays in imitation of Latin comedy the step was a small one. In 1480 Jacob Wimpfeling's *Stilpho,* the first school comedy by a

German, was produced at Heidelberg; and in 1498 Johannes Reuchlin published his *Scenica Progymnasmata* (*Dramatized School Lessons*), or *Henno,* a witty Latin farce that has the length of a *Fastnachtsspiel* but the form of classical drama—five acts, each with two scenes, and a chorus at the end. The union of the *Fastnachtsspiel* and classical form was continued and sharpened by two Hollanders who were active in Germany: Georg Macropedius (1475–1558) and Knuyt van Sluyterhoven (1462–1510). By 1501, Konrad Celtis had brought to light the six imitations of Terence by Hrotsvitha of Gandersheim (ca. 935–1001), which she wrote in order to supplant Terence in the monasteries and to inculcate the virtue of chastity, which, she claimed, the Latin poet made light of. Thus arose in Germany a Latin school comedy, which afforded the humanistic circles of the sixteenth century an outlet for their literary aspirations and materially affected the development of the vernacular drama by bequeathing to it a sense of form.

Toward the close of the sixteenth century German drama entered upon a new stage of its development. From the last years of this century to the middle of the following one, Germany was repeatedly visited by companies of English players (who soon found German imitators), the so-called *Englische Komödianten* (English Comedians). These actors brought with them not only the theatrical effects of the Elizabethan theater, but also the histrionic art of the English stage; and above all, they brought the comic personage of the English drama, the clown or *Pickelhering,* as he soon came to be called in Germany. The original English actors naturally played in English and, in the serious parts of their dramas (crude versions of the crudest plays of George Peele, Robert Greene, Christopher Marlowe, and Thomas Kyd, with the later addition of inaccurate versions of Shakespeare's plays), had to depend upon their pantomimic abilities to communicate with the public. But the music and the costumes, the bloodcurdling scenes and the buffoonery with which the productions were liberally spiced, made up for the disadvantages of the foreign language, and at an early date the role of the clown was either entirely in German or interspersed with as much broken German as the actor could command. When these English troupes found German imitators, the English comic figure was retained. The repertories of the German companies consisted in the main of translations, or rather of mangled stage versions, of popular English dramas, and later of French and Italian ones. The plays were in prose and constructed solely with a view to stage effectiveness; they had little intrinsic value, except insofar as they opened new horizons to the German drama. One of those horizons was comedy, which was the staple of the interludes between acts of productions by the *Englische Komödianten,* and which was epitomized in the figure of *Pickelhering.*

In the medieval nativity play, the confusion of the shepherds when the angel visited them by night and their subsequent pilgrimage to Bethlehem provided comic relief. Such scenes were the beginning of the interlude, which by the end of the sixteenth century was becoming a convention in Germany—either when inserted between the acts of a serious drama, or when run parallel with a static scene in the play proper. Among the authors who wrote new drama in the style of the *Englische Komödianten,* replete with comic interludes, were Jakob Ayrer (1540–1605) and Duke Heinrich Julius of Braunschweig (1564–1613). A transitional figure, Ayrer wrote sixty-nine plays, thirty-six of which are grouped together as *Fastnachtsspiele.* In his tragedies he borrowed from the *Komödianten* their sensationalism—like them, he made the most of scenes of bloodshed and murder; and he introduced the figure of the jester in its popular, clownish form, modeled after the English *Pickelhering,* with the name *Hans Wurst* (Jack Sausage). Ayrer's comic interludes grow in importance in his work until they become an actual secondary plot.

Duke Heinrich Julius of Braunschweig brought English players to his court, maintained a theater, and wrote eleven plays for it in which his clown, named *Johann Bouset,* played a major role. The Duke's tragedies were crude efforts, senseless and bloody and written in bombastic, baroque prose; it is the comic interludes in these tragedies—written in varying dialects—that constitute the Duke's important contribution to German drama. He also wrote four free-standing comedies, in the best known of which, *Vincentius Ladislaus,* both the exaggerated language and the false pretensions of the braggart soldier are objects of satire. The Duke found an emulator in Landgrave Moritz von Hessen (1572–1632), who also brought in English players, maintained a stage, and wrote German and Latin plays, but none of his texts has been preserved. Two additional authors deserve mention: Martin Böhme (a.k.a. Martin Bohemus), who wrote comic episodes in his native Silesian dialect and wove them into his main dramas with great success; and Johann Rist (1607–67), who owed his considerable reputation as a dramatist in the seventeenth century to his interludes—in which peasants spoke the *Plattdeutsch* (Low or North German) dialect of their native Holstein—and not to some thirty allegorical plays.

The next important event in the evolution of the interlude in the seventeenth century was at the same time its climax: the appearance of Andreas Gryphius's *Die geliebte Dornrose* (*The Beloved Hedgerose,* 1660). This play can and does exist independently, for, although written in Silesian dialect and intended for performance act-by-act between the acts of the *Singspiel* (musical) *Verliebtes Gespenst* (*The Ghost in Love,* 1660), it is self-contained, being a greater poetic achievement and revealing higher technical skill than the more dignified play (written in elegant, High-German verse to celebrate the marriage of the Duke of Lignitz-and-Brieg) to which it was meant to serve as accompaniment. Indeed, the term "interlude" seems inadequate when applied to a comedy of such quality and proportions. Gryphius (1616–64) wrote two other comedies, both in prose and both intended for the stage: *Horribilicribrifax oder wählende Liebhaber* (*Horribilicribrifax, or the Selective Lovers,* ca. 1633) and *Absurda Comica oder Herr Peter Squentz* (*The Absurd Comedy, or Master Peter Squentz,* ca. 1648; this work may have been performed as an afterpiece instead of during the intervals between acts of a tragedy). The first, and better, play is a satire on the military, influenced by Renaissance satirists as well as by Shakespeare; the second is a version of the "Pyramus and Thisbe" scene from *A Midsummer Night's Dream.*

The ramshackle structure of Gryphius's comedies was common to those German plays that were not entirely in the learned tradition. Such ramshackle structure was the result of authors' failure to become good playwrights, that is, artificers who could adapt to dramatic form the narrative material on which they drew. Since the Middle Ages the principal literary tradition had been narrative— even in the old morality and mystery plays. What secular drama existed was cultivated in the schools according to the scholarly classical tradition, i.e., it was well-ordered and formal. If the two traditions had been successfully amalgamated, there would have been the basis for a national tragedy and comedy. (Gryphius did not successfully amalgamate the two traditions in his tragedies, either, for they are a product of international classicism rather than a development with national roots. Written for the most part in alexandrines, they are bombastic book dramas rather than stage plays, and like Gryphius's comedies, were performed only by amateurs.) But the great achievement of the Elizabethans had no counterpart in Germany: in England, as nowhere else in Europe, a fusion of native art and learned tradition took place that formed the basis of Shakespearean comedy. Indeed, the distinctive qualities of German plays were not concentration, intensity, cohesion, but diffuseness, profuseness, discursiveness. Not only did the narrative habit prove too strong for German dramatists, then, but at the same time they were unaware of the opportunity deriving from a fusion of the two traditions—the secular-dramatic and the religious-narrative.

The theorist Martin Opitz (1597–1639) contributed to this lack of awareness. His treatise *Buch von der deutschen Poeterey* (*Book of German Poetics*, 1624) was based on Aristotle and on the work of two well-established, more recent critics, the Italian-born Frenchman Julius Caesar Scaliger (1484–1558) and the Hollander Daniel Heinsius (1580–1655). Ignoring the "German" drama of Hans Sachs and Jakob Ayrer, and repudiating English influences, Opitz formulated a drama based on classical and French patterns. He also reaffirmed the general artistic precept of the period: that art, in this case drama, served a moral purpose, providing a concrete, idealized example of behavior in fortune or misfortune. Comedy and tragedy were differentiated according to subject matter, a dichotomy that was to be enforced until the time of Lessing and that Gryphius himself observed. Only kings and the most noble persons were worthy of tragedy; only the royal will, violence, fires, incest, and similar topics were fit for presentation in tragedy. Comedy, by contrast, was obliged to portray figures of low birth and their activities, such as weddings, games, and deceptions. Opitz's attention to classical antiquity as a source of materials and values, as well as his disavowal of indigenous German drama, affected both tragedy and comedy from the seventeenth century until far into the eighteenth. And his strictures reaffirmed the notion that German drama is the property of the learned, thus enforcing the idea that drama—tragedy *and* comedy—is serious and is first and last a tool for moral edification, not for popular amusement.

The most prolific dramatist of the seventeenth century was Christian Weise (1642–1702), who wrote no fewer than fifty-five plays (all for nonprofessional school theaters), only about half of which were published. Weise's tragedies were polite and weak, but his comedies were sprightly and gently satirical. They are the true precursors to the work of Lessing almost a century later, since their language and characterization reflect the reason-based, middle-class ethos; Weise was one of the earliest German authors to portray the middle classes realistically. A typical play of his was the *Liebes-Alliance* (*Alliance of Love*, 1703), a marriage comedy in which two elderly people, each seeking to marry someone younger, find one another instead, leaving the natural union of the youngsters to take place by itself. The drama of the Enlightenment in the eighteenth century did not at first follow Weise's lead. The Enlightenment as a whole developed rather slowly in the disjointed German-language territory, which was exhausted physically as well as bewildered intellectually and culturally by the ravages of the Thirty Years' War. The fact is, there was not one noteworthy drama written in German territory in the thirty years following Weise's death in 1702.

When the drama reappeared, it was in the dress of the French classicism of Corneille, Racine, Molière, and their followers; Leipzig had become the German center for the emulation of French culture. When the East Prussian rationalistic critic Johann Christoph Gottsched (1700–66) came to Leipzig in 1723, he was able to establish himself very quickly as dictator of German-letters-in-the-French-style for his generation. His *Versuch einer critischen Dichtkunst vor die Deutschen* (*Attempt at a Critical Poetics for Germans,* 1730) set down the rules of literature in general and drama in particular in the tradition of Aristotle, Horace, Scaliger, Opitz, and Boileau. His chief models were Corneille, Racine, Destouches (whom he preferred, together with Regnard, Dufresny, and Marivaux, to Molière), and their Danish disciple, Ludwig Holberg; his chief target was the English drama, which he deplored for its "unnatural and manifest rulelessness." Gottsched demanded close observance of the unities of time, place, and action, and avoidance of all esoteric or extreme language, characters, or action—particularly the ribaldry and buffoonery of the clown figure, *Pickelhering* or *Hanswurst*. He sought thereby to codify aesthetic rules and transform the German stage into a morally oriented instrument of education for the cultured classes. Since he found no German models, Gottsched sought translations of French classical dramas. Together with several friends and his wife, Luise Adelgunde Viktoria (1713–62), he published six volumes of these translations, plus some original German dramas (among them sentimental comedies, modeled after the French *comédie larmoyante,* by his wife;[4] and his own *Der sterbende Cato* [*The Dying Cato,* 1732], a sententious tragedy modeled after F. M. C. Deschamps's *Caton d'Utique* [1715] and Joseph Addison's *Cato* [1713]), over the years 1740–45 in *Deutsche Schaubühne, nach den Regeln der alten Griechen und Römer eingerichtet* (*The German Stage, Arranged according to the Rules of the Ancient Greeks and Romans*). Having established himself as an authority, Gottsched found his practical prophetess in Caroline Neuber (1697–1760), wife of Johann Neuber, the head of a troupe of actors. Through her he was able to translate his dramatic theory into stage reality.

Gottsched was significantly responsible for the revival of literary drama in Germany. He raised the literary sights in areas besides drama, used the German language with increased logic and clarity, revived the concept of form, helped to enlarge the repertoire, and furthered the acceptance of the professional theater. But the very hands that laid the foundation of serious drama in Germany shattered the basis of the native comic tradition. Gottsched's, and the Neubers', banishment of *Hanswurst* from the stage (to which he never really returned) was an attack upon the spirit of comedy itself, incarnate in the figure of the clown—be his name *Harlekin, Hanswurst,* or *Pickelhering*—a living reminder of those ancient rites from which the whole art of comedy had sprung in the first place. Gottsched's action represents that persistent attempt to give prestige to the stage, to make it an instrument of moral and intellectual edification, which succeeded only too well in Germany and elsewhere. (We shall see another example of this in Schiller's 1784 address entitled "Die Schaubühne als eine moralische Anstalt betrachtet" ["The Stage Considered as a Moral Institution"]—the same Schiller, paradoxically, who is responsible for the discerning epigraph to this introduction.) What was intended to be a subversive force, a wholesome irritant in the body social and politic, cuts a sorry figure as the champion of municipalities and the state, as Caroline Neuber describes comedy:

> Our efforts have all consistently been in this direction: to uphold in our productions the strictest morality; to steer clear of the shallowness of buffoonery and the ignobility of sexual suggestiveness; and to achieve what should be the real and rational goal of the stage—not so much the rousing of spectators to laughter as the instruction of their minds and souls.

To be fair to Gottsched, the failure of a national comedy to take root in Germany (as opposed to Austria: see the "Brief Survey of Austrian Comedy" that follows this introduction) can be attributed as much to the absence of "social culture" in that country as to the banishment of *Hanswurst* from the stage and to the imposition of artificial rules as well as reformist aims on dramatists. By social culture I mean a society as homogeneous as England's, with its well-defined code of manners, or a capital city comparable, as a locus of dramatic energy and comic extraction, to Paris or Venice. At a time when a tradition of comedy might have been established in Germany, its cultural centers were small *Residenzstädte* (seats of court), university towns, or commercial hubs whose theaters were shallowly rooted in a nondescript public and whose inhabitants offered few models to the comic dramatist. Eccentricities existed, no doubt, but of too intimate, if not too freakish, a kind to stand translation into dramatic terms. Comedy is a metropolitan art, and only if citizens form part of a large-scale agglomeration of their fellow creatures can they be sure of not recognizing themselves upon the stage, but rather smile at what they fondly conceive to be the foibles of others.

With the creation of *Minna von Barnhelm* (1767), Gotthold Ephraim Lessing (1729–81) introduced a new era in German comedy. Lessing accepted Gottsched's banishment of *Hanswurst* from the stage, but what he could not accept was the virtual banishment of all laughter as well from the sentimental comedies that Gottsched and Caroline Neuber championed. What Lessing wanted was a new kind of comedy, a "true comedy," which, in his *Abhandlungen von dem weinerlichen oder rührenden Lustspiele (Essays on the Tearful or Sentimental Comedy,* 1754), he defined as one that

> portrays vice as well as virtue, ridiculous as well as respectable behavior, because only through the mixture of the two does comedy come close to resembling human life. Farces want only to make the spectators laugh; sentimental comedies want only to touch their hearts; the true comedy wants to do both.

To a certain extent, *Minna von Barnhelm* was Lessing's "true comedy": formally comic in that the audience knows that love will triumph in the end; seriously sentimental in that the conflict between the pride of the Prussian Major von Tellheim and the love of his Saxon sweetheart, Minna (the name in German means "the loving woman"), drives these all-too-human characters to extremes, especially Tellheim, whose exaggerated sense of honor and excessive emotionalism go against the Enlightenment's emphasis on the application of reason and moderation in all matters; and dramatically realistic in that the action has as its background the conflict between Prussia and Saxony in the Seven Years' War (1756–63) and in that the characters are closely observed *Germans*. But our response to *Minna* is smiling assent to Lessing's depiction of human imperfection, not laughter at his ridicule of vice, for there is little such ridicule in the play. The contemporary reviews are full of praise, not for the play's wit and humorousness, but for its realistic German quality, its *Nationalcharakter* (national character). These are serious, patriotic matters, not comic, aesthetically removed ones. In a comedy national characteristics are artistically valuable only if they are made the object of *ridicule,* as in the rare German examples of Heinrich Borkenstein's *Der Bookesbeutel (The Briefcase,* 1742), with its rough humor and satire based on Hamburg life, or August von Kotzebue's *Die deutschen Kleinstädter* (*Small German Townsfolk,* 1803), a satire on the modes and manners of provincial life in late-eighteenth-century Germany. Or those national characteristics are valuable if they are treated as broadly funny in themselves, as in some Irish and Yiddish plays.

But in *Minna von Barnhelm,* which was stimulated by Lessing's own military experiences in the Seven Years' War, national characteristics—Tellheim's Prussian rigidity, Minna's Saxon warmth, and Riccaut's French raffishness—are means to the desired end of German national consciousness. By having the love of the enterprising Saxon baroness overcome the potentially tragic sense of honor of the Prussian major—it was an undeserved blemish on that honor and his consequent impoverishment that compelled Tellheim, for Minna's sake, to call off their engagement—and by marrying not only them but also the Prussian sergeant major (Paul Werner) and the Saxon lady's maid (Franziska), Lessing allegorically pleads for the unification of a Germany torn by regional hostilities; by making Frederick the Great save the happiness of Minna and Tellheim like a *deus ex machina,* Lessing pays homage to the power and leadership of this king as well as to the greatness of his small Prussian state, which was victorious over all of Europe in the Seven Years' War; and through the garrulous and dishonest, if nonetheless amusing, Frenchman he protests against the French influence on German Enlightenment civilization. Goethe himself called attention to the nationalistic aspect of the play when he wrote, in *Dichtung und Wahrheit* (*Poetry and Truth,* 1811–13), that *Minna* was "the most genuine product of the Seven Years' War, the first theater piece with a specifically contemporary content based on significant human affairs."

What effect, then, did Lessing's example have on subsequent German comedy? In technical matters such as dialogue and exposition there is no question but that *Minna von Barnhelm* strongly influenced younger dramatists, and that this influence was beneficial. For the development of a genuine German comedy, however, Lessing's play could be of little benefit. In fact, merely because it was held aloft as the best German comedy, it must have deterred self-conscious authors from the writing of comedy and thereby hobbled the progress of the comedic form in Germany. They would have had either to write another *Minna* (i.e., not a truly funny comedy) or to run the risk of being considered merely popular dramatists, authors of *divertissements,* like Kotzebue (1761–1819), of whom Goethe disapproved and who for the most part remains unappreciated in his own country. Goethe himself tried his hand at dramatic satires and comic skits for social occasions, particularly during his *Sturm-und-Drang* (Storm-and-Stress) period and his first years in Weimar, but, like Schiller, who wrote no comedies at all, he thought of comedy solely as entertainment, as something too lacking in depth for a serious mind.

From the *Sturm und Drang* up to the time of romanticism and its immediate aftermath in Germany, when we get comedy, it comes in the form of the serious, sometimes bitter social satire of J. M. R. Lenz (*Der Hofmeister* [*The Private Tutor,* 1773] and *Die Soldaten* [*The Soldiers,* 1775]); the highly successful sentimental comedies of F. L. Schroeder (1744–1816) and A. W. Iffland (1759–1814) as well as the prolific Kotzebue; the fairy-tale satires of Ludwig Tieck, the best known of which are *Der gestiefelte Kater* (*Puss in Boots,* 1797) and *Die verkehrte Welt* (*The World Upside Down,* 1798); and the nihilistic fantasies *Scherz, Satire, Ironie und tiefere Bedeutung* (*Spoof, Satire, Irony, and Profounder Significance,* 1822), by Christian Dietrich Grabbe, and *Leonce und Lena* (*Leonce and Lena,* 1836), by Georg Büchner. In other words, apart from the wishful thinking of sentimental comedy, we get plays that reflect, through their staunchly satiric, ironic, or nihilistic stance toward the world, the fundamentally serious bent of the German mind and that mirror the fragmented and politically unsettled state of German society at the time—a society whose lack of political and social unity rendered it too weak and too dispersed for confidently comic kidding.

There are exceptions to the above, but they are exceptions that prove the rule: the aforementioned satirical comedies by Borkenstein and Kotzebue, and the regional or folk comedies, often in dialect (and therefore untranslatable), stimulated by romanticism's nationalistic revival of interest in Germany's past as preserved in remote, picturesque villages or in the culture of historic cities. From southwest Germany came Georg Daniel Arnold's *Der Pfingstmontag* (*Whitmonday,* 1816), Johann Heinrich de Noel's *Der verlorene Sohn* (*The Prodigal Son,* 1811), and Gottlieb Friedrich Wagner's (1774–1839) *Die Schulmeisterwahl zu Blindheim* (*Choosing Blindheim's Schoolmaster*). From Berlin in the east came Julius von Voss's *Stralower Fischzug* (*Stralow's Catch of Fish,* 1821), Karl von Holtei's (1798–1880) *Wiener in Berlin* (*Viennese in Berlin*), and Louis Angely's (1788–1835) *Fest der Handwerker* (*The Workmen's Holiday*); from Hamburg in the northwest, Johann Gottwerth Müller's *Siegfried von Lindenberg* (1779) and Jakob Heinrich David's (1811–39) *Eine Nacht auf Wache* (*A Night on Watch*). And from central Germany came the Frankfurt playwright Karl Malss (*Herr Hampelmann oder die Landpartie nach Königstein* [*Mr.*

Hampelmann, or the Trip to Königstein, 1832]) and the Darmstadt writer Ernst Elias Niebergall (*Des Burschen Heimkehr oder der tolle Hund* [*The Student's Homecoming, or The Crazy Dog,* 1837]).

Heinrich von Kleist (1777–1811)—himself a tragic dramatist of singular intensity—wrote *Der zerbrochene Krug* (*The Broken Pitcher,* 1807), a kind of folk comedy that simultaneously has ties with the sixteenth-century *Fastnachtsspiel,* which reached its culmination in the seventeenth-century *Geliebte Dornrose* (the lovers Ruprecht and Eve recall Korngold and Dornrose from Gryphius's play, and Kleist's comedy shares with a number of *Fastnachtsspiele* as well as *Der geliebte Dornrose* its peasant setting and courtroom trial), and with the rest of its author's *oeuvre. Der zerbrochene Krug*'s examination of deceit in human behavior is not so far removed, in the end, from the spirit of Kleist's tragedies, which, like all his plays, were written subsequent to his *Kantkrise* (Kant crisis) in 1801 and which all, in some form or another, dramatized the Kantian notion that "pure reason" cannot penetrate the essence of things, that the intellect cannot determine what is truth and what merely appears to be truth, that all perception is finally subjective. This notion—which for Kleist shattered the Enlightenment belief in the power of reason to comprehend the universe and to perfect life on earth—was at the heart of German romanticism, which abandoned the outer world in favor of the inner in the belief that reality was created by the imagination, that higher consciousness was gained through the unconscious, and that the generally valid was reached by way of the most individual. But whereas the romantics escaped from objective reality into a world of fairy-tale fantasy, literary satire, or nationalistic folklore, Kleist incorporated the recalcitrance of that reality into his dramas and in this sense showed some affinity for the classicism of Goethe and Schiller, which attempted to reconcile spirit and matter by harmonizing the inner and outer worlds.

Die Familie Schroffenstein (*The Schroffenstein Family* or *The Feud of the Schroffensteins,* 1803), for example, was an intense tragic treatment of a Romeo-and-Juliet dilemma, a somber drama of error and misunderstanding whose theme of the fallibility of human knowledge was to recur in the rest of Kleist's plays. In *Penthesilea* (1808), he displayed how a misunderstanding of an outer situation can distort one's already disturbed inner feelings, as the Amazonian queen Penthesilea slays Achilles and drinks his blood in the belief that he scorns her love, then realizes what she has done and commits suicide. In two of Kleist's plays, only a noble and supreme effort on the part of the protagonists can prevent tragedy. The knight Wetter vom Strahl at first disdains the love of the titular character of *Das Kätchen von Heilbronn oder die Feuerprobe* (*Cathy from Heilbronn, or The Trial by Fire,* 1808) because he cannot see a dream in the right light; only after he almost causes Kätchen's death does he recognize that his former fiancée, Kunigunde, is a witch and consent to marry Kätchen, who, in a fairy-tale ending, is revealed to be the long-lost Princess of Swabia. Tragedy is avoided in Kleist's *Prinz Friedrich von Homburg* (*Prince Friedrich of Homburg,* 1811) when the Prince realizes that the Elector is correct in sentencing him to death for disobeying orders in battle; it is due to this realization on the Prince's part that the Elector pardons him and grants him the hand of his niece, Princess Natalia, in marriage. This play was probably the first to depict the effect of hidden wishes, of the unacknowledged desires of the unconscious, upon human behavior.

In addition to *Der zerbrochene Krug,* Kleist wrote one other comedy that depends on deception and misunderstanding for its humor: his adaptation of Molière's *Amphitryon* (1807), in which the situation of mistaken identity is shown as potentially tragic, but is ultimately resolved—at least on the surface—by Jupiter's revelation of the part he played in Amphitryon and Alcmene's marital problems: a metaphysical comedy of errors, one might call this play. *Der zerbrochene Krug* itself was freely invented as a literary interpretation of a French painting, Dubucourt's *La cruche cassée,* as etched by Jean Jacques Le Veau. The play takes place in the Dutch village of Huysum, where the village judge, Adam, is alarmed when Walter, a government inspector, arrives to supervise his jurisdiction. In the case at hand a peasant woman, Martha Rull, accuses Ruprecht, a young farmer engaged to her daughter, Eve, of breaking a water jug in Eve's room during a nocturnal visit. Despite Adam's subterfuges, the investigation reveals that he himself broke the jug when, interrupted by Ruprecht in his attempts to seduce Eve, he escaped through the window. Adam loses his office to his clerk, Light, and the reunited lovers will soon be married.

Despite the Dutch setting, *Der zerbrochene Krug* depicts contemporary German village life by means of convincingly realistic characters and in a blank verse that, although highly stylized, contains everyday speech rhythms, rural imagery, and colloquialisms. The humor arises mainly from the ironic position of the judge, convicting himself, but it also comes from facetious wordplay, coarse references to bodily functions, and fighting among the characters. The familiar and serious search for the truth in Kleist's work is dramatized here by the court inquiry, which covers most of the action. But for once in his *oeuvre* the errors result not from the passive fallibility of human perception but from the protagonist Adam's deliberate, and amusing, villainy. The failure of this great comedy in its first performance at Weimar on 2 March 1808 is usually attributed to Goethe's division of its thirteen consecutive scenes into three acts as well as to stilted acting and is thought to have contributed to Kleist's suicide three years later together with his deteriorating health, his limited finances, and his increasing sense of existential isolation.

In his aberration into the comic field, Kleist is typical of the authors of great German comedy, which is an affair of brilliant individual efforts on the part, often enough, of the most unlikely persons. *Minna von Barnhelm,* for instance, was the work of a man who spent a large part of his life becoming the foremost literary critic in Europe and the remainder in theological strife, and whose *Miss Sara Sampson* (1755), a *bürgerliches Trauerspiel* or domestic tragedy, was the first of those plays of middle-class life and social problems (themselves the offshoot of an English development occasioned by George Lillo's *The London Merchant* [1731]) which, since the end of the eighteenth century, have formed a constant element in the dramatic literature of northern Europe. *Leonce und Lena* came from the hand of Büchner, best known as the author of *Dantons Tod* (*Danton's Death,* 1835) and *Woyzeck* (1836), tragedies of violent originality, and a man destined to die, in exile, at the age of twenty-three. Unlike Italy and France, say, Germany has not produced a single great writer of comedy alone, of *comedies.* Furthermore, little familial resemblance can be detected among the best German comedies—they are individual to an extreme, radical. The German comic dramatists are bound by no preconception of what a comedy ought to be and have bequeathed us, as a result, no body of comedies that we can term "classical." We might say of German comedy what Valéry said of a contemporary's work: "Ses accidents sont admirables, mais sa substance est peu de chose" ("The exceptions are admirable, but the whole is of little consequence").

Part of that inconsequential whole can be attributed to the movement known as *Das junge Deutschland* (Young Germany), a revolt against the abstraction and idealism of romanticism that championed social and political awareness and that may be seen as a precursor of realism and naturalism. *Das junge Deutschland* was in fact more a political movement than a literary one (to the detriment of the literature it produced), and from the revolutions of 1830 to those of 1848 its members struggled to create a unified, democratic

Germany. That struggle is reflected in the historico-political comedies produced during this period: among them, R. E. Prutz's satirical comedy *Die politische Wochenstube* (*The Political Childbed*,
1843), directed mainly against the forces of reaction; Karl
Gutzkow's *Zopf und Schwert* (*Sword and Column*, 1843), a historical comedy of intrigue that endorses the liberalism of King Frederick William I of Prussia; Heinrich Laube's *Die Karlsschüler* (*The
Students of Karl School*, 1846), a "literary" comedy about the
young Schiller's conflict with the Duke of Württemberg that, like
other works from *Das junge Deutschland,* barely masks its concern
for contemporary problems under a story from another time and
place; and Gustav Freytag's *Die Journalisten* (*The Journalists,*
1852), a political comedy that depicts the rivalry between two
newspapers during a big election. *Die Journalisten* is still one of the
better-known German comedies, but it is difficult to comprehend
why: the play's topicality has long since worn off, and what is left is
rather pedestrian and unfunny.[5]

Friedrich Hebbel (1813–63) is yet another serious German playwright whose work in comedy seems more like an aberration than a
natural development. But his comedies have one characteristic in
common with his otherwise realistic tragedies: overschematization.
In Hebbel's view, tragedy is universally inevitable because God has
produced a polarized world; great individuals are doomed to conflict with society precisely because they are individuals and are
great. The attempt on the part of the individual to assert himself
against the historical drift of the social order results in destruction,
but the synthetic or productive result of the conflict between society and the individual is the raising of humanity another step
toward a higher plane of existence. Thus, ultimately, Hebbel's dramatic theory is optimistic, not pessimistic, since it mandates that a
progressive world history replace fate as a force greater than the
individual.

According to Hebbel, comedy and tragedy are essentially two
different forms of the same idea. The difference derives from their
portrayal of character: unlike the protagonists of tragedies, comic
figures are neither great nor self-conscious. The characters in *Der
Diamant* (*The Diamond,* 1841) are not in conflict with the historical
drift of the social order; except for one, they are all just unconscio-
nably greedy and therefore in conflict with one another's greed.
Each is out for himself, and each is unaware of or unconcerned
about how he should ethically behave so as to fit into the larger
scheme of things—that is, until the end of the play, when everyone
repents. Hebbel thought that, with *Der Diamant,* he had given the

German people a comedy in the same class with *Der zerbrochene Krug,* but his play has neither the witty sprightliness of Kleist's nor the thematic plenitude of Grillparzer's *Weh dem, der lügt!* (see the "Brief Survey of Austrian Comedy"). The same can be said for his other full-length comedy, *Der Rubin (The Ruby,* 1849), whose fairy-tale form nevertheless manages to avoid the shrillness that pervades *Der Diamant.*

The outstanding writer of naturalistic comedy was Gerhart Hauptmann (1862–1946), but he is typically German in that his comedies make up only a small portion of his collected works, among which the following naturalistic tragedies stand out: *Vor Sonnenaufgang (Before Sunrise,* 1889), *Einsame Menschen (Lonely Lives,* 1891), *Die Weber (The Weavers,* 1892), *Florian Geyer* (1896), *Fuhrmann Henschel (Drayman Henschel,* 1898), and *Rose Bernd* (1903). Because of a fundamental weakness of will and lack of conviction, Hauptmann's heroes often capitulate before the apparent imponderables of biological and environmental forces. In *Die Weber* the playwright created, not an individual hero, but a collective one, sorely tried by hostile social and economic circumstances; this collective hero is also unsuccessful in its revolt against its oppressors because it lacks sufficient strength of purpose and unity. Hauptmann's demands for reform, like those of most naturalists, were thus outweighed by a determinism that, skeptical about the possibility of improvement and overwhelming in its documentation of exploitative living and working conditions, admitted little more than a warm but ineffectual compassion for the suffering masses in Germany's industrial cities.

Unlike the protagonists of Hauptmann's naturalistic tragedies, Mother Wolff of *Der Biberpelz (The Beaver Coat,* 1893), his best comedy, is capable of surviving because she does not suffer her poverty in passivity but instead maintains herself by resorting to all kinds of trickery and cunning, unaware of the immorality of her actions. A washerwoman married to a ship's captain, Mother Wolff dreams of opening an inn of her own on the outskirts of Berlin in the late 1880s. To augment her family's meager income she poaches, pilfers wood, and sells a beaver coat she has stolen from her employer, Krueger, to the bargeman and fence Wulkow. The justice of the peace and head of administration, Wehrhahn, busy with self-advancement, bureaucratic rigmarole, and the persecution of the liberal-democratic scholar Dr. Fleischer, bungles the investigation of the stolen coat and lets Mother Wolff go undetected. He simply cannot see this thief for what she is: a thief.

Der Biberpelz is generally recognized as one of the three great German comedies, along with *Minna von Barnhelm* and *Der zerbrochene Krug.* Like these two plays, *Der Biberpelz* is a *Charakterkomödie* (comedy of character), since it is dependent more on the skillful delineation of interesting characters than upon the sure handling of intricacies of plot; also, like *Minna* and *Krug,* Hauptmann's comedy has its serious side. The character of Wehrhahn is a satire on German, in particular Prussian, officialism, which Carl Zuckmayer was to satirize as well in his antimilitaristic (but somewhat long-winded) play *Der Hauptmann von Köpenick* (*The Captain of Köpenick,* 1931), and which Hauptmann, like his character Dr. Fleischer, knew from firsthand experience in the Berlin suburb of Erkner as a young outsider whose left-of-center politics attracted the attention of the pompous, disdainful local official Oscar von Busse, the prototype of Wehrhahn. In Erkner, too, the playwright met in Marie Heinze, his own *honest* washerwoman, the model for Mother Wolff, whose feisty character may be a comic delight but whose thieving, grasping way of life is not. *Der Biberpelz* is not exclusively a satire, however, of either Wehrhahn's officiousness or Mother Wolff's proletarian materialism. It is also a picaresque folk comedy, rich in texture and replete with flavorsome dialect in the original German.

As a satire, *Der Biberpelz* can claim kinship with the work of such lesser naturalistic playwrights as Ludwig Fulda, whose *Kameraden* (*Comrades,* 1894) was a satire on the "new woman," and Max Dreyer, whose *Der Probekandidat* (*The Teacher on Trial,* 1899) satirized a school system that forces a young advocate of Darwinism out of his job. As folk comedy, *Der Biberpelz* has connections with *Heimatkunst* (vernacular art), a movement that loomed most conspicuously in the early years of the twentieth century and that cultivated the reproduction of the life and atmosphere of the province. This was, of course, no new phenomenon in German literature, for, as I have previously discussed, through the early decades of the nineteenth century there had run a strong vein of such regionalism, originally introduced and fostered by the romantics. Every district had taken pride in its own literary production, from the *Plattdeutsch*-speaking lands in the north to the Bavarian and Swabian highlands in the south. (Gerhart Hauptmann and his older brother, Carl [1858–1920], were staunch upholders of the *Heimatkunst* of Silesia.)

But whereas this production had in the past been regarded as standing somewhat apart from the mainstream of the national literature, the new *Heimatkunst* was proclaimed by its advocates to be an essential and constant element in that literature, in counteraction to the leveling influence of the great cities—indeed, they argued that no writer should deny his soil. In Bavaria, Josef Ruderer and Ludwig Thoma contributed to a specifically Bavarian satirical comedy: notable are *Die Fahnenweihe* (*The Presentation of the Colors*, 1894) by the former, and, by the latter, *Die Lokalbahn* (*The Branch Line*, 1902, about the political inadequacies of timid, small-town liberals) and *Moral* (*Morality*, 1908, which shows how a prostitute commands protection from the top citizens listed in her little black book). In North Germany, Fritz Stavenhagen produced the peasant comedies *De duetsche Michel* (*The German Michael*, 1905) and *De ruge Hoff* (*The Peaceful Farm*, 1906). And in Austria, Karl Schönherr, following the example of Ludwig Anzengruber (see the "Brief Survey of Austrian Comedy"), painted realistic pictures of Tyrolean rustic life in such plays as *Erde* (*Earth*, 1908), a comedy about a mountain peasant whose love of life and the soil makes him refuse to die.

It is significant that Gerhart Hauptmann's sequel to *Der Biberpelz* was a tragicomedy, *Der rote Hahn* (*The Red Cock*, a.k.a. *Arson*, 1901), in which Mother Wolff outsmarts herself, commits arson, and comes to a grievous end. In time Hauptmann began to see the first play more and more in terms of his prevailing conviction that true comedy is invariably tragicomedy, and he followed it not only with *Der rote Hahn* but also with two more tragicomedies: *Peter Brauer* (written 1910 but not published until 1921) and *Die Ratten* (*The Rats*, 1911), in which rats gnaw away at the foundation of the tenement in which the poor characters live, just as human "rats" gnaw away at the social and economic foundations of their families. True comedy is, indeed, invariably tragicomedy in a realistic-naturalistic, and later expressionistic-absurd, drama that from the late nineteenth century on into the twentieth has been preoccupied with human suffering and world cataclysm. It is too difficult to depict such a world with unrelieved seriousness, and it is somewhat irresponsible to impose a wholly comic vision on it; such absolute and disparate forms no longer seemed, and seem, relevant to serious playwrights.

Bernard Shaw recognized that "Ibsen was the dramatic poet who firmly established tragicomedy as a much deeper and grimmer entertainment than tragedy," and most modern dramatists have built upon Ibsen's foundation. Seriousness in German comedy is nothing new, of course, but seriousness of a socially, if not revolutionarily, committed kind appears to be. In fact, however, it does not begin with Gerhart Hauptmann. He was simply the first heir of a German tragicomic tradition that developed from romantic irony and left its mark on the plays of J. M. R. Lenz (in particular *Der Hofmeister* and *Die Soldaten*) and Georg Büchner (especially *Woyzeck*), two near-twentieth-century sensibilities who happened to live, respectively, in the late eighteenth and early nineteenth centuries and whom the expressionists claimed as major influences on their work. I am thinking mainly of Frank Wedekind (1864–1918), who, in such plays as *Frühlings Erwachen* (*Spring Awakening*, 1891), *Der Kammersänger* (*The Tenor*, 1899), and *Der Marquis von Keith* (*The Marquis of Keith*, 1901), bridged the gap between Hauptmann's tragicomic naturalism and the grotesquery of the new expressionists; and of Carl Sternheim (1878–1942), whose trilogy of satirical comedies—*Die Hose* (*The Underpants*, 1911), *Die Kassette* (*The Strongbox*, 1912), and *Der Snob* (*The Snob*, 1914)—like the majority of his work, pillories the farcical and hypocritical nature of the way of life practiced by the German bourgeoisie.

Expressionism represented a revolt against modern society in all its forms—against capitalism, militarism, technology, and the general shallowness of life lived by bourgeois conventions. Expressionist writers opposed the materialism of the age with an appeal to the supremacy of the spirit in man and a new emphasis on the freedom of the individual to live his life in the light of his innermost convictions. One group of expressionists called for political and social reform, for transformation of a society on the brink of destruction, while another group—the "seekers after God"—concerned itself with the ecstasies of religion; common to both was the vision of a new world and a new man. As the expressionists increasingly became unconcerned with concrete dramatic situations, their art inclined toward abstraction: the characters in their plays turned into types and their language grew so intensely subjective, so exaggeratedly ecstatic, as to be almost incomprehensible. It was against this abstraction and subjectivity that the dramatists of *Die neue Sachlichkeit* (the new matter-of-factness) reacted. This movement is broadly characterized by a desire for hard-nosed, pragmatic realism, for a new look at the facts of life to be attained through a functional, unsentimental, ironic literary style. *Die neue Sachlichkeit* rejected expressionism's dreamy visions and called instead for control of the crucial dynamics of everyday living in the interest of achieving rational sociopolitical goals. Carl Zuckmayer (1896–1977) and Bertolt Brecht (1898–1956) stand out among the writers of socially realistic comedy.

Zuckmayer is best known for the satiric comedy *Der Hauptmann von Köpenick*, which he called *ein deutsches Märchen* (a German fairy tale). This play is based on the true story of an unemployed ex-convict who hoodwinked the Prussian military by donning a captain's uniform and commandeering a company of soldiers. *Der Hauptmann von Köpenick* pokes relentless fun at the German love of uniforms and condemns the inhumanity of officialdom, but behind the comedy there lies the tragedy of an individual who yearns—and deserves—to be integrated into the life of his community. Similarly, *Der fröhliche Weinberg* (*The Merry Vineyard,* 1925), written in the broad Rhenish dialect, hilariously depicts the lighthearted community of the Rhineland vineyards, but at the same time it mockingly laments the German nationalism that emerged between the wars. These two comedies, together with *Des Teufels General* (*The Devil's General,* 1946), a drama about the gradual and horrible realization on the part of a passionate flyer that he has blindly served the devil, Hitler—and the first play by a German to investigate the problem of guilt acquired through passivity in the face of Nazi evil—constitute the basis of Zuckmayer's reputation.

About Brecht it need only be said that he saw in comedy one of the necessary means for creating distance and objectivity in the theater, and thereby insight into the problems of contemporary existence; yet, paradoxically, he took up comedy with thoroughness in only two plays: *Mann ist Mann* (*A Man's a Man,* 1926) and *Herr Puntila und sein Knecht Matti* (*Mr. Puntila and His Hired Man Matti,* 1941). The comic characters of these two undervalued works are in fact closer to the ideal of Brecht's epic theater than the majority of characters in his best-known plays. That ideal places the focus not on the psychology of the individual but on the sociology of existence: man molding and being molded by the society of other men. *Mann ist Mann* in particular may be one of Brecht's more successful works because we do not demand the individuality, complex realism, or private psychology from its comic grotesques that we seem to demand from the characters in the subsequent, "straighter" parable plays, *Der gute Mensch von Sezuan* (*The Good Person of Setzuan,* 1940) and *Der kaukasische Kreidekreis* (*The Caucasian Chalk Circle,* 1945), and that we in fact get from the titular figures of the dramas thought to be Brecht's greatest, *Mutter Courage und ihre Kinder* (*Mother Courage and Her Children,* 1941) and *Leben des Galilei* (*Galileo,* 1943). We enjoy the laughs in *Mann ist Mann* at the same time that we see evil in the play as the result of specific conditions in society, not as the inherent product of human imperfection.

After 1945, the leadership in German-language tragicomedy (which could as easily be called grotesque, ironic, or absurd comedy) passed into the hands of a Swiss, Friedrich Dürrenmatt (1921–1990). Power and death are the two themes that dominate such "comedies" of his as *Es steht geschrieben* (*Thus It Is Written,* 1947, an early version of *Die Wiedertäufer* [*The Anabaptists,* 1967]),

Romulus der Grosse (*Romulus the Great,* 1949), *Die Ehe des Herrn Mississippi* (*The Marriage of Mr. Mississippi,* 1952), *Der Besuch der alten Dame* (*The Visit* or *The Elderly Lady's Visit,* 1956), *Die Physiker* (*The Physicists,* 1962), and *Der Meteor* (*The Meteor,* 1966). For Dürrenmatt, man in the end is reduced to a ridiculous creature because he is subject to the ultimate meaninglessness of death; death may appear to be life's culmination, but it is really only life's final futility. In keeping with so bitter a view, the playwright employs a bitter but vitally comedic sense of irony. If Dürrenmatt believes that life in the final analysis is insignificant, he believes equally that man is most often corruptible, especially when he possesses power. The possession of power places the individual in the precarious position to use or not use it, and its use, in Dürrenmatt's dark if comic vision, frequently results in evil.

Dürrenmatt's deep pessimism combined with amused detachment is shared not only by authors of his own generation such as Wolfgang Hildesheimer (especially in the grotesque satires *Die Uhren* [*The Clocks,* 1959] and *Landschaft mit Figuren* [*Landscape with Figures,* 1959]), Tankred Dorst (most notably in the absurdist farces *Die Kurve* [*The Curve,* 1960] and *Freiheit für Clemens* [*Freedom for Clemens,* 1960]), and Günter Grass (whose *Die bösen Köche* [*The Wicked Cooks,* 1961] is a transparent caricature of present-day political leaders as absurd cooks making a mess of the world), but also by authors of the next generation, of whom Botho Strauss (b. 1940) is representative. His farcical *Die Hypochonder* (*The Hypochondriacs,* 1972), for example, mixes elements of the absurd and the grotesque with parodies of detective and horror stories to illustrate the impossibility of genuine communication in a bourgeois capitalist society; the title refers to the chronic state of people in such a society. Strauss and his contemporaries might agree with Friedrich Dürrenmatt when he writes that "the tragic is still possible even if pure tragedy is not. We can achieve the tragic out of comedy. We can bring it forth as a frightening moment, as an abyss that opens suddenly." The implication is that German comic writers of the twentieth century, not so unlike their German comic forebears, are really tragedians in disguise, tragedians who, abandoned by the tragic muse, nevertheless continue to pursue it in comic form.

Notes

1. *Narren* literature, the best known example of which is Sebastian Brant's narrative poem *Das Narrenschyff* (*Ship of Fools,* 1494), ridiculed every type of

human vice and folly that the fifteenth century had to offer—many that we would not now regard as blameworthy at all—and thereby gave a faithful picture of the moral uncertainty that, in the age of the Reformation, was the inevitable consequence of the clash of the old order of things with the new.

2. Hans Sachs as a genial old man became one of the great figures of German comedy in *Die Meistersinger von Nürnberg* (1868), Richard Wagner's tribute to German folk art and satirical defense of his own artistic ideals against the persistent attacks of critics and pedants.

3. The beginnings of a serious drama of a somewhat secular nature in Germany (after the religious drama of the Middle Ages, into which secular elements were gradually introduced and in which the language of the people little by little took the place of Latin) can be seen in the Low or North German play *Theophilus* of the fourteenth century and in the *Spiel von Frau Jutten* (*Play about Mrs. Jutta*), written about 1480 (printed 1565) by Dietrich Schernberg, a Thuringian priest. Both dramas are forerunners of the Reformation *Volksbuch* (chapbook) of *Dr. Johann Faust* (1587); both depict the tragedy of man's temptation and fall at the hands of evil powers.

4. Mrs. Gottsched was joined in the writing of German *comédies larmoyantes* by such authors as Johann Christian Krüger (1722–50); Christian Fürchtegott Gellert (1715–69); Johann Elias Schlegel (1719–49), whose sentimental comedies *Die stumme Schönheit* (*The Speechless Beauty*, 1747) and *Der Triumph der guten Frauen* (*The Triumph of the Good Women*, 1748) were the best ones the German stage had to offer at the time; and Christian Felix Weisse (1726–1804), whose *Amalia* (1765) was discussed by Lessing in the twentieth essay of his *Hamburgische Dramaturgie* (*Hamburg Dramaturgy*, 1767–69).

5. Two Austrians produced sociopolitical comedies under the influence of *Das junge Deutschland*: Friedrich Hahn, with *Verbot und Befehl* (*Suppression and Regulation*, 1848), and Eduard von Bauernfeld, with *Das kategorische Imperativ* (*The Categorical Imperative*, 1850).

A Brief Survey of Austrian Comedy

Austrian comedy is as replete with tradition as German comedy is bereft of it. Comedy in Austria is much less an affair of spontaneous enterprise, and, while it has often been the work of highly problematic personalities—among whom I would number Franz Grillparzer, Arthur Schnitzler, Hugo von Hofmannsthal, and Ferdinand Raimund—the shadow cast by tradition in this country has dimmed the intense light of individual genius seen in Germany. The tradition of comedy in Austria is, to begin with, bifurcated, and one must distinguish between the popular variety (which emerged from the twin influences of the Jesuit school-comedy-of-serious-intent and the *Englische Komödianten* and culminated in the late nineteenth century in the plays of Raimund and Nestroy) and the more sophisticated variety of which Schnitzler and Hofmannsthal are representative.

The stream of popular or folk comedy flows continuously from the early eighteenth century, and its source can be found in Josef Anton Stranitzky (1676–1726), who was strongly influenced by the Italian *commedia dell'arte* and who acquired in 1712 the lease of the Theater am Kärntnertor, the first permanent public theater in Vienna, where he was the mainstay until his death. Stranitzky's creation of *Hanswurst* as a jolly, beer-drinking peasant eventually appeared in some form or other in most Viennese folk comedies, and the Austrian *Hanswurst* proved to be far more tenacious than his German counterpart. He might change his name and his guise, but he refused to be ousted from the theater, and many of the transformations that the *Volkskomödie* underwent were due to attempts to procure for him liberty of speech and action. In his changing form one can detect the Viennese citizenry reacting to the social and political changes around them and weighing, in the scales of laughter, the cultural and moral values that filtered down to the popular stage from higher literary or intellectual spheres.

The *Wiener Volkskomödie* reached its height as a combination of folk comedy and magical farce in the plays of Ferdinand Raimund (1790–1836) and Johann Nestroy (1801–62), most of which are untranslatable because of their use of Viennese dialect as a chief source of wit. (Some are adaptable, however: Nestroy's *Einen Jux will er sich machen* [*He Wants to Have a Fling* or *One Last Fling*, 1842] became the basis of Thornton Wilder's *The Matchmaker*, which itself later became the musical *Hello, Dolly!*.) Raimund became the master of gracious and morally uplifting fantastication with such fairy-tale plays as *Der Barometermacher auf der Zauberinsel* (*The Barometer-Maker on the Magic Isle*, 1823), *Der Diamant des Zauberkönigs* (*The Diamond of the King of Magic*, 1824), *Das Mädchen aus der Feenwelt, oder der Bauer als Millionär* (*The Girl from Fairyland, or the Millionaire Farmer*, 1826), and *Der Alpenkönig und der Menschenfeind* (*The Alpine King and the Misanthrope*, 1828). Nestroy, by contrast, became the master of fantastic spoof, of ecstatic ridicule, in such satirical folk plays as *Die Verbannung aus dem Zauberreich oder dreissig Jahre aus dem Leben eines Lumpen* (*Banishment from the Magic Kingdom, or Thirty Years in the Life of a Bum*, 1828), *Der böse Geist Lumpazivagabundus oder das liederliche Kleeblatt* (*The Evil Spirit Lumpazivagabundus, or the Untidy Trio*, 1833), and *Das Mädel aus der Vorstadt oder Ehrlich währt am längsten* (*The Girl from the Suburbs, or Honesty Wins in the End*, 1841). Rooted in a metropolitan life of a specific, stable kind and written for the entertainment of a public that was conscious of its individuality and delighted in seeing its own reflection upon the stage, the *Wiener Volkskomödie* acquired a unique quality not found in the comedy of Germany.

That quality was enhanced by the plays of Ludwig Anzengruber (1839–89), a native Viennese who took the earthy characters of Raimund and Nestroy's magical-farce tradition and put them into realistic environments. *Die Kreuzelschreiber* (*The X-Markers*, 1872) uses the *Lysistrata*-situation of wives on strike in humorously depicting a political battle between ecclesiastical and peasant interests. *Der G'wissenwurm* (*The Worm of Conscience*, 1874) deals amusingly with the vain attempts of greedy people to fleece a farmer of his property by exploiting his guilty conscience. And *Der Doppelselbstmord* (*The Double Suicide*, 1875) gaily transplants the Romeo-and-Juliet problem to a Tyrolean village and resolves it happily. Anzengruber's dialect comedies of peasant life (and his "problem plays" on the same subject) could be called a bridge, in German drama as a whole, between the realism of Friedrich Hebbel and the naturalism of Gerhart Hauptmann.

In stark contrast to the *Volkskomödie* stands Franz Grillparzer's only comedy, *Weh dem, der lügt!* (*Woe to the Liar!*, 1837), which, thematically, is closely related to his tragedies—among them *König Ottokars Glück und Ende* (*The Rise and Fall of King Ottokar*, 1825),

Ein treuer Diener seines Herrn (*A Faithful Servant of His Master,* 1828), and *Libussa* (written 1825–48, produced 1874)—and which, like all his work, reflects the classicism of Goethe and Schiller rather than the contemporary movements of romanticism and *Jungdeutschland,* to which Grillparzer felt distinctly hostile. Not without reason, *Weh dem, der lügt!* has been labeled one of the four great German(-language) comedies, together with Gotthold Ephraim Lessing's *Minna von Barnhelm* (1767), Heinrich von Kleist's *Der zerbrochene Krug* (*The Broken Pitcher,* 1807), and Gerhart Hauptmann's *Der Biberpelz* (*The Beaver Coat,* 1893). Indeed, like Lessing, Kleist, and Hauptmann, Grillparzer (1791–1872) was a deadly serious man who spent most of his life concerned with deadly serious matters, his tragedies among them, and whose seriousness underpins his comic writing as well. So serious was Grillparzer that, after *Weh dem, der lügt!* was hooted from the Burgtheater stage in Vienna on 6 March 1838 and then suppressed by the authorities, he bitterly withdrew from society and refused to allow his remaining three plays—the political tragedies *Ein Bruderzwist in Habsburg* (*Family Strife in Hapsburg,* written 1825–48, produced 1872), *Libussa,* and *Die Jüdin von Toledo* (*The Jewess of Toledo,* written 1837–51, produced 1872)—to be produced or published in his lifetime.

Like *Minna von Barnhelm, Weh dem, der lügt!* preaches moderation and compromise—in this case, in the pursuit of and obedience to the truth, which Bishop Gregory of Chalons instructs the kitchen-boy Leon to speak at all times, even when lying or deceit would be more practical, such as during Leon's attempt to rescue Gregory's nephew Atalus, who is being held hostage in the Rhine Province by the barbarian Count Kattwald. And as in *Minna,* the power of love asserts itself as a theme of ever increasing importance, first as a factor motivating the behavior of the leading female character, Edrita, Kattwald's daughter, and then as a phenomenon sufficiently valuable in itself to provide the play with a satisfying conclusion: the union of Edrita and Leon and her conversion to Christianity. Like *Der zerbrochene Krug* and *Der Biberpelz, Weh dem, der lügt!* treats the themes of misunderstanding and deception and hints at the subjectivity of all truth. But unlike *Der zerbrochene Krug* and *Der Biberpelz,* and again like *Minna, Weh dem, der lügt!* is not particularly funny, however much its overall form is comic— i.e., however much it ends happily and harmoniously.

Comedy, or perhaps I should say laughter, arises from effects of incongruity, which depend on contrast and disparity; and there is no comic contrast within Leon, the play's main character. This becomes clear when one compares him with Adam, the central figure in *Der zerbrochene Krug*. Unlike Leon, Adam is untruthful, and his every deception reveals the truth about his own untruthfulness, which stands in drastic incongruity to his position as a judge. Leon's resolution to abide by Bishop Gregory's mandate always to tell the truth produces a correspondence between character and duty that, though it is neatly interwoven with the love-motif and makes the happy ending possible, is not conducive to comic effects. There *are* scenes of comic contrast between the clever, charming Leon and the uncultured barbarians east of the Rhine,[1] but they tend to be rather broad, and this broadness only gets magnified by the stiff, overliterary verse that Grillparzer puts into the mouths of his characters. Kleist also has the characters in *Der zerbrochene Krug* speak classical blank verse, but he is careful to make their language earthy, even racy, and full of ingenious quibbles, and thus comically incongruous with the poetic form in which the play is cast; just as there is a comic contrast within the character of Adam, then, there is a comic contrast built into the speeches that he and the rest of the characters give.

Hugo von Hofmannsthal (1874–1929) represents the fusion of the native *Volkskomödie* of Austria with the tradition of Molière, of the comedy of character. Hofmannsthal adapted two of Molière's plays—*Le mariage forcé (The Forced Marriage)* and *Le bourgeois gentilhomme (The Would-Be Gentleman)*—and in his original comedies (all in prose, some in Viennese dialect), among them *Christinas Heimreise (Christina's Journey Home*, 1910), *Der Schwierige (The Difficult Man*, 1921), and *Der Unbestechliche (The Incorruptible Man*, 1932), he creates a gentle satire of contemporary social conditions. Like his coeval Arthur Schnitzler (1862–1931) in such plays as *Anatol* (1893) and *Reigen (Hands Around* or *La Ronde*, 1897), Hofmannsthal gave a new texture to the traditional material of European comedy, bringing to it an extreme sensitivity to the nuances of human relationships, an urbanity of mind imparted by life in the highly civilized community of Vienna, and an ironic awareness of the discrepancy between the individual personality and the mask that society compels it to assume.

Impatient, like many of the current generation, with the artifice of fine writing as exemplified in the work of Hofmannsthal and Schnitzler, Wolfgang Bauer (b. 1941) has written plays whose tone and language hark back to the tradition of the *Wiener Volkskomödie*. Like Raimund and Nestroy, Bauer writes in dialect—in the earthy, even rude, Austrian vernacular that is far removed from the polite standard German of the conventional theater—and in such works as *Magic Afternoon* (1968; originally titled in English by the author) and *Change* (1969; originally titled in English by the author) he treats urban scenes from the latter half of the twentieth century with the same satirical wit that Nestroy applied to nineteenth-century scenes from the life of the *Volk*. But there is a deep anguish beneath the cheerful nihilism with which the playwright depicts the lives of disaffected, apathetic youth, and in this sense he shares the tragicomic vision of his German contemporaries.

Note

1. These scenes, with their portrayal of a mere kitchen-boy, a lowly servant, as the embodiment of civilization—and French civilization at that—and of his aristocratic masters as either untutored louts (Count Kattwald and his would-be son-in-law, Galomir) or hopeless snobs (Atalus), were alarming in their sociopolitical implications for the largely upper-middle-class and patrician Burgtheater audience in 1838, only a decade away from the revolution that would threaten their position and prospects; and the play's caricature of the nobility is often cited as the major reason for the failure of its world premiere. Grillparzer might have replied that the contrast in *Weh dem, der lügt!* between the civilized French and the primitive inhabitants east of the Rhine was meant to suggest to the Viennese audience their own presumed cultural superiority over their German neighbors.

German-Language Comedy

Minna von Barnhelm

A Comedy in Five Acts

by
GOTTHOLD EPHRAIM LESSING

Translated by
Bert Cardullo

Translated from the following edition:
Lessing, Gotthold Ephraim. *Minna von Barnhelm.* In *Gesammelte Werke in zwei Bänden,* edited by Otto Mann, vol. 1. Gütersloh: Sigbert Mohn Verlag, 1966.

Characters

Major von Tellheim
Minna von Barnhelm
Count von Bruchsal, her uncle
Franziska, her maid
Just, Tellheim's servant
Paul Werner, former sergeant major in Tellheim's battalion
Innkeeper
Lady in Mourning
Orderly
Servants
Riccaut de la Marlinière

The scene alternates between two adjacent rooms of an inn.

Act 1

SCENE 1

JUST. [*Seated in a corner, sleeping and talking in his sleep.*] Bugger of a landlord! You, us?—Go to!—On guard! [*He goes through the motions of drawing his sword and in doing so wakes himself up.*] Bah! I can't even close my eyes without getting into a fight with him. I wish he'd been on the receiving end of half the blows I've dealt him!—But look, it's light out; I've got to find the master. As far as I'm concerned, he'll not set foot in this damned house again. Where did he spend the night, I wonder?

SCENE 2
JUST *and* INNKEEPER

INNKEEPER. Good morning, Herr Just, good morning! You're up early, or should I say, you're still up so late?

JUST. You can say what you damned well like.

INNKEEPER. I wasn't saying anything but "Good morning," and surely, Herr Just, you ought to say "Thank you" to that.

JUST. Thanks a lot!

INNKEEPER. Everyone feels a bit touchy when they don't get their proper rest. But never mind. So the major didn't come in last night, and you waited up for him?

JUST. You're clever, you are.

INNKEEPER. Just guessing, just guessing.

JUST. [*Turning and about to leave.*] Your servant, sir!

INNKEEPER. Oh no, Herr Just, no!

JUST. All right then, I'm not your servant!

INNKEEPER. Herr Just, I do hope that you're not still angry about yesterday. You shouldn't let the sun set on your wrath, you know.

JUST. Well, I let it, and I shall continue to do so till doomsday.

INNKEEPER. Now, I ask you, is that Christian?

JUST. It's just as Christian as throwing an honest man out of the house because he can't pay his rent right on the dot.

INNKEEPER. Well, now, who could be so godless as to do a thing like that?

JUST. A Christian innkeeper.—To think, the master, a man like that, an officer of his stamp!

INNKEEPER. And I'm the one who's supposed to have thrown him out of the house into the street? I'm afraid I have too much respect for officers to do that, and in any case too much sympathy for one who's just been discharged. I was obliged to move him to another room, that's all—it was on account of an emergency.—Don't dwell on the subject, Herr Just. [*Shouts offstage*.] Hey there!—I'll make it up to you in another way. [*Enter* SERVANT.] Bring us a bottle; Herr Just would like a drink, and make it something special!

JUST. Don't bother. Anything you offered me would turn to bile in my mouth. By God . . . No, I mustn't blaspheme when I'm sober.

INNKEEPER. [*To* SERVANT, *who enters carrying a bottle of liqueur and a glass*.] Give it to me. All right, you can go!—Now, Herr Just, here's a drop of something special: strong, but gentle, and it'll do you good. [*Fills the glass and offers it to* JUST.] Just the thing for a stomach that's been up all night!

JUST. Well, I shouldn't really.—But why should I sacrifice my health to his inhospitality? [*Takes the glass and drinks*.]

INNKEEPER. Your health, Herr Just!

JUST. [*Giving him back the glass*.] Not bad, but it doesn't make you any less of a scoundrel.

INNKEEPER. Herr Just, Herr Just!—How about another quick one? I always say, you can't stand up properly on one leg.

JUST. [*Having drunk the second glass*.] Well, I must admit it's good, very good!—Homemade, is it?

INNKEEPER. Not likely! Real Danzig brandy. The genuine article!

JUST. Now look here, innkeeper, if something like this could make me play the hypocrite, I would; but it can't and I won't, so I tell you straight to your face: you're a scoundrel.

INNKEEPER. That's the first time in my life that anyone ever called me that.—Another one, Herr Just. All good things come in threes!

JUST. All right. [*Drinks*.] Good stuff, really good stuff! But so is the truth. Truth's good stuff, too.—Innkeeper, you're still a scoundrel!

INNKEEPER. I ask you, if I was a scoundrel, would I be standing here listening to you call me one?

JUST. Yes, you would, because scoundrels seldom have any guts.

INNKEEPER. Won't you have another one, Herr Just? A four-stranded rope holds better, you know.

JUST. No, enough is enough. Besides, what's the use? If I drank the bottle down to the last drop, I wouldn't change my mind. Ugh, to have such good brandy and such rotten hospitality! Throwing out a man like my master, who's lived here day and night and spent many a pretty penny in the process, who's never in his life been a cent in debt; throwing him out just because he didn't pay his rent on time a few months, just because he wasn't spending as much as he used to—and behind his back into the bargain!

INNKEEPER. But I needed the room. It was an emergency, and I knew that the major would gladly have given it up of his own free will if only we could have waited until he got back. Was I to turn a stranger away? I ask you. Was I to shove the trade down another innkeeper's throat? And besides, I don't think they could have found another place to stay. All the inns are filled up at the moment. Is a lovely young lady like that supposed to stay out in the street? No, Herr Just, your master's too much of a gentleman to allow that! Besides, what does he lose by this? Didn't I move him to another room?

JUST. Yes, right behind the pigeon coop, with a nice view of the neighbors' chimneys . . .

INNKEEPER. Well, the view was quite good until they started building. The rest of the room is nice enough, and it's got wallpaper.

JUST. You mean it had.

INNKEEPER. It still has on one side. And you've got your little room next door, Herr Just; what's wrong with your room? There's a fireplace, which, it's true, does smoke a bit in winter—

JUST. But everything's just fine in summer.—You're not trying to harass us, are you?

INNKEEPER. Now, now, Herr Just, Herr Just—

JUST. Don't you get Herr Just excited, or else . . .

INNKEEPER. Me? Get you excited? No, that's the brandy!

JUST. To think, an officer like my master! Or perhaps you reckon that a discharged officer isn't an officer, and couldn't break your neck. Why were you innkeepers always so obliging during the war? Every officer was a worthy man then, every soldier an honest chap. Does a bit of peace make you that cocky?

INNKEEPER. Now why are you getting angry, Herr Just?

JUST. I want to get angry.

SCENE 3
TELLHEIM, INNKEEPER, *and* JUST

TELLHEIM. [*Entering.*] Just!

JUST. [*Thinking it is the* INNKEEPER *who is talking to him.*] Just?—Oh, so we're on those terms now, are we?

TELLHEIM. Just!

JUST. I thought I was Herr Just to you!

INNKEEPER. [*Becoming aware of* TELLHEIM's *presence.*] Sh! Sh! Herr, Herr, Herr Just—look behind you; your master . . .

TELLHEIM. Just, I believe you've been quarrelling. What did I tell you?

INNKEEPER. Quarrel, Your Grace? May God be my witness! Would I, Your Grace's most humble servant, take it upon myself to quarrel with one who has the honor to be in Your Grace's service?

JUST. I'd like to give that phony what for!

INNKEEPER. It's true that Herr Just was speaking out on behalf of his master, and a little heatedly. But he was right to do so. I think all the more of him for it; in fact, I admire him for it.

JUST. It's a wonder I don't knock his teeth down his throat!

INNKEEPER. It's really a shame that he's getting upset over nothing. I'm as sure as can be that Your Grace would not bring any disgrace on me for what I have done, because—it was necessary, because I had to.

TELLHEIM. Enough, sir! I owe you money; you moved me out of my room in my absence, and you must be paid. I have to find somewhere else to stay. It's all perfectly understandable!

INNKEEPER. Somewhere else? You're moving out, sir? Oh, what a wretch I am! No, never! I'd sooner have the lady move out. The major can . . . well . . . if you don't want to give her your room, the room's yours. She'll have to go; I can't help it.—I'll see to it at once, Your Grace.

TELLHEIM. My friend, please do not do two stupid things instead of one! The lady must, of course, retain possession of my room.

INNKEEPER. And to think that Your Grace thought I mistrusted you, thought I was worried about my money! As if I didn't know that Your Grace could pay whenever he wanted to! That sealed purse with the five hundred talers in it which Your Grace left in his desk—don't worry, it's in good hands.

TELLHEIM. I hope so, like the rest of my things. Just will take charge of them when he pays the bill.

INNKEEPER. Honestly, Your Grace, I was quite startled when I found that purse. Of course, I always took you for an orderly and careful man who would never allow himself to run out of money. But, well, if I'd really believed there was money in the desk . . .

TELLHEIM. You would have treated me more politely. I understand.—Please go now, sir. Leave me. I must speak with my servant.

INNKEEPER. But your Grace . . .

TELLHEIM. Come, Just, this gentleman is apparently not going to permit me to tell you what to do while we are in his house.

INNKEEPER. I'm going, Your Grace! My whole establishment is at your service.

SCENE 4
TELLHEIM *and* JUST

JUST. [*Stamping his foot and spitting after the* INNKEEPER.] Pah!
TELLHEIM. What's the matter?
JUST. I'm fairly choking with rage!
TELLHEIM. Well, at least you're not choking on your own blood.
JUST. And you, sir, I just don't know you any more. Let me die
before your very eyes if you aren't the guardian angel of this
cunning, merciless dog! In spite of the gallows, in spite of the sword
and the wheel, I'd have—I'd have strangled him with my own hands
and torn him to pieces with my own teeth.
TELLHEIM. Animal!
JUST. I'd rather be an animal than be a man like him.
TELLHEIM. But what do you want?
JUST. All I want is for you to understand how much you're being
insulted.
TELLHEIM. And then?
JUST. I want you to have your revenge on him.—No, this fellow's
not worth the bother to you.
TELLHEIM. Would you rather I told you to avenge me? That was
my plan from the start. I hadn't intended to let him see me again,
and he was to receive his payment from you. I know that you can
throw down a handful of money with a pretty disdainful air.
JUST. Ha, ha! That would have been a good way of paying him off.
TELLHEIM. But one which I'm afraid we shall have to put off for
the time being. I haven't a penny of ready cash, and I don't know
how to get any.
JUST. No ready cash? What about that little purse with the five
hundred talers which the innkeeper found in your desk?
TELLHEIM. That is money which was put in my safe keeping.
JUST. Not the five hundred talers that your old sergeant major,
Paul Werner, gave you four or five weeks ago?
TELLHEIM. The very same. They belong to Paul Werner. Why
shouldn't they?
JUST. You mean to say you haven't used them yet? You can do
what you like with them, sir; I'll take responsibility.
TELLHEIM. Really?
JUST. I told Werner how long the paymaster general was taking to
settle your claim. He heard . . .
TELLHEIM. That I would certainly be reduced to beggary, if I
weren't already. I'm very grateful to you, Just.—And this piece of
news permitted Werner to share his bit of poverty with me. I'm glad
to have got to the bottom of it.—Now listen to me, Just: give me

your bill as well; our partnership is at an end.

JUST. Eh? What?

TELLHEIM. Quiet! Someone is coming.

SCENE 5
A LADY IN MOURNING, TELLHEIM, *and* JUST

LADY. I beg your pardon, sir.

TELLHEIM. Whom are you looking for, madam?

LADY. Precisely the worthy man with whom I have the honor to be speaking. You do not recognize me anymore? I am the widow of your former captain.

TELLHEIM. For heaven's sake, madam, but you are changed!

LADY. I have just risen from my sickbed, to which I had retired because of my sorrow at my husband's death. I am sorry to have to bother you so early, Major Tellheim. I am going to the country, where a kindhearted, though not exactly prosperous, friend has offered me a haven for now.

TELLHEIM. [*To* JUST] Go, leave us alone.

SCENE 6
LADY IN MOURNING *and* TELLHEIM

TELLHEIM. Speak freely, madam! You have no need to be ashamed of your misfortune in my presence. Can I be of service to you in any way?

LADY. Major . . .

TELLHEIM. I sympathize with you, madam! How can I be of service to you? You know that your husband was my friend—I repeat, my friend; and this is a title with which I have always been very sparing.

LADY. Who knows better than I how well you deserved his friendship, and how well he deserved yours? You would have been the last person in his thoughts, your name the last word on his lips, had not the stronger bonds of nature reserved that sad privilege for his unfortunate son and for his unfortunate wife.

TELLHEIM. Please stop, madam! I would gladly weep with you, but today I have no tears. Spare me! You come upon me at a moment when I might easily be led to rail against Providence.—Oh, my honest Marloff! Quickly, madam, what is your command? If I am in a position to help you, if I am . . .

LADY. I must not leave without fulfilling his last wish. He remembered just before his death that he was in your debt and made me swear to discharge this debt with the first money I should receive. I sold his equipment, and I have come to redeem his note.

TELLHEIM. What, madam? It is for this that you have come?

LADY. For this. Please let me pay you the money.

TELLHEIM. Madam, I beg you, no! Marloff owed me money? That can scarcely be so. Let me see. [*Takes out his notebook and looks at it.*] I see nothing here.

LADY. You must have mislaid his note, and in any case, the note itself is of no importance. Permit me . . .

TELLHEIM. No, madam, I am not in the habit of mislaying things of that sort! If I do not have it, then that is evidence that I never had it, or that it was cancelled and returned to him.

LADY. Major Tellheim!

TELLHEIM. Most certainly, madam: Marloff owed me nothing. In fact I cannot even recall that he was ever in my debt. On the contrary, madam, I regard myself as having been left in his debt. I have never been able to pay off my debts to a man who for six years shared my happiness and my misfortune, my honor and my peril. I shall not forget that he has left a son. He shall be my son as soon as I can be his father. The confusion in which I find myself at the moment . . .

LADY. Generous man! But please do not think too lowly of me, major, and take the money. In this way I shall at last be put at ease.

TELLHEIM. What do you need to set you at ease beyond my assurance that this money does not belong to me? Or do you want me to steal from my friend's now fatherless child? Steal, madam, that's what it would be in the truest sense of the word. The money belongs to him, and you should invest it for him!

LADY. I understand you; and please forgive me if I have not yet learned to accept favors. But how did you know that a mother will do more for her son than for her own life? I am going now . . .

TELLHEIM. Go, madam, go! Farewell! I shall not ask you to send me news of yourself, for such news might come at a time when I could not act on it. But I forgot one thing, madam. Marloff still had money coming to him from our former regiment. His claim is just as valid as my own. If mine is settled, then his will be too. My word on it.

LADY. Oh, sir!—No, I would rather say nothing.—To grant future favors is, in God's eyes, to have granted them already. May God keep you, and may you accept my tears in gratitude! [*Exit.*]

SCENE 7

TELLHEIM

TELLHEIM. Poor woman! I must not forget to destroy that note.

[*Takes a piece of paper from his wallet and tears it up.*] After all, who can guarantee that my own need might not one day make me put it to use?

SCENE 8
JUST *and* TELLHEIM

TELLHEIM. Are you here?

JUST. [*Wiping his eyes.*] Yes!

TELLHEIM. You have been crying?

JUST. I have been writing out my bill in the kitchen, and the kitchen is full of smoke. Here it is!

TELLHEIM. Give it to me.

JUST. Have a bit of mercy on me, sir. I know people don't have any on you, but . . .

TELLHEIM. What do you want?

JUST. Well, I'd expected to die before getting the sack from you.

TELLHEIM. I have no further use for you; I now have to learn to look after myself without servants. [*Opens the bill and reads.*] "The major owes me: three and a half months pay at six talers per month—that makes twenty-one talers. From the first of the month I have paid out the following sums for him: one taler, seven groschen, and nine pfennigs. Sum total, twenty-two talers, seven groschen, and nine pfennigs."—Fine, Just, I think I should also pay you for the whole of the current month.

JUST. Look at the other side first, would you, major?

TELLHEIM. There's more? [*Reads.*] "I owe the major: advanced on my account to the surgeon, twenty-five talers. For room and board during my convalescence, thirty-nine talers. Advanced to my father, whose house was burned down and plundered, not to mention the two horses given to him, fifty talers. Sum total, one hundred and fourteen talers. Deduct the twenty-two talers, seven groschen, and nine pfennigs brought forward, and I remain in the major's debt to the tune of ninety-one talers, sixteen groschen, and three pfennigs."—Just, you're mad!

JUST. I'm ready to believe that I've cost you a great deal more than that, but it would have been a waste of ink writing it all down. I can't pay you, and if you want to take my uniform away from me—which I also haven't yet paid for—then I'd rather you just let me kick the bucket in some military hospital.

TELLHEIM. What do you take me for? You don't owe me anything, and I'll give you a recommendation to one of my friends, who will look after you better than I can.

JUST. I don't owe you anything, yet you still want to get rid of me?

TELLHEIM. Because I don't want to owe *you* anything.

JUST. Oh, just because of that? As sure as I know that I'm in your debt, I'm just as sure you don't owe me a penny, and just as sure that you shan't get rid of me. You can do what you like, major: I'm going to stay with you; I've got to stay with you.

TELLHEIM. And also because of your obstinacy, your defiance, your wild and impetuous behavior toward everyone who you think has no right to interfere with you; because of your malicious spite, your vindictiveness . . .

JUST. You can paint me as black as you like, I still won't think any worse of myself than of my dog. One evening last winter, at twilight, I was walking along a canal and heard something whining. I climbed down the bank, reached toward the voice, thinking that I was rescuing a child, and pulled a poodle out of the water. Well, that's all right too, I thought. The poodle followed me, though, and I don't particularly like poodles. I chased him away, but it was no use. I beat him, but it was no use. I refused to let him into my room at night; he slept outside the door. When he got too close to me, I gave him a kick; he would cry out, look at me, and then wag his tail. I've never given him a thing to eat, yet I'm the only one he obeys and the only one who can touch him. He runs along in front of me and does his tricks without being asked. He's an ugly poodle, but a very good dog. If he goes on like this, I'll have to stop disliking him.

TELLHEIM. [*Aside.*] Exactly as I'll have to do with him! No, there *are* no completely inhuman people! Just, we'll stay together.

JUST. Certainly!—And you wanted to get on without a servant? You forget your wounds and that you've only got the use of one arm. You can't even get dressed by yourself. You can't do without me, and—not to sing my own praises, major—I am a servant who, if worst comes to worst, can beg and steal for his master.

TELLHEIM. Just, we are not staying together.

JUST. All right, all right!

SCENE 9
SERVANT, TELLHEIM, *and* JUST

SERVANT. Hey, buddy!

JUST. What is it?

SERVANT. Can you show me the officer who was living in that room until yesterday? [*Pointing to the side from which he has just come.*]

JUST. Yes, I can. What've you got for him?

SERVANT. What we've always got when we haven't got anything: a greeting. My mistress has heard that the officer was forced out of his room on her account. My mistress knows how to conduct herself, and so I'm to beg his pardon.

JUST. All right, beg his pardon; there he is.

SERVANT. Who is he? I mean, what do you call him?

TELLHEIM. My friend, I have already heard your mission. It is an unnecessary piece of courtesy on the part of your mistress, which I nevertheless accept, as I should. Please pay her my respects.— What is your mistress's name?

SERVANT. What's her name? Oh, she's called "madam."

TELLHEIM. And her last name?

SERVANT. I've never heard that, and it's not my business to ask. You see, I arrange things so that I change masters about every six weeks. As far as I'm concerned, to hell with their names!

JUST. Bravo, mate!

SERVANT. I only started with the mistress a few days ago, in Dresden. I think she's looking for her fiancé here.

TELLHEIM. Enough, my friend. I wanted to know your mistress's name, not her secrets. Now go!

SERVANT. Brother, that's not my kind of master!

SCENE 10
TELLHEIM *and* JUST

TELLHEIM. Just, I want you to arrange to get us out of this place. I find myself more receptive to the courtesy of this strange woman than I am to the rudeness of the innkeeper. Here, take this ring; it's the one valuable thing I have left and the one thing I never thought I'd have to put to this use!—Pawn it. Raise four hundred talers on it; the innkeeper's bill can't be more than thirty talers. Pay him and then move my things.—Right, where to? . . . Wherever you like. The cheaper the inn the better. You can meet me in the café next door. I'm leaving now; see that you do a good job.

JUST. Don't you worry about that, major.

TELLHEIM. [*Returning.*] And most important of all, don't forget my pistols, which were hanging behind the bed.

JUST. I won't forget anything.

TELLHEIM. [*Returning again.*] One more thing: be sure to take your poodle along. You hear, Just? [*Exit.*]

SCENE 11
JUST

JUST. My poodle will not remain behind. He'll see to that.—Hm, so the master had this valuable ring, and carried it in his pocket instead of on his finger.—Well, innkeeper, we're not as poor as we seem to be. I know what! I'll pawn this pretty little ring with the innkeeper himself. He'll be angry, I know, because we're not going to spend all the money in his place.—

SCENE 12
PAUL WERNER *and* JUST

JUST. Well, if it isn't Werner! Hello, Werner! Welcome to the big city.

WERNER. Cursed village! I can't possibly get used to it again. Cheer up, children, cheer up! I bring fresh money. Where's the major?

JUST. He must have passed you. He just went downstairs.

WERNER. I came up the back stairs. How is he? I would have been here last week, but . . .

JUST. Well, what held you up?

WERNER. Just, have you heard of Prince Heraclius?

JUST. Heraclius? Not that I know of.

WERNER. Haven't you heard about the great hero in the East?

JUST. I do know of three wise men from the East, who run about with the stars around New Year's.

WERNER. Man, I think you must read the papers just as little as you read the Bible.—You don't know Prince Heraclius, the great man who has conquered Persia and is now going to overrun the Turks? Thank God there's some place left in the world where there's a war on! I kept hoping it would break out here again. But everybody's still sitting 'round licking their wounds. No, once a soldier, always a soldier, I say! But listen, Just. [*Looking around shyly to make sure no one is listening.*] Confidentially, I'm going to Persia to fight a campaign or two against the Turks under the leadership of His Royal Highness, Prince Heraclius.

JUST. You?

WERNER. Me! As sure as I'm standing here. Our ancestors used to fight the Turks, and we would too if only we were honest men and good Christians. I know that a campaign against the Turks can't be half as much fun as one against the French, but then the rewards are greater, in this life and the next. Did you know that the Turks all have swords encrusted with diamonds?

JUST. I wouldn't travel a mile, let alone all the way to Turkey, to have my head split open by a sword like that. You surely aren't crazy enough to leave your beautiful farm, are you?

WERNER. I'm taking it with me!—Didn't you know?—My farm

has been sold.—

JUST. Sold?

WERNER. Sh!—Here are the three hundred I got yesterday upon the sale. They're for the major.

JUST. And what is he supposed to do with them?

WERNER. What do you think he's supposed to do with them? Use them up, gamble them away, drink them down, whatever he likes. The man's got to have some money, and it's bad enough he's having all this trouble getting his own. I know what I'd do if I were in his place. I'd think, "The devil take the lot of them! I'm going with Paul Werner to Persia."—Hell! Prince Heraclius must have heard of Major Tellheim, even if he doesn't know his old sergeant major, Paul Werner. That incident at Katzenberg alone—

JUST. Shall I tell you about it?

WERNER. *You* tell *me?*—I'm well aware that a good battle plan is something beyond your comprehension, and I'm not going to throw my pearls before swine.—Take the three hundred talers and give them to the major. Tell him to keep them for me. I've got to go to the market now; I've brought forty bushels of rye with me, and he can have what I get out of that, too.

JUST. Werner, I know you mean well, but we don't want your money. Keep your talers, and you can have the other five hundred back as soon as you like; we haven't touched them.

WERNER. Really? The major still has money of his own, has he?

JUST. No, he hasn't.

WERNER. Well, has he borrowed some, then?

JUST. No.

WERNER. Then what are you living on?

JUST. Credit, and when we can't get any more credit and they throw us out, we shall pawn what we've still got left and move on.— Listen, Paul, we've got to get even with the innkeeper here.

WERNER. If he's done something to the major, I'm with you!

JUST. What if we wait for him when he comes out of the tobacco shop this evening and give him a good working over?

WERNER. This evening?—Wait for him?—Two against one?—No, that's not right.

JUST. Suppose we burn down his house around him?

WERNER. Burn it down? You know, it's easy to tell you were with equipment-and-supply and not in the infantry. Pah!

JUST. How about seducing his daughter? Although it's true she's quite ugly . . .

WERNER. And she'll stay ugly for a long time! Anyway, you don't need my help for that. But tell me what's going on. What's happened?

JUST. Come with me and you'll hear something that'll surprise you!

WERNER. Has all hell broken loose around here or something?

JUST. You said it. Now let's go!

WERNER. That suits me just fine! To Persia, then! To Persia!

Act 2

SCENE I
The Lady's Boudoir
MINNA VON BARNHELM *and* FRANZISKA, *her maid*

MINNA. [*In her négligée, looking at her watch.*] Franziska, we got up very early. We're going to have more time on our hands than we know what to do with.

FRANZISKA. Well, I don't know who can get any sleep in these big cities, what with the coaches, night watchmen, drums, cats, and corporals—there's no end of rattling, rolling, shouting, swearing, and meowing, just as if the night were made for anything but peace.—Would you like a cup of tea, madam?

MINNA. No, I don't feel like tea.

FRANZISKA. I'll get them to make some of our chocolate.

MINNA. Yes do, for yourself.

FRANZISKA. Only for myself? I'd just as soon talk to myself as drink alone.—Well, it's certainly going to be a long day. Out of sheer boredom we shall have to smarten ourselves up and then choose the dress in which we're going to make our first assault.

MINNA. Why do you talk of assaults when you know that I have only come here to demand a surrender?

FRANZISKA. And that officer we turned out, the one we sent our apologies to—he doesn't seem to have the best of manners, otherwise he would at least have asked for the honor of being allowed to pay his respects to us.

MINNA. Not all officers are Tellheims. To tell you the truth, I only sent him my apologies so that I could have the chance to ask him about Tellheim.—Franziska, my heart tells me that our journey will be successful, that I shall find him.

FRANZISKA. Your heart, madam? I shouldn't put too much trust in my heart if I were you. The heart likes to tell us what we want to hear. If our mouths were as ready to say what our hearts wanted them to, we'd long ago have got into the fashion of wearing locks on our mouths.

MINNA. Ha, ha! You and your mouths with locks on them! That's a fashion I'd approve of!

FRANZISKA. It's better to keep even the prettiest teeth hidden than to have your heart leaping out over them every few minutes.

MINNA. Really? Are you so reserved?

FRANZISKA. No, madam, but I wish I were. People talk very seldom about the virtues they possess and most often about the ones they lack.

MINNA. You know, Franziska, that's a very good observation you've made!

FRANZISKA. Made? Do you really *make* something that just occurs to you?

MINNA. And do you know why I think it's such a good observation? Because it has a lot to do with my Tellheim.

FRANZISKA. Do you ever come across anything that doesn't have some connection with him?

MINNA. His friends and enemies alike say that he is the bravest man in the world. But has anyone ever heard him talk about his bravery? He has the most honest heart on earth, but does he go around proclaiming his honesty and high ideals?

FRANZISKA. What virtues does he talk about, then?

MINNA. He doesn't talk about any, because he lacks none of them.

FRANZISKA. That's just what I wanted to hear.

MINNA. Wait a minute, I do remember one thing. He often talks about economy. You know, in strictest confidence, Franziska, I think he's a bit of a spendthrift.

FRANZISKA. There's one virtue he doesn't have, madam. I've also heard him talk a lot about his sincerity and faithfulness where you are concerned. Does that mean he's a bit of a flirt?

MINNA. You beast!—But you're not serious, are you, Franziska?

FRANZISKA. How long is it since he wrote to you?

MINNA. Oh, he's only written to me once since the armistice!

FRANZISKA. Another complaint against peace! Wonderful! Peace is supposed to make good all the evil caused by the war, but it also seems to destroy whatever good the war brought about. Peace ought not to be so obstinate!—And how long have we been at peace, anyway? Time really drags when there's so little news. There's not much point in having proper postal service again—nobody ever writes, because nobody has anything to write about now that the war is over!

MINNA. "Peace has come," he wrote to me, "and I am approaching the fulfillment of my wishes." But that he should have written only once . . .

FRANZISKA. By doing so, he forces us to rush to the fulfillment of those wishes of his—if we can only find him.—And when we do, we'll make him pay for this! But supposing he had in the meantime fulfilled his wishes, and we were to find out here . . .

MINNA. [*Anxiously, quickly.*] That he was dead?

FRANZISKA. Dead to you, madam; in the arms of another.

MINNA. Oh, you torture me! Just you wait, Franziska, he'll pay you back for that! But go on talking, or we shall fall back to sleep.— His regiment was disbanded after the armistice. Who knows where he stood in all the confusion there must have been over records and accounts? Who knows whether he was posted to another regiment in some distant province? Who knows what the circumstances . . . There's a knock.

FRANZISKA. Come in!

SCENE 2
INNKEEPER, MINNA, *and* FRANZISKA

INNKEEPER. [*Thrusting his head in.*] May I come in, gracious ladies?

FRANZISKA. Is it the innkeeper?—Please come in.

INNKEEPER. [*A feather pen behind his ear, a sheet of paper in one hand, and an inkwell in the other.*] I come, madam, to wish you a most humble good morning—[*To* FRANZISKA.] and you too, my dear.

FRANZISKA. What a polite man!

MINNA. We thank you.

FRANZISKA. And wish you a good morning, too.

INNKEEPER. May I take the liberty of asking how Your Graces rested on your first night under my miserable roof?

FRANZISKA. Well, the roof isn't all that bad, but the beds could have been better.

INNKEEPER. What? Don't tell me that you didn't sleep well! Perhaps you were overtired from the journey.

MINNA. Perhaps.

INNKEEPER. Of course, that's what it was! For otherwise . . . In the meantime, if there is anything that is not completely as it should be for Your Graces' comfort, Your Graces have only to tell me.

FRANZISKA. Very good, sir, very good! And incidentally, we are not stupid and an inn is the last place where you should be stupid. We'll let you know how we'd like everything to be.

INNKEEPER. There's one more thing—[*He takes the pen from behind his ear.*]

FRANZISKA. Well?

INNKEEPER. I am sure that Your Graces are familiar with the regulations that, in their wisdom, our police have made.

MINNA. I'm afraid I am completely unfamiliar with them, sir.

INNKEEPER. We innkeepers are directed not to put up any stranger, no matter what his social class or sex, for more than twenty-four hours without handing in a report to the proper authority giving his name, home address, profession, the business that brings him here, the proposed duration of his stay, etc.

MINNA. Very well.

INNKEEPER. Would Your Graces object, therefore—[*He goes to a table and prepares to write.*]

MINNA. Not at all.—My name is . . .

INNKEEPER. One moment, if you please. [*Writes.*] "Date: arrived here at the King of Spain Inn on the 22nd of August, *anni currentis.*"—Now your name, madam?

MINNA. Fräulein von Barnhelm.

INNKEEPER. [*Writes.*] "Von Barnhelm."—And you come from where, madam?

MINNA. From my estates in Saxony.

INNKEEPER. [*Writes.*] "Estates in Saxony."—Saxony! Ha, ha! Saxony, madam, Saxony?

FRANZISKA. Well, and why not? I take it that it isn't a sin around here to come from Saxony.

INNKEEPER. A sin? Oh, heaven forbid! That would be a brand-new sin to have to add to the list!—So you come from Saxony? Saxony, dear old Saxony!—But if I'm right, madam, Saxony isn't exactly what you would call small, and it has several—how should I call them—districts, provinces. Our police like us to be very precise.

MINNA. I understand. I'm coming from my estates in Thuringia.

INNKEEPER. From Thuringia! Yes, that's better, madam, that's much more precise.—[*Writes and then reads aloud.*] "Fräulein von Barnhelm, coming from her estates in Thuringia together with a lady-in-waiting and two servants."

FRANZISKA. A lady-in-waiting, is that me?

INNKEEPER. That's right, my dear.

FRANZISKA. Now, sir, I think you'd better change that to lady's *maid.*—You said that the police like you to be very precise, and there might be a misunderstanding, which could cause me trouble when my banns are read. For I really am still a maid, and my name is Franziska, surname Willing. Franziska Willing. I'm from Thuringia; my father used to be a miller on one of the lady's estates.

Our village was called Klein-Rammsdorf. My brother owns the mill now. I went to court when I was still very young and was brought up with madam here. We are the same age, twenty-one next Candlemas. Madam and I were taught exactly the same things. It is important that the police should know exactly who I am.

INNKEEPER. Very well, my child, I'll make a note of that in case anyone should inquire.—Now, madam, what is your business here?

MINNA. My business?

INNKEEPER. Is Your Grace perhaps seeking something from His Majesty, the King?

MINNA. Oh, no!

INNKEEPER. Or from the High Court of Justice?

MINNA. No, not that either.

INNKEEPER. Or . . .

MINNA. No, No. I'm here solely on a personal matter.

INNKEEPER. Fine, madam, but what is that personal matter?

MINNA. It concerns . . . Franziska, do you know, I think we're being cross-examined.

FRANZISKA. Sir, surely the police would never insist on knowing a young lady's secrets.

INNKEEPER. Oh certainly, my dear, the police want to know everything, absolutely everything, and especially secrets.

FRANZISKA. What shall we do, madam?—Now listen, sir: it has to stay between us and the police.

MINNA. [*Aside.*] Whatever is the fool going to tell him?

FRANZISKA. We've come to steal an officer from the King—

INNKEEPER. How's that? What? My dear child!

FRANZISKA. Or to let ourselves be stolen away by the officer. It's all the same.

MINNA. Franziska, are you mad?—Sir, this saucy girl is pulling your leg.

INNKEEPER. Well, I hope not! I mean, as far as my humble person is concerned, she can joke as much as she likes, but when it comes to the authorities . . .

MINNA. Do you know what, sir! I really don't know what to do about all this. I should have thought that you'd leave this filling out of forms until my uncle arrives. I told you yesterday why he didn't arrive with me. He had an accident with his coach a couple of miles from here and was determined that I not be delayed another night, so I came on ahead. At the very most he'll only take a day more than I did to get here.

INNKEEPER. All right then, madam, we'll wait for him.

MINNA. He will be able to answer your questions better than I can. He knows to whom he has to tell things, how much to tell, and what he may conceal.

INNKEEPER. So much the better! It's true, you can't ask a young woman [*Giving a meaningful look to* FRANZISKA.] to treat a serious matter seriously among serious people.

MINNA. And the rooms for my uncle, are they ready?

INNKEEPER. Absolutely, madam, absolutely, except for one . . .

FRANZISKA. From which you have had to turn out another honest man?

INNKEEPER. Lady's maids from Saxony, madam, seem to be a wonderfully compassionate lot.

MINNA. It's true, sir, what you did was not right. It would have been better had you not taken us in at all.

INNKEEPER. How so, madam, how so?

MINNA. I hear that the officer who was turned out on our account—

INNKEEPER.—was only a discharged officer, madam.

MINNA. Even so!

INNKEEPER. Who's on his last legs.

MINNA. That makes it worse! He's bound to be a very deserving fellow.

INNKEEPER. But I tell you, he is discharged.

MINNA. The King cannot possibly know of every deserving man who served him.

INNKEEPER. Oh, yes he does; he knows them, all of them.

MINNA. But he can't reward them all.

INNKEEPER. They'd all be rewarded if they had lived properly. But as long as the war was on, these gentlemen lived as if it were going to last forever and as if the idea of other people's wealth and property had been abandoned for good. And so now all the inns are full of them, and a landlord has to be pretty careful. I've managed to get on pretty well with this one. If he didn't actually have any money left, he had valuables, and he could easily have stayed on for another two or three months. Still, it's all for the best that he's leaving.—By the way, madam, do you know anything about jewels?

MINNA. Not especially.

INNKEEPER. I'm sure Your Grace does. I must show you a ring, a valuable ring. You know, you have a very beautiful one on your own finger, and I must say that I'm surprised, because the more I look at it the more it looks just like the one I have.—See for yourself, see for yourself! [*He takes the ring out of its case and hands it to* MINNA.] What luster! The center diamond alone weighs over five carats!

MINNA. [*Looking at the ring.*] Where am I? What do I see? This ring—

INNKEEPER. —at a fair estimate is worth fifteen hundred talers.

MINNA. Franziska, have a look!

INNKEEPER. I didn't hesitate for a moment to lend four hundred on it.

MINNA. Don't you recognize it, Franziska?

FRANZISKA. It's the very same!—Sir, where did you get this ring?

INNKEEPER. Surely you have no claim on it, my dear.

FRANZISKA. No claim on it?—Madam's name is engraved on the inside of that ring. Show him, madam.

MINNA. This is it! This is it!—How did you come by this ring, innkeeper?

INNKEEPER. Me? In the most honorable fashion in the world.— Madam, madam, surely you don't want to cause me disgrace and misfortune. How should I know where the ring originally came from? I do know that during the war a lot of things changed hands very often, with or without the knowledge of the rightful owner. War's war, after all. More than one ring has come over the border from Saxony.—Give it back to me, madam, please give it back!

MINNA. First answer this: from whom did you get it?

INNKEEPER. From a man who I should never have thought was capable of such a thing. From an otherwise very good man.

MINNA. From the best man under the sun, if you got it from its rightful owner.—Hurry, bring this man to me! They have to be one and the same, or at least your man must know where mine is.

INNKEEPER. Who, madam? Who's that?

FRANZISKA. Are you deaf? Our major.

INNKEEPER. Major, that's right, he is a major, the man who had this room before you, and he's the one I got the ring from.

MINNA. Major von Tellheim?

INNKEEPER. Von Tellheim, yes! Do you know him?

MINNA. Do I know him! He was here? Tellheim here? Living in this room? And it was he who pawned the ring with you? How did he get into such a predicament? Where is he? Does he owe you money?—Franziska, bring me the strongbox! Open it! [FRANZISKA *places the box on the table and opens it.*] How much does he owe you? Does he owe money to anyone else? Bring all his creditors to me. Here's cash, ready money. And it all belongs to him!

INNKEEPER. What is all this?

MINNA. Where is he, where is he?

INNKEEPER. He was still here an hour ago.

MINNA. You horrible man, how could you be so unkind to him, so harsh, so cruel?

INNKEEPER. Forgive me, Your Grace—

MINNA. Hurry, bring him to me.

INNKEEPER. His servant may still be here. Does Your Grace want me to look for him?

MINNA. Do I? Hurry, run! If you do me this service, I'll overlook your bad treatment of the major.

FRANZISKA. Hurry, sir, fast! Move, be quick! [*Pushes him out.*]

SCENE 3
MINNA *and* FRANZISKA

MINNA. I've got him back, Franziska! You see, now I've got him back! I'm so happy I don't even know where I am! Rejoice with me, dear Franziska. But then, why should you? Still you ought to, you *have* to rejoice with me. Come, dear, I'll give you gifts and then you'll be able to join me in my happiness. Tell me, Franziska, what shall I give you? What would you like best of all the things I own? Take whatever you want, but rejoice with me. I can see you won't take anything. Wait a minute! [*She reaches into the strongbox.*] There you are, dear Franziska [*She gives her money.*], buy yourself something you'd like. Ask me for more if that's not enough. Only rejoice with me! Oh, it's so sad to have to rejoice alone! Come, take it!

FRANZISKA. I'd be stealing it from you, madam; you're drunk, drunk with happiness.

MINNA. Now, girl, I may be a bit tipsy, but I want you to take it anyway. [*She presses the money into her hand.*] And don't thank me!—Wait a minute; it's a good thing I thought of it. [*She puts her hand into the strongbox again and takes out some more money.*] And this, dear Franziska, set this aside for the first poor wounded soldier we run into.

SCENE 4
INNKEEPER, MINNA, *and* FRANZISKA

MINNA. Well, is he coming?

INNKEEPER. What a miserable, rude fellow he is!

MINNA. Who?

INNKEEPER. His servant. He refuses to go and fetch him.

FRANZISKA. Bring the wretch in here. I know all of the major's servants. Which one was it?

MINNA. Bring him here, quickly. When he sees us, he'll go. [*Exit* INNKEEPER.]

SCENE 5

MINNA *and* FRANZISKA

MINNA. I can hardly wait. But Franziska, why are you still so cold? You still don't want to rejoice with me?

FRANZISKA. I would like to, from the bottom of my heart, if only . . .

MINNA. If only?

FRANZISKA. We have found the major again, but how have we found him? From all that we hear, things are not going well for him. He must be unhappy, and that makes me sad.

MINNA. Makes you sad?—Let me hug you for those words, my dearest friend! I will never forget what you said! I am merely in love, but you are goodness itself.

SCENE 6

INNKEEPER, JUST, MINNA, *and* FRANZISKA

INNKEEPER. I managed to bring him, but it wasn't easy.

FRANZISKA. A stranger! I don't know him.

MINNA. My friend, are you in the service of Major von Tellheim?

JUST. Yes.

MINNA. Where is your master?

JUST. Not here.

MINNA. But you know where to find him?

JUST. Yes.

MINNA. Will you bring him here quickly?

JUST. No.

MINNA. You would be doing me a favor.

JUST. Ha!

MINNA. And your master a service.

JUST. Maybe, maybe not.

MINNA. What makes you think that?

JUST. Aren't you the strangers who sent their regards to him this morning?

MINNA. Yes.

JUST. I'm right, then.

MINNA. Does your master know my name?

JUST. No, but he dislikes over-polite ladies as much as he dislikes excessively rude landlords.

INNKEEPER. Are you referring to me?

JUST. Yes.

INNKEEPER. You don't need to take out your frustrations on madam, here. Go get your master, and hurry.

MINNA. [*In a low voice to* FRANZISKA.] Give him a little something.

FRANZISKA. [*Trying to press money into* JUST's *hand*.] We're not asking you to do this service for nothing.

JUST. And I'm not asking you for money without doing you a service.

FRANZISKA. Fair exchange.

JUST. But I can't help you. My master has told me to move his things out. That's what I'm doing, and I'd be grateful if you didn't hold me up any longer. When I'm finished, I'll tell him that you want him. He's next door in the café, and when he gets tired of being there, he'll probably come up here. [*Starts to leave*.]

FRANZISKA. Wait a moment. Madam is the major's—sister.

MINNA. Yes, yes, his sister.

JUST. I know better than that. The major hasn't got any sisters. Twice in six months, he sent me on an errand to his family in the Kurland.—Of course, there are sisters, and then there are sisters!

FRANZISKA. You scoundrel!

JUST. Don't you have to be one in order to get people to stop bothering you? [*Exit*.]

FRANZISKA. Devil!

INNKEEPER. Well, I told you. Let him go. I know now where his master is. I'll fetch him myself at once.—But madam, I ask you most humbly to apologize to the major for me for my being put in the unfortunate position of having to inconvenience, against my will, a man of his worth.

MINNA. Just go quickly, innkeeper. I will see that everything turns out all right. [*Exit* INNKEEPER.] Franziska, run after him and make sure that he doesn't mention my name! [*Exit* FRANZISKA.]

SCENE 7
MINNA *and, afterwards,* FRANZISKA

MINNA. I've got him back!—Am I alone?—I should make use of this time. [*She folds her hands*.] Now I'm not alone! [*Looking up*.] A single, thankful thought directed toward heaven is the perfect prayer!—I have found him, I have found him! [*She flings her arms wide*.] I am so happy, oh so happy! And what can be more pleasing to God's eyes than a joyful creature? [*Enter* FRANZISKA.] Back again, Franziska?—You feel sorry for him? I don't feel sorry for him. Unhappiness is good, too. Perhaps heaven took everything away from him in order to give it all back in the form of me!

FRANZISKA. He may be here at any moment, and you're still in your négligée, madam. Why don't you hurry and get dressed?

MINNA. Please go. From now on he will see me like this more often than he will see me all dressed up.

FRANZISKA. You certainly know best, madam.

MINNA. [*After brief reflection.*] That's right.

FRANZISKA. A beautiful woman is most beautiful without make-up.

MINNA. But do we have to be beautiful?—I suppose it's necessary for us to think that we are beautiful.—No, as long as he thinks I'm beautiful!—Franziska, if all girls feel as I do at this moment, then we are—strange young creatures. At once delicate and proud, virtuous and vain, sensual and pious. You can't understand me, and I don't think I even understand myself. Joy makes you dizzy, giddy.

FRANZISKA. Pull yourself together, madam. I hear someone coming—

MINNA. Pull myself together? Shall I receive him without showing my feelings?

SCENE 8

TELLHEIM, INNKEEPER, MINNA, *and* FRANZISKA

TELLHEIM. [*Seeing* MINNA *and at once rushing up to her.*] Oh, my Minna!

MINNA. [*Going toward him.*] Oh, my Tellheim!

TELLHEIM. [*Stopping suddenly and turning back.*] Forgive me, madam—but to find Fräulein von Barnhelm here—

MINNA. Surely it can't be entirely unexpected. [*As she moves nearer to him, he withdraws further.*] Am I to forgive you because I am still your Minna? Or is heaven to forgive you because I am still Fräulein von Barnhelm!

TELLHEIM. Madam! [*He looks at the* INNKEEPER *and shrugs his shoulders.*]

MINNA. [*Growing aware of the* INNKEEPER, *she motions to* FRANZISKA *to get rid of him. To* TELLHEIM.] Sir . . .

TELLHEIM. Perhaps we are both mistaken . . .

FRANZISKA. Innkeeper, who's this you've brought us? Come along, quickly, let's go and find the right one.

INNKEEPER. Isn't he the right one? He must be!

FRANZISKA. Oh no, he mustn't! Hurry up, let's go; I haven't said good morning to your daughter yet.

INNKEEPER. [*Without budging.*] Oh, don't honor us!

FRANZISKA. [*Taking hold of him.*] Come and show me the menu. I want to know what we're going to have.

INNKEEPER. The first thing you're going to have . . .

FRANZISKA. Quiet, quiet! If madam finds out beforehand what she's eating for lunch, it spoils her appetite. Come, you can tell me in private what's on the menu. [*Forces him to leave with her.*]

SCENE 9
TELLHEIM *and* MINNA

MINNA. Well, are we still making a mistake?

TELLHEIM. I wish to heaven we were! But there is only *one* Minna, and that's you.

MINNA. What a lot of fuss! Why shouldn't the whole world hear what we have to say to each other?

TELLHEIM. You here? What are you looking for here, madam?

MINNA. I'm no longer looking for anything. [*Runs to him with open arms.*] I have found everything I wanted.

TELLHEIM. [*Backing away.*] You were looking for a happy man, worthy of your love, and you have found—a wretched one.

MINNA. So you don't love me anymore; do you love someone else?

TELLHEIM. A man who could love someone else could never have loved you.

MINNA. You remove but *one* thorn from my flesh. If I have lost your love, who cares whether I have lost it to your indifference or to another woman's charms?—You no longer love me, and yet you do not love another?—Unhappy the man who loves no one at all!

TELLHEIM. True, madam. The man who is unhappy must abandon all love. He deserves his misfortune if he is unable to do so, if he can permit himself to stand by and watch while those he loves participate in his misfortune.—Ever since reason and necessity bade me forget Minna von Barnhelm, what an effort I have made to do so, to achieve this difficult victory over myself. I had just begun to hope that this effort would not forever be in vain—and you appear, madam!

MINNA. Do I understand you correctly? One moment, sir, and let us see where we are before we say anything more!—Would you answer me just one question?

TELLHEIM. As many as you like, madam.

MINNA. Will you answer me without quibbling or evading the issue? With nothing but a simple "yes" or "no"?

TELLHEIM. I will—if I can.

MINNA. You can.—Good: forgetting for the moment the effort you made to forget me, do you still love me, Tellheim?

TELLHEIM. Madam, this question . . .

MINNA. You promised to answer only "yes" or "no."

TELLHEIM. But I did add, "If I can."

MINNA. You can; you must know what is going on in your own heart. Do you still love me, Tellheim? Yes or no?

TELLHEIM. If my heart . . .

MINNA. Yes or no!

TELLHEIM. Well, yes!

MINNA. Yes?

TELLHEIM. Yes, yes, except . . .

MINNA. Stop!—You still love me: that's enough for me.—What kind of tone am I using? A hostile, melancholic, contagious one.—I shall speak in my own tone again. Now, my beloved, unhappy one, you still love me and you still have your Minna, so why are you unhappy? Just let me tell you what a vain and foolish creature your Minna was—and is. She allowed herself to dream that she was your whole happiness, and she still allows herself this conceit. Quickly, show her the cause of your unhappiness and let her see how much of it she can counterbalance. Well?

TELLHEIM. Madam, I am not in the habit of complaining.

MINNA. Good for you. I certainly cannot imagine a quality, after boastfulness, that would please me less in a soldier than complaining. But there is a certain cold, disinterested way in which you can speak about your bravery, on the one hand, and your misfortune, on the other.

TELLHEIM. In the end it's still boasting and complaining, though.

MINNA. Argue, argue, argue! In that case you should never have said you were unhappy. Either be completely quiet about the matter or be totally open in discussing it!—So reason and necessity bade you forget me? I am a great admirer of reason, and I have a whole lot of respect for necessity; but tell me, if you would, how reasonable this reason is, how necessary this necessity.

TELLHEIM. Very well, madam, then listen to me. You call me Tellheim, and this is indeed my name. But you imagine when you say it that I am the same Tellheim you knew in your native country, a man in the bloom of youth, full of prospects, full of ambition, and completely in control of his body and his soul; a man to whom every frontier of honor and happiness was open and who, even if he was not yet worthy of you, hoped to grow more worthy each day of your heart and hand.—I am as far from being this Tellheim as I am from being my own father. Both are part of the past. I am Tellheim the discharged soldier, with his honor wounded, Tellheim the cripple and the beggar. You promised yourself to the other Tellheim, madam; do you wish to keep your word to this one?

MINNA. That sounds very tragic! But, sir, until I find the other one again—I am really rather fond of Tellheims, as you can see— this one will do for the moment.—Give me your hand, dear beggar! [*Takes his hand.*]

TELLHEIM. [*Putting his other hand in front of his face and turning away from her.*] This is too much!—Where am I?—Let me go, madam! Your goodness tortures me!—Let me go!

MINNA. What has come over you? Where do you want to go?

TELLHEIM. Away from you!

MINNA. Away from me? [*Draws his hand to her breast.*] Dreamer!

TELLHEIM. I will die of despair right here if you don't let me go.

MINNA. Away from me?

TELLHEIM. Yes, away from you, never, never to see you again! Or at least in my position I am quite resolved, very firmly resolved, to do nothing ignoble, nor to allow you to do anything rash.—Let me go, Minna! [*Tears himself away from her and exits.*]

MINNA. [*Calling after him.*] Minna let you go? Tellheim! Tellheim!

Act 3

SCENE I
The Parlor

JUST. [*A letter in his hand.*] Do I have to come back into this damned house again?—A note from my master to the young lady who says she's his sister.—I hope there's nothing brewing between them! Otherwise there'll be no end of carrying notes back and forth. I'd really like to get rid of this note, but I don't want to have to go up to the room. That woman asks so many questions, and I don't like answering them!—Wait a minute, the door's opening. How lucky! It's the lady's maid!

SCENE 2
FRANZISKA *and* JUST

FRANZISKA. [*Calling back through the door through which she has just come.*] Don't worry, I'll be careful! [*She catches sight of* JUST.] Look out, here's someone getting in my way already! There's no way around this brute, though.

JUST. Your servant.

FRANZISKA. I wouldn't want a servant like you.

JUST. It's only a manner of speaking, you know!—I was just bringing a note from my master to your mistress, the young lady—his sister. Wasn't that it? Sister?

FRANZISKA. Give it to me! [*Snatches the note out of his hand.*]

JUST. "Would you be so good," my master says, "as to give it to her? And afterwards would you be so good," my master says—I don't want you to think that *I* am asking for anything!

FRANZISKA. Go on.

JUST. My master knows what's what. He knows that the way to a young lady is through her maid—at least, that's what I think is going through his mind! "Would the young maid be good enough," my master says, "to let him know whether he might have the pleasure of speaking with the young maid for a quarter of an hour?"

FRANZISKA. Do you mean me?

JUST. You'll excuse me if I'm referring to you by the wrong title.—Yes, you! Just a quarter of an hour, but alone, absolutely alone, in secret, tête-à-tête. He has something very important to tell you.

FRANZISKA. Well, I've got a few things to tell him, too! Let him come and I'll meet with him.

JUST. But when can he come? When is it most convenient for you? This evening?

FRANZISKA. What do you mean? Your master can come when he wants to, and now be off with you!

JUST. With pleasure! [*Starts to leave.*]

FRANZISKA. Wait a minute, there's just one more thing. Where are the major's other servants?

JUST. The other ones? They're here, there, everywhere.

FRANZISKA. Where's William?

JUST. The valet? The major let him take a trip.

FRANZISKA. Oh? And Philip, where is he?

JUST. The gamekeeper? The major left him in good hands.

FRANZISKA. Doubtless because the major's not doing any hunting at the moment. But what about Martin?

JUST. The coachman? He took a ride.

FRANZISKA. And Fritz?

JUST. The footman? He's been given a promotion.

FRANZISKA. Where were you, then, when the major was with us in Thuringia at his winter quarters? Were you not yet in his service?

JUST. Oh yes, I was a groom, but I was in the hospital at the time.

FRANZISKA. A groom? And what are you now?

JUST. A bit of everything—valet, gamekeeper, footman, and groom.

FRANZISKA. Well, I declare! Letting so many good people go and keeping the worst one of all! I'd like to know what your master sees in you.

JUST. Perhaps he thinks I'm an honest person.

FRANZISKA. People who have only honesty to recommend them don't get very far.—Now William, there was a man! And your master let him go off on a trip?

JUST. Yes, he let him—he couldn't stop him.

FRANZISKA. How so?

JUST. William'll cut a good figure on his travels; he took the master's whole wardrobe with him.

FRANZISKA. What? You mean he made off with it?

JUST. Well, you couldn't exactly say that; but after we left Nuremberg, he just didn't bother to follow us with it.

FRANZISKA. What a rogue!

JUST. He was quite a chap—could cut your hair, shave you, chat with you . . . and charm you, couldn't he?

FRANZISKA. But still, I wouldn't have let the gamekeeper go if I had been the major. Even if I couldn't use him as a gamekeeper, he was still a hard-working sort of fellow.—Who has charge of him now?

JUST. The Commandant of Spandau.

FRANZISKA. The fort? Surely there can't be much hunting on the ramparts.

JUST. Well, Philip isn't actually hunting there.

FRANZISKA. What's he doing then?

JUST. He's pushing a wheelbarrow.

FRANZISKA. Pushing a wheelbarrow?

JUST. But only for three years. He hatched a little plot among the soldiers in my master's company and was going to take six deserters through the lines.

FRANZISKA. I can't believe it! The devil!

JUST. Oh, he's a hard-working chap, all right. He knows every highway, byway, and footpath for fifty miles 'round, and can he ever shoot!

FRANZISKA. It's lucky the major still has his good old coachman.

JUST. Has he still got him?

FRANZISKA. I thought you said that Martin had taken a ride somewhere. I suppose he'll be back, won't he?

JUST. You think so?

FRANZISKA. Where has he gone?

JUST. It's about ten weeks since he rode off with the master's one and only horse, which he had taken out to water.

FRANZISKA. And he hasn't come back yet? Oh, the scoundrel!

JUST. Of course he may have taken a drop more to drink than his horse!—He was a proper coachman, he was! He'd driven in Vienna for ten years. The master won't get another like him. Why, when the horses were at full gallop, he only had to say "Whoa," and they stood stock-still. And what's more, he was a trained horse-doctor!

FRANZISKA. After all that, I'm afraid to ask about the footman's promotion.

JUST. No, no, that's a fact. He's a drummer in a garrison regiment.

FRANZISKA. I thought he'd be all right!

JUST. Fritz fell in with a bad lot, never came home at night, ran up debts everywhere in the master's name, and got into all kinds of dirty business. In short, the major saw that he really wanted to rise in the world [He pantomimes hanging.], so he helped him along the way. The drum-roll that he now plays at others' executions will be the same drum-roll he hears at his own!

FRANZISKA. What a wretch that Fritz is!

JUST. But he was a perfect footman, that's certain. Give him a fifty-pace head start, and my master couldn't overtake him with his fastest horse. If Fritz gave the gallows a thousand-pace head start, though, I'd bet my life he'd still catch up with it.—They were all good friends of yours, were they? William, Philip, Martin, and Fritz? Well, Just, the last of them, bids you good day! [Exit.]

SCENE 3
FRANZISKA and, afterwards, the INNKEEPER

FRANZISKA. [Looking earnestly after him.] I deserved that. Thank you, Just. I set too low a price on honesty, and I won't forget the lesson you've taught me. Oh, how unlucky the major is! [Turns and is about to go into MINNA's room when the INNKEEPER enters.]

INNKEEPER. Wait a minute, my dear.

FRANZISKA. I don't have time right now, sir.

INNKEEPER. Just one little moment!—Still no more news of the major? Surely he hasn't left.

FRANZISKA. What else?

INNKEEPER. Didn't your mistress tell you? When I left you down in the kitchen, my dear, I happened to come back into this room.

FRANZISKA. You just happened to, on purpose, so that you could do a bit of eavesdropping.

INNKEEPER. My dear child, how could you think such a thing of me? There's nothing worse than an inquisitive innkeeper.—I hadn't been here long when the door of madam's room suddenly burst open. The major rushed out and the young lady followed him, but in quite a state, exchanging glances—oh, you had to be there to appreciate it. She grabbed hold of him, he tore himself away, she grabbed him again. "Tellheim!"—"Madam, let me go!"—"Where are you going?"—He dragged her with him to the head of the stairs, and I was afraid they were going to fall down, but he slipped out of her clutches at the last moment. The young lady stood there calling after him and wringing her hands. Then suddenly she turned 'round, ran to the window, from the window back to the stairs, and from there she started pacing back and forth in this room. I was standing right in front of her and she passed me by three times without seeing me. Finally she seemed to see me but, God help us, I think the young lady took me for you, my dear. "Franziska," she cried, looking at me, "am I happy now?" Then she looked straight up at the ceiling and cried out again, "Am I happy now?" After that she wiped the tears from her eyes, smiled, and asked me yet again, "Franziska, am I happy now?"—Honestly, I didn't know what to do. Next thing she does is run to her door; there she turned to me once more and said, "Come along, Franziska; who's making you sad now?"—And in she went.

FRANZISKA. You must have dreamt it.

INNKEEPER. Dreamt it? No, no, my child, one doesn't dream in such detail. Yes, I'd give a lot—not that I'm nosey, mind you—but I'd give a lot to have the key to that.

FRANZISKA. The key? To our door? That's on the inside, sir. We took it in last night and locked up; we're scared and don't want to tempt anyone.

INNKEEPER. I don't mean a key like that. What I mean, my dear, is a key to everything I saw, something to explain the events I witnessed.

FRANZISKA. Ah, yes!—Well, adieu, sir.—By the way, are we going to eat soon?

INNKEEPER. I almost forgot what I really wanted to say.

FRANZISKA. And what's that? Make it quick, though!

INNKEEPER. The young lady still has my ring; I call it mine, in any event.

FRANZISKA. It's in safe keeping, I can assure you.

INNKEEPER. I'm not worried about that; I just wanted to remind you. You see, I don't even want it back again. I can easily guess how she recognized the ring and why it looked to her so like her own. She's the best one to look after it. I don't want it anymore, and I'll charge the young lady's account with the five hundred talers I lent on it. That's all right, my dear, isn't it?

SCENE 4

PAUL WERNER, INNKEEPER, *and* FRANZISKA

WERNER. There he is!

FRANZISKA. Five hundred talers? I thought it was only four hundred.

INNKEEPER. That's right, four hundred and fifty, only four hundred and fifty. That's what I'll do then, my dear, charge it to the young lady's account.

FRANZISKA. Well, sir, we'll have to see.

WERNER. [*Coming up behind her and then clapping her on the shoulder.*] Little lady, little lady!

FRANZISKA. [*Startled.*] Hey!

WERNER. Don't be frightened, little lady!—I see that you're pretty and a stranger here, and pretty strangers have to be warned.—Little lady, beware of this man! [*Points at* INNKEEPER.]

INNKEEPER. What an unexpected pleasure! Herr Paul Werner! Welcome to my inn, welcome! Still the same old jolly, funny, honest Werner.—You beware of me, my dear? Ha, ha, ha!

WERNER. Keep out of his way, whatever you do!

INNKEEPER. Out of my way? Am I so dangerous? Ha, ha, ha!—Just listen to that, my dear! How do you like the joke?

WERNER. People like him always pass the truth off as a joke.

INNKEEPER. The truth! Ha, ha, ha! It gets better and better, doesn't it, my dear? He really knows how to joke! Me, dangerous? Me?—Now twenty years ago there might have been something to that. Yes, child, then I was dangerous, as many could attest; but now . . .

WERNER. There's no fool like an old fool!

INNKEEPER. That's the trouble: when we get old, we're not dangerous anymore. You'll be in the same boat one day, Herr Werner!

WERNER. I've never heard anything like it!—Young lady, you know that I wasn't talking about *that* sort of danger. One devil was cast out, and seven others have taken its place inside him.

INNKEEPER. Listen to him, just listen to him! See how he's managed to bring the subject 'round again! One joke after another, and always something new! Oh, he's a splendid man, our Paul Werner! [*Whispering to* FRANZISKA.] And a wealthy man, too, and a bachelor. He has a beautiful farm about three miles from here. He made a little pile in the war, you see! And he was a sergeant major in the major's regiment. Oh, this is a friend of the major's! He's a real friend, one who would die for him!

WERNER. Yes, and you're a friend of my major's—one he should have killed!

INNKEEPER. What! How's that?—No, Herr Werner, that's not a nice joke at all. Me not a friend of the major's?—No, that's a joke I don't understand.

WERNER. Just told me a few nice things about you.

INNKEEPER. Just? I thought I recognized the voice of Just in this. Just is an evil-speaking, mean fellow. But right here there's a nice young thing who can tell you whether I'm a friend of the major's or not, whether I haven't done him a few services! And why shouldn't I be a friend to the major? Isn't he a worthy man? It's true he had the misfortune to be discharged, but what does that matter? The King cannot possibly know of all the worthy men who served him, and even if he did know them, he couldn't reward all of them.

WERNER. God's the one making him talk like that! Now Just— there's certainly nothing special about Just, but a liar he's not. And if what he told me was true . . .

INNKEEPER. I don't want to hear anything about Just! As I said, this lovely child here can speak for me!—[*Whispering to* FRANZISKA.] You know, my dear, the ring!—Tell Herr Werner. That way he'll get to know me better. And so that it won't appear as if you're just saying things to please me, I'll leave. But you'll have to repeat her words to me, Herr Werner; you'll have to repeat them and then tell me whether Just isn't a dirty slanderer.

SCENE 5
PAUL WERNER *and* FRANZISKA

WERNER. Well, little lady, so you know my major?

FRANZISKA. Major von Tellheim? Certainly I know him; he's a good man.

WERNER. Isn't he a good man? Are you perhaps a friend of his?

FRANZISKA. From the bottom of my heart.

WERNER. Really? You know, little lady, when you say that, you seem twice as pretty to me.—But what are these services that the innkeeper says he did for the major?

FRANZISKA. I'm sure I don't know, unless he's trying to take credit for something that happened for the good in spite of his rotten behavior.

WERNER. So it was true, then, what Just told me? [*Turning to the side where the* INNKEEPER *has exited.*] Lucky for you that you left!—He really turned the major out of his room? Imagine playing a trick like that on a man like that, simply because the idiot thought the major didn't have any money left! The major, no money!

FRANZISKA. What, you mean the major does have money?

WERNER. Piles of it! He doesn't know how much he's got. He doesn't know who owes him what. I owe him money myself, and I've brought a bit of it with me. Look, little lady, in this purse [*Taking a purse from his pocket.*] there are five hundred talers. And in this little roll [*He takes the roll from his other pocket.*], three hundred. All his money!

FRANZISKA. Really? Then why does the major have to pawn things? He pawned a ring.

WERNER. Pawned? Don't you believe it! Perhaps he just wanted to get rid of a piece of junk.

FRANZISKA. But it's not junk! It's a valuable ring that he received from a very dear person.

WERNER. That's it, then: from a very dear person. Of course! A thing like that often reminds you of something you'd rather not be reminded of. So you get rid of it.

FRANZISKA. What are you saying?

WERNER. Some funny things happen to a soldier when he's in winter quarters. There's nothing to do, so out of boredom and to amuse himself, he strikes up acquaintances that he intends only for the winter, but that his acquaintances, the kind hearts, assume are for life. The next thing you know, someone's popped a ring on his finger; he himself doesn't even know how it got there. And as often as not, he'd gladly cut off his finger just to get rid of that ring.

FRANZISKA. Oh, and do you think this happened to the major?

WERNER. I'm sure of it. Especially in Saxony. If he had had ten fingers on each hand, all twenty would have had rings on them.

FRANZISKA. [*Aside.*] This sounds very odd; I'll have to look into it.—Herr Werner . . .

WERNER. Little lady, if it's all the same to you, I'd rather you called me sergeant major.

FRANZISKA. All right, sergeant major, but I've got a note here from the major to my mistress. I'll just take it in quickly and come right back. Will you be good enough to wait? I'd very much like to chat with you some more.

WERNER. Do you like having a chat, little lady? By all means, go ahead and deliver your note. I like a chat, too, and I'll wait here for you.

FRANZISKA. Oh yes, please wait! [*Exit.*]

SCENE 6
WERNER

WERNER. That's not a bad little lady! But I should never have promised to wait, because the most important thing is to find the major. So, he doesn't want my money and would rather pawn things. That's typical.—I've just thought of something. When I was in town two weeks ago, I visited Marloff's widow. The poor woman was ill and was lamenting the fact that her dead husband owed the major four hundred talers, which she didn't know how she was going to pay back. I was going to visit her again today and tell her that I could lend her the three hundred talers I got upon the sale of my farm, plus another two hundred. I wanted at least some of my money to be safe in case things don't work out in Persia.—But she's gone, and I'm certain she hasn't been able to pay the major.—Yes, that's what I'll do, and the sooner the better. The little lady mustn't take this the wrong way, but I just can't wait for her at the moment. [*Exits deep in thought and almost collides with* TELLHEIM, *who enters at the same time.*]

SCENE 7
TELLHEIM *and* WERNER

TELLHEIM. Lost in thought, Werner?

WERNER. Ah, there you are. I was just coming to call on you in your new quarters, major.

TELLHEIM. So that you could bombard my ears with curses against my old landlord? Please spare me that!

WERNER. Yes, I would probably have done that as well. But what I really wanted to do was to thank you for looking after the five hundred talers for me. Just gave them back to me. I must admit that I would have been grateful if you could have kept them for me a bit longer. But you've moved to new quarters that neither of us knows anything about. Who knows what it's like there? The money might be stolen from you, and then you'd have to replace it; it couldn't be helped. And I can't give you that kind of responsibility.

TELLHEIM. [*Smiling.*] Since when have you been so careful, Werner?

WERNER. It's something you learn. You can't be too careful with your money these days.—And there was another thing, Major, concerning Frau Marloff; I've just come from her. Her husband owed you four hundred talers, and she sends three hundred in partial payment. She'll give you the rest next week. It could be that

I'm the cause of her not sending the whole sum, because she owed me a taler and eighty groschen, and as she thought I had come to pester her about it—which was probably the case—she paid me out of the money she'd set aside for you. It's easier for you to wait a week for your hundred talers than it is for me to wait that long for my few groschen.—There you are! [*Hands him the roll of money.*]

TELLHEIM. Werner!

WERNER. Why are you staring at me like that?—Take it, sir!

TELLHEIM. Werner!

WERNER. What's the matter? What's upset you?

TELLHEIM. [*Bitterly, striking himself on the forehead and stamping his foot.*] That . . . that the whole four hundred talers aren't there.

WERNER. But, major, didn't you understand what I said?

TELLHEIM. It's just because I did understand you! Why is it that on this day the finest people torment me the most?

WERNER. What did you say?

TELLHEIM. You're only half the problem.—Leave me, Werner! [*He pushes aside the hand in which* WERNER *holds the money.*]

WERNER. As soon as I've got rid of this!

TELLHEIM. Werner, supposing I was to tell you that Frau Marloff had been here early this morning?

WERNER. So?

TELLHEIM. And that she doesn't owe me anything?

WERNER. Really?

TELLHEIM. That she paid her husband's debt down to the last penny? What would you say to that?

WERNER. [*Pausing for a moment.*] I'd say that I'd lied and that lying is a dirty business, because you can get caught at it.

TELLHEIM. And would you feel ashamed of yourself?

WERNER. But what about the person who forced me into lying, what about him? Shouldn't he also be ashamed of himself? Now look, major, if I didn't come straight out and tell you that I don't like the way you're carrying on, I'd be lying again, and I don't want to lie anymore.

TELLHEIM. Don't be angry, Werner! I recognize your goodness of heart and your affection for me, but I don't need your money.

WERNER. You don't need it? You'd rather sell some things and pawn others and have people talking about you?

TELLHEIM. I don't care if people know that I have nothing left. No one should wish to appear more wealthy than he is.

WERNER. But why should he appear poorer?—As long as your friends have means, you have means, too.

TELLHEIM. It would not be proper for me to be in your debt.

WERNER. Wouldn't be proper?—Don't you remember that day when the sun and the enemy were making things hot for us and your groom had got lost with the canteens, and you came to me and said, "Werner, have you got anything to drink?" And I handed you my water bottle, which you took and drank from? Was that proper? Upon my poor soul, if a drink of stagnant water at that time wasn't worth more than all this rubbish! [*Taking out the purse containing five hundred talers and offering* TELLHEIM *both that and the previous three hundred.*] Please take it, major! Imagine that it's water. God made money for everybody, too.

TELLHEIM. You're torturing me. You heard me: I do not want to be in your debt.

WERNER. First it wasn't proper to be in my debt, and now you don't want to be? Well, that's something different again. [*Somewhat angrily.*] You don't want to be in my debt, but supposing you were already in my debt, major? Or don't you owe anything to the man who warded off the blow that would have split your head in two, or who another time chopped off the arm that was going to put a bullet through your heart? How can you get further into this man's debt? Or is my neck worth less than my purse? If that's your way of thinking, then upon my soul, it's a pretty poor way!

TELLHEIM. Why are you talking to me like this, Werner? We are alone now, and I can speak frankly; if a third party were listening to our conversation, it would sound like a lot of hot air. I'll gladly admit that I have you to thank for saving my life on a couple of occasions. But, my friend, wouldn't I have done exactly the same for you, had the opportunity arisen?

WERNER. Had the opportunity arisen? Who has any doubts about that, major? Haven't I seen you risk your life a hundred times for the commonest soldier in a jam?

TELLHEIM. Very well!

WERNER. But . . .

TELLHEIM. Why can't you understand me? I say, it is not proper for me to be in your debt; I do not wish to be in your debt. At least not under the circumstances in which I find myself at the moment.

WERNER. Ah ha! You want to wait until things get better. You want to borrow money from me another time, when you don't need it, when you've got money and I haven't any.

TELLHEIM. No one should borrow if he doesn't know how he's going to pay the money back.

WERNER. But a man like you won't always be wanting.

TELLHEIM. Tell the world that!—And anyway, the last person to borrow money from is someone who needs it himself.

WERNER. Oh, and that's me, is it? What do I need money for? As a sergeant major, I'm well provided for.

TELLHEIM. You need it so that you can become more than a mere sergeant major. So that you can make your way in a career in which even the worthiest man cannot succeed if he has no money.

WERNER. Be more than a sergeant major? I wouldn't dream of it. I'm a good sergeant major and I might become a bad captain and certainly an even worse general. I've seen that happen in other men.

TELLHEIM. Please don't make me think anything that is unworthy of you, Werner! I wasn't exactly pleased to hear from Just that you've sold your farm and want to go off on some expedition again. I would rather not have to believe that it's not so much the career you enjoy as the wild, dissolute life that, unfortunately, goes along with it. A man should be a soldier in order to fight for his country or for a cause, not to serve as a mercenary one day here and the next day there. That's no better than being a butcher's boy.

WERNER. Well, you're right, major. I'll follow your advice and stick with you. You know best in these matters.—But major, please take my money for the time being. Sooner or later all your business will be settled and you'll get piles of money. Then you can pay me back with interest. Take it from me, I'm only doing it for the interest.

TELLHEIM. I don't want to hear another word about your money!

WERNER. Upon my soul, I'm only doing it for the interest! Sometimes I think, "What's going to happen to me in my old age, when I'm hacked to bits, when I'm penniless, when I have to go begging?" Then I conclude, "No, I won't have to go begging; I'll go to Major Tellheim: he'll share his last penny with me; he'll look after me for the rest of my life; he'll see that I die as an honest man."

TELLHEIM. [*Taking* WERNER's *hand.*] And, my friend, don't you still believe this?

WERNER. No, I don't believe it anymore. If someone won't accept something from me when he needs it and I have it, then he won't give me anything when he has it and I need it.—That's all! [*Starts to exit.*]

TELLHEIM. Werner, don't drive me out of my mind! Where are you going? [*Holds him back.*] Suppose I were to assure you, on my honor, that I still have some money, that I will tell you when I have no more, and that you will be the first and only person from whom I borrow any? Will that satisfy you?

WERNER. How could it not?—Give me your hand on it, major!

TELLHEIM. There, Paul! [*They shake hands.*]—I'm glad that's

over with. I came here in the first place to speak with a particular
girl.

SCENE 8
FRANZISKA, *coming out of* MINNA's *room*; TELLHEIM; *and*
WERNER

FRANZISKA. [*Coming out.*] Are you still here, sergeant major?—
[*She sees* TELLHEIM.] And you're here too, major? I'll be with you
both in an instant. [*Goes quickly back into the room.*]

SCENE 9
TELLHEIM *and* PAUL WERNER

TELLHEIM. She's the one! And it sounds as if you know her, too,
Werner.

WERNER. Yes, I know the little lady.

TELLHEIM. Yet if I remember correctly, when I was in winter
quarters in Thuringia, you were not with me.

WERNER. No, I was seeing about some equipment in Leipzig.

TELLHEIM. Then how do you know her?

WERNER. Our acquaintanceship is still in its infancy: it dates
from today. But a young acquaintanceship is a warm one.

TELLHEIM. So have you also met her mistress?

WERNER. Is her mistress a young lady? She told me that you
knew her mistress.

TELLHEIM. Haven't you figured it out? I met them both in
Thuringia.

WERNER. Is the young lady beautiful?

TELLHEIM. Yes, very beautiful.

WERNER. Rich?

TELLHEIM. Very rich.

WERNER. Is the young lady as friendly with you as the girl was?
That would be splendid!

TELLHEIM. What do you mean?

SCENE 10
FRANZISKA, *coming out of the room again with a letter in her
hand*; TELLHEIM; *and* PAUL WERNER

FRANZISKA. Major . . .

TELLHEIM. My dear Franziska, I haven't had the chance yet to
bid you welcome.

FRANZISKA. I'm sure you've already done so in your thoughts. I know that you like me. And I like you, too. And it isn't nice to sneak up on people who like you.

WERNER. [*Aside.*] Ha, I understand! That's right!

TELLHEIM. What is my fate, Franziska? Have you given her the letter?

FRANZISKA. Yes, and this one is for you. [*Hands him the letter.*]

TELLHEIM. An answer?

FRANZISKA. No, your own letter back.

TELLHEIM. What? She wouldn't read it?

FRANZISKA. She wanted to, but—we can't read handwriting very well.

TELLHEIM. You're teasing me!

FRANZISKA. And we think that letter-writing is not intended for those who can communicate by word-of-mouth whenever they want.

TELLHEIM. What an excuse! She must read it. It contains my vindication, all the reasons and grounds—

FRANZISKA. Madam would like to hear them from your own lips and not read about them.

TELLHEIM. Hear them from my own lips? So that her every word, her every facial expression will confuse me? So that I shall see in each look she gives me how great my loss is?

FRANZISKA. No mercy!—Take it! [*Gives him the letter.*] She will expect you at three. She wants to take a ride and look at the town. You are to go with her.

TELLHEIM. Go with her?

FRANZISKA. And what will you give me if I let you two go alone? I want to stay at home.

TELLHEIM. All alone?

FRANZISKA. In a nice closed carriage.

TELLHEIM. Impossible!

FRANZISKA. Yes, yes; in a carriage you will have to face the music, major. You can't escape there. That's why we've arranged it like that. In short, major, you will come at three sharp.—Well? You wanted in addition to speak with me privately. What have you got to say to me?—[*As she catches sight of* WERNER.] But then we are not alone.

TELLHEIM. Oh yes, Franziska, we would be alone. But since your mistress has not read the letter, I don't have anything to say to you yet.

FRANZISKA. Oh, so we would be alone? You have no secrets from the sergeant major?

TELLHEIM. No, none.

FRANZISKA. And yet it seems to me that there are some you should have.

TELLHEIM. What do you mean?

WERNER. Why should he, little lady?

FRANZISKA. Especially secrets of a certain kind.—All twenty, sergeant major? [*Holding up both hands with the fingers spread apart.*]

WERNER. Sh, sh! Little lady, little lady!

TELLHEIM. What's going on?

FRANZISKA. "And the next thing you know, someone's popped a ring on your finger," eh, sergeant major? [*She mimes placing a ring on her finger as she speaks.*]

TELLHEIM. What are you two talking about?

WERNER. Little lady, little lady, surely you know a joke when you hear one.

TELLHEIM. And you, Werner, surely haven't forgotten what I have so often told you: there is a certain point beyond which you should never joke with women.

WERNER. Upon my soul, I guess I forgot.—Little lady, please . . .

FRANZISKA. Well, if it was a joke, I'll forgive you this time.

TELLHEIM. If I really have to come, Franziska, please see that your mistress reads the letter beforehand. That will spare me the pain of having once more to think things and say things that I would so like to forget. There, give it to her. [*He gives the letter back to her, and in so doing becomes aware that it has been opened.*] Do my eyes deceive me, Franziska, or has this letter been opened?

FRANZISKA. Perhaps it has. [*Looks at it.*] That's right, it has been opened. I wonder who did that? But we really haven't read it, major, honestly. And we don't want to read it, because the writer is coming in person. Do come, major, but you know what? Don't come as you are now, in boots, with your hair scarcely combed. Of course you hadn't expected us, so we excuse your appearance up to now. But before you call on my mistress, put on a pair of shoes and make sure your hair's neatly combed. As it stands, you look much too bellicose, much too Prussian!

TELLHEIM. Thank you, Franziska.

FRANZISKA. You look as if you had camped out last night.

TELLHEIM. You may not be wrong by much.

FRANZISKA. We're going to get dressed, too, and then we shall eat. We would be happy to invite you to join us, but we fear that your presence might hinder us from eating; and we are not so much in love that we have lost our appetites.

TELLHEIM. I'm going. Franziska, please prepare her a little so that I don't appear despicable in her eyes or my own.—Come, Werner, you shall eat with me.

WERNER. Here in the inn? I shouldn't enjoy a bite.

TELLHEIM. No, in my room.

WERNER. I'll follow you at once, but first I want a word with the little lady.

TELLHEIM. That's fine with me! [*Exit.*]

SCENE II

PAUL WERNER *and* FRANZISKA

FRANZISKA. Well, sergeant major?

WERNER. Little lady, when I come back again, shall I be dressed up, too?

FRANZISKA. Come as you please, sergeant major; my eyes won't hold anything against you. But my ears will have to be even more on guard than they have been.—Twenty fingers, and all full of rings! Eh, sergeant major?

WERNER. No, little lady, that was just what I wanted to tell you: I made that cock-and-bull story up off the top of my head! There's not a bit of truth in it. I think one ring is enough for anybody. And I've heard the major say hundreds and hundreds of times that it's a rotten kind of soldier who would lead a girl on. That's what I think too, little lady. You can depend on it! Now I must go join him. Goodbye, little lady! [*Exit.*]

SCENE 12

MINNA *and* FRANZISKA

MINNA. Has the major gone again already?—Franziska, I think I am now calm enough for him to have stayed.

FRANZISKA. And I can make you even calmer.

MINNA. So much the better! His letter, oh, his letter! Every line told me what an honorable, noble man he is. Each refusal to have me bespoke his love for me. I suppose he noticed that we had read the letter. It doesn't matter as long as he comes. He is coming, isn't he?—There appears to me to be just a little too much pride in his behavior, Franziska. He doesn't want to owe his good fortune to his beloved, and that is pride, unforgivable pride! If he lets his pride get the better of him, Franziska—

FRANZISKA. You'll give him up?

MINNA. Now see here! Are you feeling sorry for him again

already? No, my dear, you don't give up a man because of one flaw; but I *have* thought of a trick to give him back some of his own medicine.

FRANZISKA. Oh, you must really have calmed down, madam, if you're thinking of playing tricks again.

MINNA. I have; but come, you have a part to play in this as well. [*They go into her room.*]

Act 4

SCENE I
MINNA'*s boudoir*
MINNA, *richly but tastefully dressed, and* FRANZISKA. *They are just getting up from the table, which is being cleared by a* SERVANT.

FRANZISKA. You surely can't have had enough to eat, madam.

MINNA. You don't think so, Franziska? Perhaps I wasn't hungry when I sat down at the table.

FRANZISKA. We had agreed not to mention him during the meal; perhaps we ought to have undertaken not to think of him as well.

MINNA. You're right: I was thinking of nothing but him.

FRANZISKA. I noticed that. I started to talk about a hundred different things, and each time you answered me as if you were in another world. [*A second* SERVANT *enters with coffee.*] Here comes something that will bring you out of your melancholy. Good, dear coffee!

MINNA. I'm not melancholy; I was just thinking about the lesson I'm going to teach him. Do you understand what to do, Franziska?

FRANZISKA. Oh yes, but it would be better if he saved us the trouble.

MINNA. You'll see that I know him through and through. The man who now refuses me because I am wealthy will fight the whole world for me as soon as he hears that I am poor and forlorn.

FRANZISKA. [*Very earnestly.*] And a thing like that has to gratify to no end even the best-developed ego.

MINNA. Don't moralize! You used to accuse me of being frivolous, and now it's of having a big ego. Just leave me alone, my dear Franziska. By now you should be able to wrap your sergeant major around your little finger, too, you know.

FRANZISKA. My sergeant major?

MINNA. Yes, even if you completely deny it, it's still true. I haven't seen him yet, but from everything you've told me about him, I'd prophesy that you're going to marry him.

SCENE 2
RICCAUT DE LA MARLINIÈRE, MINNA, *and* FRANZISKA

RICCAUT. [*Offstage.*] *Est-il permis, monsieur le Major?*

FRANZISKA. What is that? Is it coming toward us? [*Moves toward the door.*]

RICCAUT. *Parbleu,* I 'ave made ze mistake!—*Mais non*—I 'ave not made ze mistake—*c'est sa chambre.*

FRANZISKA. Madam, this man obviously thinks that Major von Tellheim still occupies this room.

RICCAUT. Zat eez right! *Le Major de Tellheim; juste, ma belle enfant, c'est lui que je cherche. Où est-il?*

FRANZISKA. He isn't staying here anymore.

RICCAUT. *Comment?* Before twenty-four hour 'e still 'ere. And eez not residing any longer? Where 'e reside?

MINNA. [*Coming up to him.*] Sir—

RICCAUT. Ah, madame—mademoiselle—Your Grace, forgive—

MINNA. Sir, your mistake is a pardonable one, and your surprise quite natural. The major was kind enough to give up his room to me, a stranger who did not know where she could find other accommodation.

RICCAUT. *Ah, voilà de ses politesses! C'est un très galant homme que ce Major!*

MINNA. I am ashamed to say that I do not know where he has moved in the meantime.

RICCAUT. Your Grace not know? *C'est dommage; j'en suis fâché.*

MINNA. Of course, I should have made inquiries, since I am quite sure that his friends will go on looking for him here.

RICCAUT. I am very much of 'is friend, Your Grace.

MINNA. Franziska, do you perhaps know where the major has moved?

FRANZISKA. No, madam.

RICCAUT. I am needing to speak wis 'im. I come to bring 'im a *nouvelle* zat will make 'im very 'appy.

MINNA. That makes me even more sorry. But I hope to speak to him myself, perhaps soon, and if it is not important from whose mouth he hears the news, then I am happy to offer my services, sir.

RICCAUT. I understand.—*Mademoiselle parle français? Mais*

sans doute; telle que je la vois!—La demande était bien impolie; vous me pardonnerez, mademoiselle.

MINNA. Sir—

RICCAUT. No? You do not speak French, Your Grace?

MINNA. Sir, in France I would try to speak it. But why should I do so here? I can tell that you understand me, and I also understand you. You may speak French or German, however you see fit.

RICCAUT. Good, good! I can myself explain in German, too.— *Sachez donc, mademoiselle*—I must tell Your Grace that I come from eating wis ze minister . . . minister of . . . minister of . . . 'ow eez calling 'imself, ze minister . . . in ze long street . . . on ze big square?

MINNA. I am a complete stranger here.

RICCAUT. Well, ze minister of ze War Department. I dine zere at midday—I dine *à l'ordinaire* wis 'im—and zen we start to talk about Major Tellheim. *Et le ministre m'a dit en confidence, car Son Excellence est de mes amis, et il n'y a point de mystères entre nous*—'Is Excellency, vat I wish to say, 'as told me in confidence, zat ze case of our major eez on ze point of ending, and ending good. 'E 'as made a report to ze King, and ze King 'as resolved *tout à fait en faveur du major.*—"*Monsieur,*" *m'a dit Son Excellence, "vous comprenez bien, que tout dépend de la manière, dont on fait envisager les choses au Roi, et vous me connaissez. Cela fait un très joli garçon que ce Tellheim, et ne sais-je pas que vous l'aimez? Les amis de mes amis sont aussi les miens. Il coute un peu cher au Roi ce Tellheim, mais est-ce que l'on sert les rois pour rien? Il faut s'entr'aider en ce monde; et quand il s'agit de pertes, que ce soit le Roi, qui en fasse, et non pas un honnête-homme de nous autres. Voilà le principe, dont je ne me dépars jamais.*"—Vot say Your Grace? Is 'e not a good man? *Ah, que Son Excellence a le coeur bien placé!* 'E assured me *au reste,* zat if ze major 'as not already received *une lettre de la main*—a letter from ze royal 'and—zat 'e must *infailliblement* receive one today.

MINNA. Indeed, sir, this news will be most welcome to Major von Tellheim. I only wish that I might tell him the name of the friend who is taking such an interest in his good fortune.

RICCAUT. Your Grace vish my name? *Vous voyez en moi*—Your Grace see in me *le Chevalier Riccaut de la Marlinière, Seigneur de Pret-au-vol, de la Branche de Prensd'or.* Your Grace is very surprised zat I come from such a great family, *qui est véritablement du sang royal.*—*Il faut le dire: je suis sans doute le cadet le plus aventureux, que la maison a jamais eu.* I am serving since I am eleven years old. An *affaire d'honneur* forced me to run away. Zen I served 'Is 'Oliness ze Pope, ze Republic of San Merino, ze crown of Poland, and in 'Olland, till at last I come 'ere. *Ah, mademoiselle, que je voudrais n'avoir jamais vu ce pays-là.* If only I could 'ave stayed in 'Olland, zen I would be now at least a colonel. But 'ere I remain a *capitaine,* and now a discharged *capitaine,* too.

MINNA. That's a great misfortune.

RICCAUT. *Oui, mademoiselle, me voilà reformé, et par-là mis sur le pavé!*

MINNA. I have great sympathy for you.

RICCAUT. *Vous êtes bien bonne, mademoiselle.*—No, zere's no justice in what 'as 'appened 'ere. To discharge a man like me! A man 'oo furzermore 'as lost all 'is money since! I 'ave gambled more zan twenty zousand francs away. What do I 'ave now? *Tranchons le mot; je n'ai pas le sou, et me voilà exactement vis-à-vis du rien.*

MINNA. I am very sorry.

RICCAUT. *Vous êtes bien bonne, mademoiselle,* but as ze proverb goes, each misfortune brings 'is brozer wis 'im; *qu'un malheur ne vient jamais seul:* zat is what 'appens to me. What can an *honnête-homme* of my *extraction* do for resources but to gamble? Always I 'ave played wis fortune, but zat was when I did not need fortune. Now I need 'er, *mademoiselle: je joue avec un guignon, qui surpasse toute croyance.* In ze last fifteen days, not a day 'as passed when I 'ave not been broken. Yesterday alone I was broken sree times. *Je sais bien, qu'il y avait quelque chose de plus que le jeu. Car parmi mes pontes se trouvaient certaines dames*—I say no more. I must be gallant to ze ladies. Zey invited me today, to give me *revanche; mais—vous m'entendez, mademoiselle*—first you must earn ze living, before you can gamble.

MINNA. Sir, I hope—

RICCAUT. *Vous êtes bien bonne, mademoiselle.*

MINNA. [*Taking* FRANZISKA *aside.*] Franziska, I really am sorry for this man. Do you think he would be offended if I offered him something?

FRANZISKA. He doesn't look as though he would.

MINNA. Good—Sir, I hear that when you gamble, you keep the bank, doubtless at places where there is something to be won. I must confess to you that I—also like to gamble . . .

RICCAUT. *Tant mieux, mademoiselle, tant mieux! Tous les gens d'esprit aiment le jeu à la fureur.*

MINNA. And that I like to win and want very much to entrust my money to a man who—knows how to gamble. Would you have any interest, sir, in letting me become your partner? In allowing me to put up a share of your bank?

RICCAUT. *Comment, mademoiselle, vous voulez être de moitié avec moi? De tout mon coeur.*

MINNA. To begin with, just a small amount—[*She goes and takes money from her strongbox.*]

RICCAUT. *Ah, mademoiselle, que vous êtes charmante!*

MINNA. Here is something I won a short time ago, fifty talers—I must say that I am ashamed it is not more . . .

RICCAUT. *Donnez toujours, mademoiselle, donnez!* [*Takes the money.*]

MINNA. Of course, I have no doubt, sir, that your gaming house is a very respected one.

RICCAUT. Oh, very respected. Fifty talers? Your Grace shall 'ave a sird interest, *pour le tiers*—certainly zat much and per'aps a little more. But wis a beautiful lady we will not make zings too precise. I congratulate me to 'ave come into *liaison* with Your Grace, *et de ce moment je recommence à bien augurer de ma fortune.*

MINNA. But, unfortunately, I shall not be able to be present when you are playing, sir.

RICCAUT. Why does Your Grace need to be present? We gamblers are 'onest people among one anozer.

MINNA. If we are lucky, sir, then I shall expect you to bring me my share. But if we are unlucky—

RICCAUT. Zen I come and get some new recruits, eh, Your Grace?

MINNA. The recruits may run out before long. So guard our money well, sir.

RICCAUT. What does Your Grace take me for? A simpleton, a block'ead?

MINNA. Forgive me, sir.

RICCAUT. *Je suis des bons, mademoiselle. Savez vous ce que cela veut dire?* I 'ave experience—

MINNA. But nevertheless, sir . . .

RICCAUT. *Je sais monter un coup—*

MINNA. [*Surprised.*] But should you?

RICCAUT. *Je file une carte avec une adresse—*

MINNA. Never!

RICCAUT. *Je fais sauter la coupe avec une dextérité—*

MINNA. But sir, surely you wouldn't.

RICCAUT. Why not, Your Grace, why not? *Donnez moi un pigeon-neau à plumer, et . . .*

MINNA. Play false? Cheat?

RICCAUT. *Comment, mademoiselle? Vous appelez cela* "cheat"?

Corriger la fortune, l'enchaîner sous ses doights, être sûr de son fait: is zat what ze Germans call "cheat"? "Cheat"! Oh, what a poor language German is, what a crude language!

MINNA. No, sir, if that is the way you think—

RICCAUT. *Laissez-moi faire, mademoiselle,* and do not worry. Why should you worry 'ow I play? Zat's enough: either Your Grace will see me tomorrow wis five hundred talers, or you never see me again.—*Votre très humble, mademoiselle, votre très humble.* [*Hurries out.*]

MINNA. [*Looking after him with astonishment and displeasure.*] I hope it will be the latter, sir, I hope it will be the latter!

SCENE 3

MINNA *and* FRANZISKA

FRANZISKA. [*Bitterly.*] I'm dumbfounded! Oh, beautiful, just beautiful!

MINNA. All right, mock me; I deserve it. [*She pauses and then continues more calmly.*] Don't mock me, Franziska; I don't deserve it.

FRANZISKA. Marvelous! You've really done a good deed, putting a rogue back on his feet!

MINNA. I thought I was helping out an unfortunate.

FRANZISKA. And the best of it is, he thinks you're one of his kind.—I must go after him and get the money back. [*Starts to leave.*]

MINNA. Franziska, don't let the coffee get too cold. Pour me a cup.

FRANZISKA. He must give it back to you. You've changed your mind; you don't want to go into partnership with him. Fifty talers! You could tell, madam, that he was begging money from you. [MINNA *meanwhile pours out her own coffee.*] But who would give that much to a beggar? And at the same time try to spare him the indignity of having had to beg for it? The generous person who pretends, out of generosity, not to recognize a beggar is in turn not recognized by the beggar. How would you like it, madam, if he looks on your gift as I-don't-know-what—[MINNA *gives her a cup of coffee.*] Are you trying to get me even more worked up? I don't want any coffee. [MINNA *removes the cup.* FRANZISKA *imitates* RICCAUT.] "*Parbleu,* Your Grace, zere's no justice in what 'as 'appened 'ere." Of course not, when they let rogues like that go running around loose without hanging them.

MINNA. [*Cold and meditative, while drinking.*] My dear girl, you get along so well with good people, but when are you going to learn to put up with the bad ones? After all, they are people too. And often they are not nearly as bad as they seem to be; you simply have to find their good side.—I imagine that this Frenchman is nothing more than vain. It's sheer vanity that makes him pretend to be a cheat: he doesn't want to feel obliged to me; he doesn't want to have to thank me. Perhaps he'll go and pay off some of his small debts and live quietly and frugally on what's left, as long as it holds out, without giving a thought to gambling. If that's the case, Franziska, then he can come back and fetch recruits any time he wants.— [*Hands her her cup.*] Here, put this away.—Tell me, shouldn't Tell-heim be here by now?

FRANZISKA. [*Shaking her head.*] No, madam, I can neither find a bad side to a good person nor a good side to a bad one.

MINNA. But is he really coming?

FRANZISKA. He'd do better to stay away!—Just because you detect a little pride in the major, the best of men, you're going to play such a cruel trick on him?

MINNA. Are you back on that subject again? I'll hear no more of it, and that's that. If you spoil my fun, if you don't say and do exactly what I told you, I'll leave you all alone with him, and then . . . That must be him now.

SCENE 4
PAUL WERNER, *with a stiff, military bearing*; MINNA; *and* FRANZISKA

FRANZISKA. No, it's just his dear sergeant major.

MINNA. *Dear* sergeant major? What is this "dear" all about?

FRANZISKA. Madam, please don't confuse the man.—Your servant, sergeant major. What news do you bring us?

WERNER. [*Ignoring* FRANZISKA *and going directly to* MINNA.] Major von Tellheim asks me, sergeant major Paul Werner, to pay his most humble respects to Fräulein von Barnhelm and to tell her that he will be here immediately.

MINNA. Where is he then?

WERNER. Your Grace will pardon him: we left our quarters before the stroke of three, but the paymaster general stopped us on the way; and since conversations with people like that go on forever, the major gave me the nod to come and report the delay to you.

MINNA. That's all right, sergeant major. I do hope, though, that the paymaster general had something agreeable to say to the major.

WERNER. Officers like that seldom do.—Has Your Grace any orders for me? [*He is about to leave.*]

FRANZISKA. Where are you off to, sergeant major? I thought we were going to have a little chat.

WERNER. [*Softly and seriously.*] Not here, little lady. It would show a lack of respect; it would be insubordinate.—Madam—

MINNA. Thank you for your trouble, sergeant major. It has been a great pleasure to meet you. Franziska has told me many good things about you. [WERNER *makes a stiff bow and exits.*]

SCENE 5
MINNA *and* FRANZISKA

MINNA. Is that your sergeant major, Franziska?

FRANZISKA. Since your tone is mocking, I won't take you up again on that "your."—Yes, madam, that is my sergeant major. I'm sure that you find him a little stiff or wooden. He even seemed that way to me just now. But I noticed that, in front of Your Grace, he felt as if he were on parade. And when soldiers are on parade, they certainly do look more like marionettes than men. But you ought to see and hear him when he's off on his own.

MINNA. Yes, I really ought to.

FRANZISKA. He must still be outside. May I go and talk to him for a little while?

MINNA. You know how reluctant I am to deny you this pleasure, Franziska, but you must stay here. You must be present while I am talking to the major. Oh, and something else occurs to me. [*She takes her ring off her finger and gives it to* FRANZISKA.] Take my ring and look after it, and give me the major's.

FRANZISKA. Why?

MINNA. [*While* FRANZISKA *is getting the major's ring.*] I don't quite know myself, but I have a feeling that I might have a use for it.—There's a knock.—Give it to me quickly! [*She puts it on.*] He's here!

SCENE 6
TELLHEIM, *in the same uniform, but otherwise dressed as* FRANZISKA *prescribed*; MINNA; *and* FRANZISKA

TELLHEIM. Madam, you will excuse my being late.

MINNA. Oh, major, we don't want to be quite so military with each other. You are here, and looking forward to the pleasure of your arrival has been a pleasure in itself!—Well? [*She looks smilingly into his face.*] Dear Tellheim, don't you think that we were being rather childish earlier?

TELLHEIM. Yes, madam, it is childish to go on struggling when you should resign yourself.

MINNA. I thought we might go for a drive, major, and take a look at the city, after which we could go meet my uncle.

TELLHEIM. What?

MINNA. You see, we haven't had a chance yet to talk about such important matters as this.—Yes, he arrives today. It is mere chance that I arrived a day ahead of him.

TELLHEIM. The Count of Bruchsal? Has he returned?

MINNA. The disturbances caused by the war drove him to Italy, but peace has brought him back home again.—Don't worry, Tellheim. Even if we thought previously that the greatest obstacle to our union would come from his side—

TELLHEIM. Our union?

MINNA. He is your friend. He has heard too many good things from too many people about you *not* to be your friend. He is dying to meet the man who has been chosen in marriage by his only heir. He is coming as uncle, as guardian, as father, to give me to you.

TELLHEIM. Madam, why didn't you read my letter? Why didn't you wish to read it?

MINNA. Your letter? Oh, yes, I remember, you did send me one. What happened to that letter, Franziska? Did we or didn't we read it? What did you write to me, dear Tellheim?

TELLHEIM. Nothing but what honor bade me.

MINNA. Which was that you should not leave an honorable girl who loves you in the lurch. Surely honor would bid you to write that. I certainly should have read the letter. But what I have not read, I can hear from you.

TELLHEIM. Yes, you shall hear it.

MINNA. No, I don't even need to hear it. It is obvious. Could you be capable of so mean a trick as not to want me now? Don't you know that I would spend the rest of my life in disgrace? My female compatriots would point their fingers at me and say, "That's the one. That's Fräulein von Barnhelm, who thought that just because she was rich, she could get the brave Tellheim—as if brave men were to be had for money!" That's what they would say, for my female compatriots are all jealous of me. They can't deny that I am wealthy, but they don't want to know that in addition I am really a rather fine person who is entirely worthy of the man of her choice. Isn't that right, Tellheim?

TELLHEIM. Yes, yes, madam, I know your compatriots. I'm sure they would envy you an officer who has been discharged, whose honor has been besmirched, and who is a cripple and a beggar into the bargain.

MINNA. And are you supposed to be all those things? I heard something of the sort this morning, if I am not mistaken. Your situation is a mixture of the bad and the good. Let us therefore look at each point more closely.—You are discharged? So I have heard, but I thought that your regiment had simply been absorbed into another. Why didn't they keep a man of your merit?

TELLHEIM. What had to happen has happened. The authorities have convinced themselves that a soldier does very little out of love for them and not much more from a sense of duty; they believe, rather, that he does everything from the standpoint of his own reputation. Why then should they feel that they owe him anything? Peace has made several people like me dispensable, and in the end no one is indispensable as far as they are concerned.

MINNA. You talk like a man who finds that the authorities, for their part, are very dispensable. And certainly this was never more true than at this moment. I am grateful to the authorities that they have renounced their claim to a man whom I would have shared with them only with great reluctance. I am your commander, Tellheim; you don't need any other master. I could scarcely have dreamt that I would have the good fortune to find you discharged!— But you are not merely discharged: you are more. Now let's see, what else is there? You are a cripple, you said. Well [*She looks him up and down.*], for a cripple you appear to be pretty much intact, and you seem strong and healthy enough to me.—My dear Tellheim, if your rationale for begging is the loss of your limbs, I predict that you'll get very little money except from good-hearted girls like me.

TELLHEIM. At the moment you sound mischievous rather than good-hearted, my dear Minna.

MINNA. And all I choose to hear in your rebuff is "dear Minna."—I don't want to poke fun anymore, because I'm aware that you are indeed a partial cripple. A bullet did take away some of the use of your right arm. But, all things considered, that's not so bad: I shall be so much the safer from your beatings.

TELLHEIM. Madam!

MINNA. What you should say is that now you have even less to fear from mine. Well, Tellheim, I hope that matters never deteriorate to the point where we want to hit each other.

TELLHEIM. You wish to laugh, madam. I am only sorry that I cannot laugh with you.

MINNA. Why not? What do you have against laughter? Can't one laugh and be serious at the same time? Dear major, laughter keeps us more reasonable than gloominess does. The proof is here at hand. Though your beloved is laughing, she judges your situation far more accurately than you do yourself. You say that your honor is besmirched because you have been discharged; you say that you are a cripple because you were shot in the arm. Is that really correct? Isn't that an exaggeration? And my view is that all exaggerations are comic. I'll bet that if we look into this beggar nonsense, it will prove to have as little substance as the rest. You've probably lost your equipment two or three times; some of your funds may have disappeared from one bank or another; you probably have no hope of being repaid for this or that advance that you made while you were in the service—but are you a beggar because of these things? Even if you had nothing left but what my uncle is bringing you—

TELLHEIM. Your uncle is bringing me nothing.

MINNA. Nothing but the ten thousand talers that you so generously advanced to our government.

TELLHEIM. If only you had read my letter, madam!

MINNA. Oh, very well, I did read it. But I am completely puzzled about what you said on this point. No one is going to try to make a crime out of what was a noble act.—Please explain to me what happened, dear major.

TELLHEIM. You will remember, madam, that I had orders to collect the levy in all the districts of your region, to collect it in cash, and to employ the utmost severity in doing so. I wished to avoid the use of force, so in the end I myself advanced the sum by which the collection fell short.

MINNA. Yes, I remember well. I loved you for this even though I had not yet met you.

TELLHEIM. Your government gave me its promissory note, and I wanted to include this among the debts that had to be settled when the armistice was signed. The note was acknowledged as valid, but my right to it was disputed. People sneered when I assured them that I had advanced the money in cash. They declared that it was a bribe from your government because I had so quickly agreed to the lowest possible sum for the levy. Thus the note was taken from me, and if it is paid, it will certainly not be paid to me. It is for this reason, madam, that I regard my honor as having been besmirched, and not because of my discharge, which I should have asked for in any case had I not received it.—You are completely serious now, madam? Why aren't you laughing? Ha, ha, ha! *I'm* laughing.

MINNA. Oh, stop this laughter, Tellheim! I beg you! It is the terrible laughter of the misanthrope! No, you are not the man to regret a good act merely because it had evil consequences for you. No, these evil consequences cannot possibly persist! The truth must come to light. My uncle's testimony, the testimony of our legislature . . .

TELLHEIM. Your uncle! Your legislature! Ha, ha, ha!

MINNA. Your laughter is killing me, Tellheim! If you believe in virtue and providence, then don't laugh! I've never heard curses that were more horrible than your laughter.—And even if the worst happens and you are thoroughly misunderstood here, you won't be misunderstood in Thuringia, Tellheim. No, we cannot, we will not misunderstand you. And if our legislature has the slightest concept of honor, then I know what they must do. But I'm being silly: why should that be necessary? Just imagine, Tellheim, that you lost the ten thousand talers during a wild night. Your unlucky card was a king, but the queen [*Pointing to herself.*] will be that much more favorable for you. Providence, believe me, always indemnifies the man who is honorable, and very often ahead of time. The deed that was to cost you ten thousand talers was the very thing that won you my heart. Were it not for this deed I should never have been eager to meet you. You know that I came uninvited to the first party at which I thought I should find you. I came only because of you. I came with the firm intention of falling in love with you—indeed, I loved you already!—with the firm intention of possessing you, even if I had found you as black and ugly as the Moor of Venice. You aren't as black and ugly, nor would you be as jealous. But Tellheim, Tellheim, you do have a lot in common with him! Oh, these wild, inflexible men who can fix their obstinate eyes on nothing but the ghost of their honor and who steel themselves against any other feeling!—Look at me, Tellheim! [TELLHEIM, *meanwhile, has been staring fixedly in front of himself, absorbed in thought.*] What are you thinking about? Can't you hear me?

TELLHEIM. [*Absent-mindedly.*] Oh yes! But tell me, madam, how did the Moor come to enter the Venetian service? Did he have no fatherland? Why did he sell his strength and his blood to a foreign country?

MINNA. [*Shocked.*] Where are you, Tellheim?—It's time now to stop. Come! [*She takes his arm.*] Franziska, have them send the carriage 'round.

TELLHEIM. [*Breaking free from* MINNA *and following* FRAN- ZISKA.] No, Franziska, I am unable to accept the honor of accompanying Fräulein Barnhelm.—Madam, I pray you, excuse me and leave me with my good sense still intact. You are doing your best to make me lose it, and I shall resist as much as I can. Since I am still in my right mind, I want you to listen, madam, to what I have firmly resolved and from which nothing in the world shall shake me. If there isn't another lucky throw left for me in the game, if the tables are not completely turned in my favor, if—

MINNA. I'm afraid I have to interrupt you, major.—We should have told him straightaway, Franziska. You never remind me of anything.—Our conversation would have been quite different, Tell-heim, if I had begun it with the good news that the Chevalier de la Marlinière just brought you.

TELLHEIM. The Chevalier de la Marlinière? Who is that?

FRANZISKA. He seems to be quite a good man, except for—

MINNA. Silence, Franziska!—He is also a discharged officer, and he has come here from service in Holland . . .

TELLHEIM. Oh, Lieutenant Riccaut!

MINNA. He assured me that he was your friend—

TELLHEIM. And I can assure you that I am not his.

MINNA. —and that one of the ministers, I forget which, had told him that your affair was close to a favorable conclusion. Apparently a letter from the King is on its way to you.

TELLHEIM. How on earth could Riccaut have been meeting with a minister? It's true that something should have been decided, because the paymaster general just now told me that the King had dismissed all the charges against me and had released me from my written pledge not to leave here until everything was settled. But that must be all there is to it. They're simply going to let me go. But they are mistaken; I will not go. I would rather die here in penury before the very eyes of my defamers.

MINNA. Obstinate man!

TELLHEIM. I need no clemency; I seek justice. My honor . . .

MINNA. The honor of a man like you—

TELLHEIM. [Heatedly.] No, madam, you may be a good judge of everything else, but not of this. Honor is not the voice of con-science, and it doesn't come from the testimony of men less noble than I—

MINNA. No, no, I know! Honor is . . . honor.

TELLHEIM. One moment, madam, you have not permitted me to finish speaking. I wanted to say that, if I am to be so unscrupulously denied that which is mine, if I do not receive complete satisfaction for my honor, then, madam, I cannot be yours. For in the eyes of the world, I am not worthy to be. Fräulein von Barnhelm deserves a man of irreproachable character. It is a vile love that does not hesitate to expose the object of its affection to scorn. And it is a contemptible man who is not ashamed to depend on a girl for his entire wealth and happiness, a girl whose own blind affection—

MINNA. Are you serious, major? [*Suddenly turning her back on him.*] Franziska . . .

TELLHEIM. Don't be angry, madam.

MINNA. [*Aside to* FRANZISKA.] Now is the moment! What do you advise, Franziska?

FRANZISKA. I advise nothing, but he is certainly making it hard for you.

TELLHEIM. [*Advancing to interrupt them.*] You are angry, madam.

MINNA. [*Scornfully.*] I am? Not in the least.

TELLHEIM. If I loved you less, madam—

MINNA. [*In the same tone as before.*] Oh, yes, that would certainly be my misfortune!—And you see, major, I do not wish to be your misfortune, either. We must remain unselfish in our love.—It's just as well that I have not been more candid. Perhaps your sympathy would have granted what your heart denies me. [*Slowly taking the ring from her finger.*]

TELLHEIM. What do you mean by that, madam?

MINNA. No, neither of us should make the other either happier or unhappier. That is the meaning of true love! I believe you, Tellheim, and you have too much honor not to recognize true love.

TELLHEIM. Are you laughing at me, madam?

MINNA. Here, take back the ring with which you pledged your love to me. [*Gives him the ring.*] There, now we'll pretend we never knew each other.

TELLHEIM. What is this I hear?

MINNA. Why are you surprised?—Take it, sir. Surely you weren't just playing coy?

TELLHEIM. [*Taking the ring out of her hand.*] Oh, God, can Minna talk like this?

MINNA. You cannot be mine because of *one* circumstance; I cannot be yours under *any* circumstances. Your misfortune is only apparent; mine is certain.—Farewell! [*Starts to exit.*]

TELLHEIM. Where are you going, my dearest Minna?

MINNA. Sir, you insult me now with such familiarity.

TELLHEIM. What is the matter, madam? Where are you going?

MINNA. Let me go. Let me hide my tears from you, you traitor! [*Exit.*]

SCENE 7
TELLHEIM *and* FRANZISKA

TELLHEIM. Her tears? And I am supposed to let her go? [*Starts to follow* MINNA.]

FRANZISKA. [*Restraining him.*] Major, surely you wouldn't follow her into her bedroom.

TELLHEIM. Her misfortune, did she not speak of her misfortune?

FRANZISKA. Yes, of course, her misfortune to lose you after—

TELLHEIM. After? After what? There's something else. What is it, Franziska? Speak, tell me.

FRANZISKA. After she . . . I was going to say . . . had sacrificed so much for you.

TELLHEIM. Sacrificed? For me?

FRANZISKA. Listen now; I will be quite brief.—It is just as well, major, that you got rid of her in this manner. Why shouldn't I tell you? It can't remain a secret much longer. We have run away! The Count von Bruchsal has disinherited my mistress because she would not accept a man of his choice. She has lost everything and renounced everything. What were we to do? We decided to search for the one who—

TELLHEIM. Enough! Come, I must throw myself at her feet.

FRANZISKA. What are you thinking of? You ought to thank your lucky stars it turned out this way.

TELLHEIM. You wretch, what do you take me for? Forgive my anger, dear Franziska, but such advice does not come from your heart.

FRANZISKA. Don't delay me any longer. I must go and see what she is doing. How easily something might have happened to her!— Please go! You may come back later if you wish to. [*Exits to* MINNA.]

SCENE 8
TELLHEIM

TELLHEIM. But Franziska!—I will await you here! No, this is more urgent! If she sees how serious I am, she cannot refuse me her forgiveness.—Now I do have need of you, honest Werner!—No, Minna, I am not a traitor! [*Exits in haste.*]

Act 5

SCENE I
The Parlor
Enter TELLHEIM *from one side,* WERNER *from the other.*

TELLHEIM. Werner, I've been looking everywhere for you! Where have you been?

WERNER. And I've been looking everywhere for you, major. I bring you some good news.

TELLHEIM. It's not your news I need at the moment, it's your money. Hurry, Werner, give me as much as you have, and then go try to borrow as much as you can.

WERNER. What major?—Well, bless my soul, didn't I say he'd only borrow from me when he himself had something to lend?

TELLHEIM. Surely you're not looking to get out of helping me?

WERNER. So that I shall have nothing to reproach him with, he takes it from me with one hand and gives it back with the other.

TELLHEIM. Don't delay, Werner!—I have every intention of repaying you, but when and how, God only knows!

WERNER. Then you don't know that the royal treasury has received orders to pay you your money? I just heard from—

TELLHEIM. What are you talking about? Why are you letting yourself be taken in? Surely you must know that if this were true, I would be the first to hear about it!—Quickly, Werner, money! Money!

WERNER. By God, with pleasure! Here's some for you! The five hundred talers and the three hundred. [*Hands him both amounts.*]

TELLHEIM. The five hundred talers, Werner, go and give to Just. He's to redeem at once the ring that he pawned this morning.—But where will you get more money, Werner? I need a lot more.

WERNER. Let me worry about that. The man who bought my farm lives in town. We were not due to close for two weeks, but he's got the money now, and he'll get a half percent discount if he turns it over early.

TELLHEIM. Good enough, dear Werner!—Don't you see that you are my only hope? I must confide everything to you. The young lady here—you saw her—is unhappy—

WERNER. Oh, that's too bad!

TELLHEIM. But tomorrow she will become my wife.

WERNER. Oh, that's very good!

TELLHEIM. And the day after tomorrow I shall leave with her. I have permission to go and I intend to go. I just want to get away from all this. Who knows where I may find good fortune? If you like, Werner, come along. We'll enlist again.

WERNER. Really? We'll enlist someplace where there's a war on, major?

TELLHEIM. Where else?—But go, my dear Werner. We can talk about this later.

WERNER. A major after my own heart! The day after tomorrow? Why not tomorrow instead?—I'll get everything in order.—Major, there's a wonderful war in Persia! What do you think about going there?

TELLHEIM. We'll consider it. Now go, Werner!

WERNER. Hurray, hurray! Long live Prince Heraclius! [*Exit.*]

SCENE 2
TELLHEIM

TELLHEIM. What has happened to me?—My soul is newly inspired. My own misfortune got me down and made me angry, shortsighted, withdrawn, indolent; her misfortune raises me up again. I look around once more as a man unconstrained and feel the strength and the will to undertake everything for her. But why am I waiting? [*Is about to go to* MINNA's *room when* FRANZISKA *comes out.*]

SCENE 3
FRANZISKA *and* TELLHEIM

FRANZISKA. So, it's you.—I thought I heard your voice. What do you want, major?

TELLHEIM. What do I want? What is your mistress doing?—Answer me!

FRANZISKA. She's just going out.

TELLHEIM. Alone? Without me? Where is she going?

FRANZISKA. Have you forgotten, major?

TELLHEIM. Have you lost your senses, Franziska?—I upset her and she was offended. I shall ask for her forgiveness and she will forgive me.

FRANZISKA. What? After you took back your ring?

TELLHEIM. I took it without knowing what I was doing!—Now that you mention the ring, where did I put it? [*Looks for it on his person.*] Here it is.

FRANZISKA. Is that it? [TELLHEIM *replaces the ring.*] [*Aside.*] If only he would look at it a little more closely!

TELLHEIM. She forced it on me with such bitterness . . . but I have forgotten her bitterness already. When one is under stress, one doesn't always weigh one's words carefully. But she won't refuse for a moment to take back my ring.—And don't I still have hers?

FRANZISKA. She's expecting to get that back.—Where is it, major? Show it to me.

TELLHEIM. [*Somewhat abashed.*] I . . . I forgot to bring it with me.—Just . . . Just is going to bring it to me at once.

FRANZISKA. I suppose that each is very much like the other. Let me have a look at this one; I love looking at such things.

TELLHEIM. Another time, Franziska. Come . . .

FRANZISKA. [*Aside.*] He simply won't see his mistake.

TELLHEIM. What did you say? Mistake?

FRANZISKA. I meant to say that it is a mistake if you think my mistress is still a good match. Her own estate is a very modest one, and her guardians could reduce it to nothing with a few selfish maneuvers. She expected to inherit everything from her uncle, but this cruel man—

TELLHEIM. Don't even mention him! Am I not the man to make good to her for everything?

FRANZISKA. Do you hear that? She's ringing for me; I must go in.

TELLHEIM. I'm going with you.

FRANZISKA. Oh for heaven's sake, no! She expressly forbade me to talk to you. At least wait and come in after me.

SCENE 4

TELLHEIM

TELLHEIM. [*Calling after her.*] Announce me to her!—Speak for me, Franziska!—I'll follow immediately after you!—What shall I say to her?—When you speak from the heart, there is no need for preparation.—The one thing that might need careful handling is her reticence, her hesitation to throw herself in her misfortune into my arms, and by contrast her eagerness to pretend to wealth, all of which she lost on account of me. But how can she excuse herself in her own eyes for this lack of trust in my honor and in her own worth? How can she?—Well, I have already excused her!—Ah, here she comes.

SCENE 5

MINNA, FRANZISKA, *and* TELLHEIM

MINNA. [*Coming out as though unaware of the major's presence.*] The carriage is waiting, isn't it, Franziska?—My fan, please!

TELLHEIM. [*Going up to her.*] Where are you going, madam?

MINNA. [*With affected coldness.*] Out, major.—I can guess the reason why you've taken the trouble to come here again—to give me back my ring in return. Very well, major, please have the goodness to hand it to Franziska.—Franziska, take the ring from the major! I'm afraid I have no time to lose. [*About to go.*]

TELLHEIM. [*Stepping in front of her.*] Madam!—What's this I hear? That I am not worthy of such a love as yours?

MINNA. So, Franziska, you have told the major . . .

FRANZISKA. Everything.

TELLHEIM. Please don't be angry with me, madam. I am no traitor. On account of me you have lost much in the eyes of the world; but in my eyes you have lost nothing. Indeed, in mine you have gained incalculably by this loss. It all happened to you so fast. You feared that it might make an extremely unfavorable impression on me, so at first you wanted to conceal it. I'm not complaining about your lack of trust in me. I know that it came from your desire to retain my affection, and this desire is a source of pride to me. You found that I too had suffered misfortune, and you didn't want to pile misfortune upon misfortune. You couldn't know how much more your misfortune would mean to me than my own.

MINNA. That's all well and good, major, but what's done is done. I have released you from your obligation; by taking back your ring you have—

TELLHEIM. —agreed to nothing!—On the contrary, I regard myself as under a greater obligation than before.—You are mine, Minna, forever mine! [*He takes out the ring.*] Here, take it for a second time as the pledge of my fidelity.

MINNA. You want me to take this ring back? This ring?

TELLHEIM. Yes, dearest Minna, yes!

MINNA. What are you asking of me? *This* ring?

TELLHEIM. The first time you took this ring from my hand, our circumstances were alike and we both enjoyed good fortune. Our circumstances are no longer fortunate, but they are at least alike once again. Equality is always the strongest bond of love.—Permit me, my dearest Minna . . . [*Seizes her hand in order to place the ring on her finger.*]

MINNA. What, by force, major? No, there is no power on earth that could make me take this ring back! Do you think perhaps that I'm in need of a ring?—You see, don't you [*Pointing to her ring.*], that I have one here that is not in the least inferior to yours?

FRANZISKA. [*Aside.*] Well, if he doesn't see it now!

TELLHEIM. [*Letting* MINNA's *hand drop.*] What does this mean? I see Fräulein von Barnhelm, but it is not her that I hear.—You are playing coy, madam. Forgive me for borrowing this expression from you.

MINNA. [*In her natural tone.*] Did those words offend you, major?

TELLHEIM. They hurt me.

MINNA. [*Touched.*] They were not meant to, Tellheim.—Forgive me.

TELLHEIM. Ah! This familiar tone tells me that you are coming to your senses, madam; that you love me, Minna.

FRANZISKA. [*Bursting out.*] The joke almost went too far.

MINNA. [*Imperiously.*] Please do not interfere, Franziska!

FRANZISKA. [*Aside and taken aback.*] Not far enough yet?

MINNA. Yes, sir, it would be a woman's frivolousness to continue pretending to be cold and disdainful. Away with all that! You deserve to find in me someone just as truthful as you yourself are.— I still love you, Tellheim, I still love you; but nevertheless . . .

TELLHEIM. Say no more, dearest Minna, say no more! [*Seizes her hand again in order to place the ring on her finger.*]

MINNA. [*Withdrawing her hand.*] But nevertheless . . . it is for this very reason that we can never marry—never!—Where can your thoughts be, major? I thought you had enough to think about with your own misfortune.—You must remain here; you must extort the fullest satisfaction. In my haste I can think of no other word but extort, and this you must do even if the most extreme destitution should consume you before the very eyes of your slanderers.

TELLHEIM. So I thought and so I spoke when I didn't know what I was thinking and saying. Anger and suppressed rage had clouded my whole soul. Love itself in the fullest glow of happiness could not dispel the gloom. But Love sent her daughter, Pity, who, being more familiar with the darkness of misfortune, dispersed the clouds and opened all the avenues of my soul once again to tender sensations. I felt the urge for self-preservation because I had something more valuable than myself to preserve and that could only be preserved by me. Please don't be insulted by this word "pity," madam. You can hear it without humiliation when you are innocent of the cause of your misfortune. I am the cause; it is on my account, Minna, that you are losing friends and relatives, fortune and fatherland. And it is through me and in me that you must find them all again, or I shall have on my conscience the ruin of the most lovable and lovely of her sex. Please don't make me even think about a future in which I would have to hate myself.—No, nothing shall keep me in this place any longer. From this moment on I shall show nothing but contempt for the injustice that has been meted out to me here. Is this country the whole world? Does the sun rise nowhere else but here? Where may I not go? What service would refuse me? And even if I have to seek employment under the farthest sky, follow me with confidence, dearest Minna. We shall want for nothing; I have a friend who will gladly help me.

SCENE 6
An ORDERLY, TELLHEIM, MINNA, *and* FRANZISKA

FRANZISKA. [*Catching sight of the* ORDERLY.] Sh, Major!

TELLHEIM. [*To the* ORDERLY.] For whom are you looking?

ORDERLY. I am looking for Major von Tellheim.—Ah! You yourself are the major. Sir, I am to give you this letter from His Majesty the King. [*He takes the letter from his bag.*]

TELLHEIM. To me?

ORDERLY. That's what it says on the envelope.

MINNA. Franziska, do you hear? The chevalier was speaking the truth after all!

ORDERLY. [*As* TELLHEIM *takes the letter.*] I must beg your pardon, major; you would have received it yesterday, but it was impossible to find you. It was only today on parade that I learned your address from Lieutenant Riccaut.

FRANZISKA. Do you hear, madam? This is the chevalier's minister.—"'Ow eez calling 'imself, ze minister on ze big square?"

TELLHEIM. I am most grateful to you for your trouble.

ORDERLY. I'm just doing my duty, major. [*Exit.*]

SCENE 7
TELLHEIM, MINNA, *and* FRANZISKA

TELLHEIM. Well, madam, what do I have here? What is the content of this letter?

MINNA. I have no right to stretch my curiosity that far.

TELLHEIM. What, do you still think of your fate as separate from mine?—But why am I waiting to open it? It cannot make me more unhappy than I am now: no, dearest Minna, it cannot make *us* more unhappy . . . but perhaps it can make us happier!—Permit me, madam. [*While he opens the envelope and reads the letter, the* INNKEEPER *slips onto the stage.*]

SCENE 8
INNKEEPER, TELLHEIM, MINNA, *and* FRANZISKA

INNKEEPER. [*To* FRANZISKA.] Psst, my dear, a word!

FRANZISKA. [*Going up to him.*]—Sir? I'm afraid we don't yet know ourselves what's in the letter.

INNKEEPER. Who wants to know about the letter?—I've come about the ring. Your mistress must return it to me at once. Just is here and wants to redeem it.

MINNA. [*Who in the meantime has approached the* INNKEEPER.] Tell Just that the ring has already been redeemed; and tell him by whom—me.

INNKEEPER. But . . .

MINNA. I take full responsibility. You may go! [*Exit* INNKEEPER.]

SCENE 9

TELLHEIM, MINNA, *and* FRANZISKA

FRANZISKA. And now, madam, it's time to stop teasing the major.

MINNA. Oh, kind intercessor! As if the knot weren't going to untie all by itself at any moment.

TELLHEIM. [*After reading the letter with the greatest excitement.*] Ah, here, too, he has remained true to himself!—Oh, madam, what justice! What kindness! This is more than I had expected! More than I deserve! My fortune, my honor, everything is restored!—Surely I am dreaming! [*Looking once more at the letter as though to reassure himself.*] No, it is not an illusion born of my desires!—Read for yourself, madam; read for yourself!

MINNA. I would not be so presumptuous, major.

TELLHEIM. Presumptuous? The letter is to me, to your Tellheim, Minna. It contains something that your uncle cannot take away from you. You must read it; please read it!

MINNA. If it makes you happy, major. [*She takes the letter and reads it.*]

"My dear Major Tellheim:

I hereby inform you that the matter that had given me concern for your honor has been cleared up to your advantage. My brother knew the particulars of your case, and his testimony has more than proved your innocence. The royal treasury has orders to restore to you the promissory note in question and to reimburse you for the sum advanced. I have also ordered that all claims made against your account by the Army Paymaster be dismissed. Please inform me if your health permits you to take up active service again. I would be sorry to lose a man of your courage and temperament.

Your most affectionate Majesty," etc.

TELLHEIM. What do you have to say to that, madam?

MINNA. [*Folding up the letter and returning it to him.*] I?

Nothing.

TELLHEIM. Nothing?

MINNA. Well, I could say that your King, who is a great man, is doubtless also a good man.—But of what concern is that to me? He is not my King.

TELLHEIM. And you have nothing else to say? Nothing about us?

MINNA. You are going back into his service; from major you will be promoted to lieutenant colonel and perhaps full colonel. I give you my heartiest congratulations.

TELLHEIM. And you don't know me any better than that?—No, since fortune is restoring so much to me—more than enough to satisfy the wishes of a reasonable man—it will depend entirely on my Minna whether in the future I belong to anyone besides her. May my whole life be dedicated to your service alone! It is dangerous to serve the mighty, and such service offers no recompense for the trouble, duress, and debasement that it brings. Minna is not one of those vain creatures who love their men only for their title and position. She will love me for myself, and for her sake I shall renounce the rest of the world. I became a soldier out of pure partisanship; I do not myself know for what political principles I fought. And it was just a whim of mine that soldiering is good for every man of honor, for a time at least, so that he may become familiar with everything that men call danger and so learn coolheadedness and determination. Only the most dire necessity could have compelled me to make a vocation out of this experiment, to make a profession out of this temporary occupation. But now that I am no longer under any sort of pressure, my sole ambition is to be a peaceful and contented human being. With you, dearest Minna, this is what I shall inevitably become; and in your company, this is what I shall constantly remain.—May the most holy bond of matrimony join us tomorrow, and then we'll seek out and find the most peaceful, pleasant, and happy place in the whole world, a little corner that has everything necessary to be a true paradise except a loving couple. There we will live; there shall all of our days . . . What's the matter, Minna? [MINNA *moves uneasily back and forth, trying to hide her emotion.*]

MINNA. [*Pulling herself together.*] You are cruel, Tellheim, to describe so charmingly a happiness that you know I must reject. My loss . . .

TELLHEIM. Your loss? What do you mean by your loss? Anything that Minna could lose would not be Minna's. You are the sweetest, loveliest, most enchanting creature under the sun, full of goodness and generosity, full of innocence and joy—mixed now and then with a little petulance, and here and there a touch of willfulness. But so much the better! So much the better! Minna would otherwise be an angel whom I should have to worship with awe and whom I could not love. [*Takes her hand to kiss it.*]

MINNA. [*Taking her hand back.*] No, sir!—What is this change that has suddenly come over you? Is this flattering, impetuous lover the cold Tellheim? Could only the return of his good fortune have kindled this fire in him?—I trust he will permit me, in this fleeting passion of his, to retain the power of reflection for us both.—When he himself was in a position to reflect, I heard him say that it was a vile love that did not hesitate to expose the object of its affection to scorn.—That is true; but I aspire to just as pure and noble a love as he does. And now, when honor calls him, when a great king solicits his services, am I to allow him to give himself up to lovesick dreams of happiness with me? Am I to permit the illustrious warrior to degenerate into an amorous swain? No, major, follow the summons of your higher destiny.

TELLHEIM. Very well! If you find the great big world more attractive, Minna, then let us remain in the great big world!—How small and pitiful such a world really is! You know only its gilded surface. But in truth, Minna, you will . . . Never mind! So be it, then! That will be our destiny. Your charms will not lack admirers, nor will my happiness want for those envious of it.

MINNA. No, Tellheim, that's not what I meant. I'm directing you back into the great big world, back onto the path of your honor, without desiring to follow you there! In that world, Tellheim will need a wife who is beyond reproach. A runaway girl from Saxony who has thrown herself into his arms . . .

TELLHEIM. [*Starting up and looking wildly around him.*] Who dares to say such things?—Oh, Minna, I tremble before myself when I imagine someone other than you speaking like that. My rage against him would know no bounds.

MINNA. You see! That is just what troubles me. You would not put up with the slightest ridicule of me, and yet day in and day out you yourself would have to endure the most bitter mockery.—In short, Tellheim, listen to the decision I have made and from which nothing in the world can sway me.

TELLHEIM. Before you finish, madam . . . I implore you, Minna . . . consider for a moment that you are about to pass a sentence of life or death over me!

MINNA. I don't need to consider any further!—As surely as I gave you back the ring with which you once pledged your faithfulness to me, and as surely as you took this same ring back, just as surely shall the unfortunate Barnhelm never become the wife of the more fortunate Tellheim.

TELLHEIM. And so you condemn me to death, madam?

MINNA. Equality is the only sure bond of love. The prosperous Barnhelm wished to have as her husband only the prosperous Tellheim. Even the unfortunate Minna might finally have let herself be persuaded to share, for better or for worse, the ill fortune of her friend.—He must have noticed, before this letter arrived and made us unequal once again, that my refusal was only feigned.

TELLHEIM. Is that true, madam?—Thank you, Minna, for not yet pronouncing the final sentence. Is it only the unfortunate Tellheim that you want? He can be had. [*Coolly.*] I realize now that it does not become me to accept this belated vindication; that it will be better if I do not seek the return of what has been deprived me through so shameful a suspicion.—Yes, I will pretend not to have received the letter. This shall be my sole response to it! [*About to tear the letter up.*]

MINNA. [*Grabbing his hands.*] What are you going to do, Tellheim?

TELLHEIM. Have you for my own.

MINNA. Stop!

TELLHEIM. Madam, I swear to you that I shall tear it up unless you change your mind. Then we shall see what further objections to me you have!

MINNA. Why this tone?—So shall I, must I, grow contemptible in my own eyes? Never! Only a worthless creature would not be ashamed to owe her entire wealth and happiness to the blind affections of a man!

TELLHEIM. False, absolutely false!

MINNA. Do you dare deny your own words when they come from my lips?

TELLHEIM. This is sophistry! So the weaker sex is dishonored by the same things that dishonor the stronger! May a man, then, permit himself everything that is proper in a woman? Which sex did nature appoint to support the other?

MINNA. Calm down, Tellheim!—I shall not be completely without support even if I must decline the honor of yours. I'll manage to get by. I have let our ambassador know that I am here, and he wishes to see me today. I hope that he will take me under his wing. But the time is getting on. Permit me, major . . .

TELLHEIM. I will accompany you, madam.

MINNA. No, major, please don't.

TELLHEIM. Your shadow shall leave you before I do! Come, madam, we will go wherever you want and to whomever you want. And everywhere, a hundred times a day, in your presence, I shall tell friends and strangers alike of the bonds that tie you to me, and of the cruel obstinacy that makes you want to sever those bonds.

SCENE 10

JUST, TELLHEIM, MINNA, *and* FRANZISKA

JUST. [*Rushing in.*] Major! Major!

TELLHEIM. Yes?

JUST. Come quickly, quickly!

TELLHEIM. Why? You come here! Tell me, what is it?

JUST. Just, listen . . . [*Whispers to* TELLHEIM.]

MINNA. [*Aside to* FRANZISKA.] Do you notice anything, Franziska?

FRANZISKA. Oh, you are a merciless creature! Watching this has been like standing on hot coals!

TELLHEIM. [*To* JUST.] What did you say?—That's impossible!— You? [*Looking wildly at* MINNA.] Say it out loud! Say it to her face! Listen, madam!

JUST. The innkeeper says that Fräulein von Barnhelm has redeemed the ring that I pawned to him. She recognized it as her own and would not give it back.

TELLHEIM. Is that true, madam? No, it can't be true!

MINNA. [*Smiling.*] And why not, Tellheim? Why can't it be true?

TELLHEIM. [*Vehemently.*] All right, then, it is true!—A terrible light suddenly dawns on me! Now I see you for the false, unfaithful woman you are!

MINNA. [*Alarmed.*] Who? Who is unfaithful?

TELLHEIM. You, whom I can no longer call by name.

MINNA. Tellheim!

TELLHEIM. Forget my name!—You came here to break with me, that much is clear!—Oh, that chance should play so willingly into your faithless hands! It restored your ring to you, and by your own cunning you contrived to give me back mine.

MINNA. Tellheim, what visions are you conjuring up? Pull yourself together and listen to me!

FRANZISKA. [*To herself.*] Now she'll catch it!

SCENE 11

WERNER, *with a bag of gold*; TELLHEIM, MINNA, FRANZISKA, *and* JUST

WERNER. Here I am, back already, major!

TELLHEIM. [*Without looking at him.*] Who sent for you?

WERNER. Here's the money! Five thousand talers!

TELLHEIM. I don't want it!

WERNER. And tomorrow, major, you can have the same amount again if you so desire.

TELLHEIM. Keep your money!

WERNER. But it's your money, sir.—I don't think you know to whom you are speaking.

TELLHEIM. Take it away, I say!

WERNER. What's the matter with you? I'm Paul Werner.

TELLHEIM. All goodness is sheer pretense, all kindness mere deceit!

WERNER. Is that aimed at me?

TELLHEIM. As you please!

WERNER. I was just carrying out your orders.

TELLHEIM. Then carry out this one as well, and go away!

WERNER. Sir! [*Angry.*] I am a man—

TELLHEIM. Oh, that's really something!

WERNER. —who has a bit of a temper.

TELLHEIM. Good! A temper is still the best thing to have.

WERNER. I beg you, major . . .

TELLHEIM. How often do I have to tell you? I don't need your money!

WERNER. [*In a rage.*] All right, then, whoever wants it can have it! [*He throws the bag of gold down and goes to one side.*]

MINNA. Oh, my dear Franziska, I should have followed your advice. I've carried the joke too far. But he need only hear me out.—[*Going up to him.*]

FRANZISKA. [*Approaching* WERNER *without answering* MINNA.] Sergeant major!

WERNER. [*Sullenly.*] Leave me alone!

FRANZISKA. Ugh! What sort of men are these?

MINNA. Tellheim!—Tellheim! [TELLHEIM *is gnawing at his fingers in rage and has turned away from* MINNA, *refusing to listen to her.*] No, this is too much!—Listen to me!—You are mistaken!—It's just a misunderstanding . . . Tellheim!—Won't you listen to your Minna!—Can you entertain such a suspicion? I wanted to break my engagement with you? And that's the reason I came here?—Tellheim!

Two SERVANTS, *who run into the room one after the other from opposite sides*; WERNER, TELLHEIM, MINNA, FRANZISKA, *and* JUST

FIRST SERVANT. Madam, His Excellency, the Count!

SECOND SERVANT. He's coming, madam!

FRANZISKA. [*Runs to the window.*] It is he! It is he!

MINNA. Is it?—Now quickly, Tellheim—

TELLHEIM. [*Suddenly coming to himself.*] Who? Who's coming? Your uncle, madam? That cruel uncle?—All right, let him come; let him! Do not be afraid! Let him just try to harm you with even so much as a glance! He has me to deal with now.—Of course it's true that you don't deserve to be defended by me.—

MINNA. Quickly, Tellheim! Put your arms around me and forget everything.

TELLHEIM. Oh, if only I thought you might regret your treatment of me!

MINNA. No, I cannot regret having obtained a glimpse of your whole heart!—What a wonderful man you are! Put your arms around your Minna, your happy Minna, who is in nothing happier than in her love for you. [*She falls into his arms.*] And now, to meet him!

TELLHEIM. Meet whom?

MINNA. The best of your unknown friends.

TELLHEIM. What?

MINNA. The Count, my uncle, my father, your father.—My flight, his displeasure, my disinheritance . . . don't you see that it was all made up? How gullible you are, my dear!

TELLHEIM. Made up?—But the ring? What about the ring?

MINNA. Where is the ring that I gave back to you?

TELLHEIM. You'll take it back?—Oh, how happy you make me!—Here, Minna! [*He takes it out.*]

MINNA. Look at it first!—Oh, there are none so blind as those who will not see!—Which ring is that? The one you gave to me, or the one I gave to you?—Isn't it the very one I didn't want to leave in the innkeeper's possession?

TELLHEIM. My God, what do I see? What am I hearing?

MINNA. Shall I take it back now? Shall I?—Give it to me! Give it here! [*She snatches it from his hand and places it on his finger.*]

Now, is everything all right?

TELLHEIM. Where am I?—[*Kissing her hand.*] Oh, you wicked angel! To torture me like that!

MINNA. This was just a demonstration, my dear husband, that you shall never play a trick on me without my playing one on you right back.—Don't you think that you tortured me as well?

TELLHEIM. You actresses! I should have known better than to be fooled by the two of you.

FRANZISKA. No, really, I don't think I could be an actress. I was trembling and shuddering and had to hold my hand over my mouth to keep it shut.

MINNA. My role didn't come easily to me, either.—But now let's go.

TELLHEIM. I still can't get over it.—How happy I feel, yet how frightened! It's like suddenly waking up from a nightmare.

MINNA. We must not delay.—I hear him coming.

SCENE 13
COUNT VON BRUCHSAL, *accompanied by several* SERVANTS *and the* INNKEEPER; MINNA, FRANZISKA, TELLHEIM, JUST, WERNER, *and the two* SERVANTS *from the previous scene*

COUNT. [*Entering.*] You arrived safely, then?

MINNA. [*Running to meet him.*] Oh, my father!

COUNT. Yes, here I am, dear Minna! [*Embracing her.*] But what's this, my girl? [*Noting* TELLHEIM.] You've been here only twenty-four hours, and you've already made friends and are beginning to entertain?

MINNA. Can you guess who it is?

COUNT. Surely not your Tellheim?

MINNA. Who else!—Come, Tellheim! [*She leads him to the* COUNT.]

COUNT. Sir, we have never met before, and yet I thought I recognized you as soon as I saw you. I hoped it would be you.—Give me your hand! You enjoy my highest esteem, and I ask for your friendship. My niece, my daughter, loves you.

MINNA. That much you know, father! And is it blind, this love of mine?

COUNT. No, Minna, your love is not blind, but your beloved . . . is mute.

TELLHEIM. [*Throwing himself into the* COUNT's *arms.*] Please let me pull myself together, father.

COUNT. Very well, my son. I see that your heart can speak even if your mouth cannot.—As a rule I do not care for officers who wear this color [*Pointing to* TELLHEIM's *uniform.*], but you are an honorable man, Tellheim; and whatever uniform an honorable man puts on, people will still like him.

MINNA. Oh, if only you knew the whole story!

COUNT. What's to prevent me from hearing it?—Where are my rooms, innkeeper?

INNKEEPER. Would your Excellency be good enough to step this way?

COUNT. Come on, Minna! Come, major! [*Exits with* INNKEEPER *and* SERVANTS.]

MINNA. Come, Tellheim!

TELLHEIM. I'll follow you in a moment, madam. I need a word first with this man. [*Turning to* WERNER.]

MINNA. And make it a good one. I think you owe it to him. Right, Franziska? [*Exit.*]

SCENE 14
TELLHEIM, WERNER, JUST, *and* FRANZISKA

TELLHEIM. [*Pointing to the bag that* WERNER *threw away.*] Pick up that bag, Just, and take it home. Go on! [JUST *picks it up and exits.*]

WERNER. [*Who has been standing sullenly in the corner and not participating in any of the foregoing.*] Well?

TELLHEIM. [*Approaching him in a friendly manner.*] Werner, when can I have the other five thousand talers?

WERNER. [*Immediately getting back into a good mood.*] Tomorrow, major, tomorrow.

TELLHEIM. I no longer need to become your debtor, but I will be your banker. You good-hearted people all need someone to look after your financial affairs. You are sort of a spendthrift, you know. . . . I'm afraid I made you angry a little while ago, Werner.

WERNER. Upon my soul, you did!—But I shouldn't have been such a fool. Now I understand everything. I really deserve a hundred lashes, and you may give them to me, major. Only no more hard feelings, please!

TELLHEIM. Hard feelings!—[*Shaking* WERNER's *hand.*] Read in my eyes all that I cannot put into words.—Hah, I'd like to meet the man who has a finer girl and a better friend than I have! Isn't that right, Franziska? [*Exit.*]

SCENE 15
FRANZISKA *and* WERNER

FRANZISKA. [*Aside.*] Yes, indeed, he is a very good man! I'll never meet another like him. And I've got to convey that to him! [*Shyly and modestly going up to* WERNER.] Sergeant major . . .

WERNER. [*Wiping his eyes.*] Yes?

FRANZISKA. Sergeant major . . .

WERNER. What do you want, little lady?

FRANZISKA. Look at me, sergeant major.

WERNER. I can't just yet; I don't know what I've got in my eye.

FRANZISKA. Do look at me, please!

WERNER. I'm afraid I've looked at you a bit too much already, little lady!—There, now I can see you. What is it?

FRANZISKA. Sergeant major—don't you need a Mrs. Sergeant Major?

WERNER. Are you in earnest, little lady?

FRANZISKA. Absolutely!

WERNER. And would you even go to Persia with me?

FRANZISKA. Wherever you like!

WERNER. Really?—Hey, major, don't boast! I've got as fine a girl and as good a friend as you have!—Give me your hand, little lady! It's a match!—In ten years' time you'll either be a general's wife or a widow!

Curtain

Select Bibliography

Aikin, Judith P. "Who Learns a Lesson? The Function of Sex Role Reversal in Lessing's *Minna von Barnhelm.*" In *Feminist Studies and German Culture: Women in German Yearbook 3,* edited by Marianne Burkhard and Edith Waldstein, 47–61. Lanham, Md.: University Press of America, 1986.

Batley, E. M. "Lessing's Dramatic Technique as a Catalyst of the Enlightenment." *German Life and Letters,* n.s. 33, no. 1 (October 1979): 9–23.

Belgardt, Raimund. "Tellheim's Honor: Flaw or Virtue? A Reinterpretation." *The Germanic Review* 42, no. 1 (January 1967): 16–29.

Bennett, Benjamin. "The Generic Constant in Lessing's Development of a Comedy of Institutions and Alienation." *German Quarterly* 56, no. 2 (March 1983): 231–42.

Boa, Elizabeth. "Der gute Mensch von Barnhelm: The Female Essence and the Ensemble of Human Relations in Lessing's *Minna von Barnhelm.*" *Publications of the English Goethe Society* 54 (1983–84): 1–36.

Brewer, E. V. "Lessing and the Corrective Virtue in Comedy." *Journal of English and Germanic Philology* 26 (1927): 1–23.

Brown, F. Andrew. *Gotthold Ephraim Lessing.* New York: Twayne, 1971.

Carroll, Joseph. "*Minna von Barnhelm* and *le genre sérieux*: A Reevaluation." *Lessing Yearbook* 13 (1981): 143–58.

Critchfield, Richard. "The Search for an Enlightened Sovereign in Lessing's Drama." *Studies in Eighteenth-Century Culture* 9 (1979): 251–67.

Dodson, Daniel B. "Gotthold Ephraim Lessing." In *European Writers: The Age of Reason and Enlightenment,* edited by George Stade, 537–62. New York: Scribner's, 1984.

Duncan, Bruce. "Hand, Heart, and Language in *Minna von Barnhelm.*" *Seminar* 8, no. 1 (March 1972): 15–30.

———. "The Implied Reader of Lessing's Theory of Comedy." *Lessing Yearbook* 10 (1978): 35–45.

Durrani, Osman. "Love and Money in Lessing's *Minna von Barnhelm.*" *Modern Language Review* 84, no. 3 (July 1989): 638–51.

Garland, H. B. *Lessing: The Founder of Modern German Literature*. 2d ed. Cambridge: Bowes and Bowes, 1949.

Gombrich, E. H. "Lessing." *Proceedings of the British Academy* 43 (1957): 133–56.

Graham, Ilse Appelbaum. "The Currency of Love: A Reading of Lessing's *Minna von Barnhelm.*" *German Life and Letters,* n.s. 18, no. 4 (July 1965): 270–78.

Guidry, Glenn A. "Money, Honor, and Love: The Hierarchy of Values in Lessing's *Minna von Barnhelm.*" *Lessing Yearbook* 14 (1982): 177–86.

Harrison, Robin. *Lessing: "Minna von Barnhelm"; Critical Guides to German Texts 4*. London: Grant and Cutler, 1985.

Heitner, Robert. "Lessing's Manipulation of a Single Comic Theme." *Modern Language Quarterly* 18, no. 3 (September 1957): 183–98.

———. "Rationalism and Irrationalism in Lessing." *Lessing Yearbook* 5 (1973): 82–106.

Hoelzel, Alfred. "Truth and Honesty in *Minna von Barnhelm.*" *Lessing Yearbook* 9 (1977): 28–44.

Jolles, Matthijs. "Lessing's Conception of History." *Modern Philology* 43, no. 3 (February 1946): 175–91.

Jones, G. L. "Reason and Reality: Some Reflections on *Minna von Barnhelm,* Lessing, and Frederick the Great." *Oxford German Studies* 10 (1979): 64–75.

Kieffer, Bruce. "Wieland and Lessing: *Musarion* and *Minna von Barnhelm.*" *Lessing Yearbook* 14 (1982): 187–208.

Kies, Paul P. "Lessing's Relation to Early English Sentimental Comedy." *PMLA* 47, no. 3 (September 1932): 807–26.

Lamport, F. J. *Lessing and the Drama.* New York: Oxford University Press, 1981.

Lehrer, Mark. "Lessing's Economic Comedy." *Seminar* 20, no. 2 (May 1984): 79–94.

Löb, Ladislaus. *From Lessing to Hauptmann: Studies in German Drama.* London: University Tutorial Press, 1974.

Lukács, Georg. "Lessing's *Minna von Barnhelm.*" *International Social Science*

Journal 19, no. 4 (1967): 570–80. First published in German in *Akzente, Zeitschrift für Dichtung,* April 1964.

Mander, Gertrude. "Lessing and His Heritage." In *The German Theatre: A Symposium,* edited by Ronald Hayman, 13–26. New York: Barnes and Noble, 1975.

Martinson, Steven D. "The Cunning of Deceit in Lessing's Major Works." *Lessing Yearbook* 14 (1982): 99–118.

Metzger, Michael M. *Lessing and the Language of Comedy.* The Hague: Mouton, 1966.

Nolte, Fred Otto. *Grillparzer, Lessing, and Goethe in the Perspective of European Literature.* Lancaster, Pa.: Lancaster Press, 1938.

Stout, Harry L. "Lessing's Riccaut and Thomas Mann's Fitelberg." *German Quarterly* 36, no. 1 (January 1963): 24–30.

Ulmer, Bernhard. "The Leitmotiv and Musical Structure in Lessing's Dramas." *The Germanic Review* 22, no. 1 (February 1947): 13–31.

Wessell, Leonhard P., Jr., and Charles M. Barrack. "The Tragic Background to Lessing's Comedy *Minna von Barnhelm.*" *Lessing Yearbook* 2 (1970): 149–61.

Whiton, John. "Tellheim and the Russians: Aspects of Lessing's Response to the Seven Years' War in *Minna von Barnhelm.*" *Lessing Yearbook* 17 (1985): 89–108.

Wilson, W. Daniel. " 'Die Dienste der Grossen': The Flight from Public Service in Lessing's Major Plays." *Deutsche Vierteljahrsschrift für Literaturwissenschaft und Geistesgeschichte* 61, no. 2 (June 1987): 238–65.

Witte, Karsten. "How Nazi Cinema Mobilizes the Classics: Schweikart's *Das Fräulein von Barnhelm* (1940)." Translated by Jan-Christopher Horak. In *German Film and Literature: Adaptations and Transformations,* edited by Eric Rentschler, 103–16. New York: Methuen, 1986.

The Broken Pitcher

A Comedy

by
HEINRICH VON KLEIST

Translated by
Bert Cardullo

Translated from the following edition:
Kleist, Heinrich von. *Der zerbrochene Krug.* In *Werke und Briefe in vier Bänden,* edited by Siegfried Streller et al., vol. 1. Berlin: Aufbau-Verlag, 1978.

Characters

Walter, Circuit Judge
Adam, Village Judge
Light, Clerk of Court
Frau Martha Rull
Eve, her daughter
Veit Tümpel, a peasant
Ruprecht, his son
Frau Bridget
A Servant, Bailiff, Maidservants, etc.

The action takes place in a Dutch village near Utrecht.

Scene: The Courtroom

SCENE I

ADAM *is sitting and bandaging his leg.* LIGHT *enters.*
LIGHT. Well, what the devil, tell me now, friend Adam!
Whatever's happened to you? How you look!

ADAM. Oh well, to stumble all you need is feet.
On this smooth floor, I ask you, where's a stump?
And yet I stumbled here; for each man has
The wretched stumbling block within himself.
 LIGHT. What's that you say? That each man has his block—?
 ADAM. Yes, in himself.
 LIGHT.   A curse on that!
 ADAM.   What do you mean?
 LIGHT. You're named after a flighty ancestor,
Who fell right at the very start of things,
And whom that selfsame fall has given fame;
You're surely not—?
 ADAM.   Well?
 LIGHT.   Likewise—?
 ADAM.   I—? I think so—!
Right here it was I took a fall, I tell you.
 LIGHT. No figurative fall?
 ADAM.   Not figurative.
I guess 'twas no fair figure that I cut.
 LIGHT. And when did all this business come to pass?
 ADAM. Right now, this moment; I was getting up
From bed. I had the dawn song on my lips,
When, crash! I stumbled right into the dawn,
And I'd not yet begun my daily rounds
Before God made me dislocate my foot.
 LIGHT. No doubt it was the left, to boot?
 ADAM.   The left one?
 LIGHT. This sound one here?
 ADAM.   Of course!
 LIGHT.   Oh, righteous God,
Who makes the way of sin so very hard!
 ADAM. The foot! What? Hard! How so?
 LIGHT.   The clubfoot?
 ADAM.   Clubfoot!
One foot is just as clubby as the other.
 LIGHT. Not so, my friend! You do your right a wrong.
The right one cannot boast of such a sprain,
And it might sooner walk a slippery road.
 ADAM.   Oh, bosh!
Where one foot ventures out, the other follows.
 LIGHT. And what has given your face such defacement?
 ADAM. My face, you say?
 LIGHT.   What, you've not faced that yet?

ADAM. Unless I'm lying, no—how does it look?
LIGHT. What, how it looks?
ADAM.   Yes, friend.
LIGHT.   Why, horrible!
ADAM. Explain yourself more plainly.
LIGHT.   Well, it's flayed,
A gruesome sight. A piece out of your cheek,
How big? I cannot judge without the scales.
ADAM. The hell you say!
LIGHT. [*Brings a mirror.*] Here, look! Convince yourself!
A sheep that with the baying dogs right on its heels
Must squeeze through thorns, won't leave more wool behind
Than you've abandoned flesh, the Lord knows where.
ADAM. Hm! Yes! That's so. It doesn't look so nice.
I see my nose has suffered.
LIGHT.   And your eye.
ADAM. Oh, not my eye, good friend.
LIGHT.   Why yes, here lies
Crossways a welt, bloodstained, God is my judge;
A raging farmhand might have dealt the like.
ADAM. That's just the eyebone there.—Well, think of that.
And all that happened and I never knew it.
LIGHT. Yes, sir! It's like that in the middle of a fight.
ADAM. What? Fighting!—With that curséd billy goat
Next to my stove I fought, I guess. That's it.
When I had lost my balance, drunk with sleep,
And, hands outstretched, was clawing at the air,
I got hold of the trousers that last night
I'd hung, all wet to dry, above the stove.
I grabbed at them, you see, fool that I was,
And thought they'd hold me up, but then the belt
Gave way, and belt and I and trousers fell,
And head first with my forehead down I crashed
Upon the stove, just where the billy goat
Sticks out his nose, right at the corner there.
LIGHT. [*Laughs.*] That's good!
ADAM.   Now damn it all!
LIGHT.   First fall of Adam
You ever took in falling *out* of bed.
ADAM. Upon my soul!—But by the way, what is the news?
LIGHT. Oh yes, there's news, all right! And I'll be hanged,
I almost had forgot it.
ADAM.   Well?

LIGHT. Make ready for an unexpected visit
From Utrecht.
    ADAM.   Oh?
    LIGHT.   The circuit judge is coming.
    ADAM. Who's coming?
    LIGHT.   Justice Walter, circuit judge.
He's out inspecting all the district courts,
And will arrive by us today.
    ADAM. Today? Have you your senses?
    LIGHT.   Sure's I'm standing here.
He was in Holla yesterday, reviewed
The court of justice in that border town.
A peasant saw the horses being hitched
To bring his carriage on to our own Huysum.
    ADAM. Today, from Utrecht, here, the circuit judge!
Inspecting us, that honest man who feathers his
Own nest yet claims to hate such goings-on.
He comes to Huysum just to torment us!
    LIGHT. If he reached Holla, he'll reach Huysum too.
You'd best beware.
    ADAM.   Go on!
    LIGHT.   I'm telling you.
    ADAM. Go on there with your fairy tales, I say.
    LIGHT. God knows, the peasant says he saw him.
    ADAM. Who knows who 'twas that blear-eyed scoundrel saw?
Those fellows can't distinguish back from front;
A head's a face to them, so long it's bare.
Just put a hat upon my stick,
A mantle draped around, two boots beneath—
Such fools will take it to be anyone you want.
    LIGHT. Well, go on doubting, in the devil's name,
Till he comes in that door.
    ADAM.   What, he, come here!—
Without his having breathed a word to us?
    LIGHT. You are so thick! As if 'twas still the same
Inspector as before, Judge Juniper!
It's Walter now who will review our court.
    ADAM. Suppose it is! Go on, leave me in peace.
The man has taken his official oath
And practices, like us, according to
Existing edicts and the precedents.
    LIGHT. Well, I assure you, yesterday Judge Walter
Appeared in Holla wholly unexpected,

Inspected records and accounts,
And then suspended both the judge and clerk.
Why? I don't know, but they are out of office.
    ADAM. Well, I'll be damned! Was that the peasant's tale?
    LIGHT. That and some more—
    ADAM.   Oh?
    LIGHT.   If you want to know.
This very day they went to see the judge,
Whom they were holding prisoner in his own house,
And found him in the granary out back,
Strung up there from a rafter in the roof.
    ADAM. What do you say?
    LIGHT.   Meanwhile some help was brought,
They cut him down, they shook and slapped and drenched him,
And barely brought him back to life.
    ADAM. They brought him back, eh?
    LIGHT.   Now his house is sealed,
With depositions sworn and things locked up,
As if he was a corpse before his time;
And add to that his judgeship's gone to someone else.
    ADAM. Well, shut my eyes!—He was a wretched cur—
Yet otherwise an honest soul, upon my life,
A chap with whom good times were to be had;
But what a low-life, yes, I have to say.
And if today Judge Walter was in Holla,
Poor man, he surely had his work
Cut out for him, I do believe.
    LIGHT. And only this affair, the peasant said,
Has kept the judge from reaching us much sooner;
But without fail he will be here by noon.
    ADAM. At noon! Good partner! Now your friendship tells.
You know just how two hands can wash each other.
I know you'd well like to be village judge,
And you deserve it, too, as much as any man.
But this is not your opportunity;
Today I hope you'll let that cup pass by.
    LIGHT. I, village judge! What are you thinking of?
    ADAM. You are a lover of effective speech,
And you have learned as much from Cicero
As any at the school in Amsterdam.
But keep ambition back today, you hear?
No doubt there'll be occasions yet to come
When you can show your skill with good results.

LIGHT. We two are fine comrades! Go on, relax.

ADAM. At proper times, you know, Demosthenes
The great was mute. Be guided now by him.
And though I am not King of Macedon,
Still in my way I can be grateful too.

LIGHT. Away with your suspiciousness, I say.
Or have I ever—?

ADAM.   Look, for my part, I,
I follow that great Greek myself. You know,
One could in time work out a mighty speech
On public funds and rates of interest:
But who would want to talk about such things?

LIGHT. That's right!

ADAM.   Of such reproach I'm wholly free,
Confound it! And whatever I have done that's wrong
Was just a prank, let's say, born of the night
And shunning daylight's prying rays.

LIGHT.   I know.

ADAM. My word! No reason, really, why a judge,
When he's not sitting on the judge's bench,
Should carry on as gravely as a polar bear.

LIGHT. I say so, too.

ADAM.   Well then, come on, good friend,
And follow me into the registry;
I'll stack the documents a bit, for they,
Like Babel's fallen tower, lie about.

SCENE 2

A SERVANT *enters. Later: two* MAIDSERVANTS.

SERVANT. God save you, Judge! Inspector Justice Walter
Sends his respects and says he'll soon be here.

ADAM. Oh, righteous heaven! Is he done already in
Holla?

SERVANT. Yes, he is here in Huysum now.

ADAM. Hey, Lisa! Greta!

LIGHT.   Quiet there, be calm.

ADAM. My friend!

LIGHT.   Please send him back respectful thanks.

SERVANT. Tomorrow we continue on to Huzzah.

ADAM. What shall I do? Let's see! [*He reaches for his clothes.*]

FIRST MAID. [*Enters.*]   I'm right here, sir.

LIGHT. Put on those trousers, will you? Are you mad?

SECOND MAID. [*Enters.*] Here, at your service, Judge.

LIGHT.   And now your coat.

ADAM. [*Looks around.*] Is that the circuit judge?

LIGHT.   No, just the maid!

ADAM. My cuffs! My coat! My collar!

FIRST MAID.   First the vest!

ADAM. What?—Coat off! Quick!

LIGHT. [*To* SERVANT.]   The circuit judge will be
Most welcome here. We shall at once
Be ready to receive him. Tell him that.

ADAM. The hell you say! Judge Adam begs to be
Excused.

LIGHT. You say excused!

ADAM.   I say excused.
Is he already on his way?

SERVANT.   He is
Still at the inn. He has sent for the smith;
The carriage needs repairs.

ADAM.   That's good. My compliments.
Our smith is very slow. But all
The same, I must excuse myself.
Just say I nearly broke my neck and legs;
You see yourself, it is a fright the way I look;
And more excitement will affect me like a purge.
Say I am sick.

LIGHT.   Have you your wits about you?—
You tell the judge we shall be glad to see him.
—Won't you?

ADAM.   Oh, hang it!

LIGHT.   What?

ADAM.   The devil take me,
It's just as if I've had a purgative.

LIGHT. That's all you need to give yourself away.

ADAM. Margreta! Hey! You bag of bones! Hey, Lisa!

BOTH MAIDS. Why, here we are. What is it?

ADAM.   Go, I say!
Fetch cheese and ham, and Brunswick sausage, butter, beer,
From out the registry! And make it quick!—
Not you. The other.—Nitwit! I mean you!
God's lightning, Greta!—Lisa, milkmaid, you
Go get it, now! [*Exit* FIRST MAID.]

SECOND MAID. Be clear about just what you want!

ADAM. And you shut up! Be gone! Get me my wig!

March! From the bookcase. Quick! Take off!
[*Exit* SECOND MAID.]
   LIGHT. [*To* SERVANT.] I hope your lord, the worthy circuit judge,
Has met with no misfortune on his trip?
   SERVANT. Well, yes, we flipped the carriage in a narrow pass.
   ADAM. Ouch, ouch! My foot's all skinned! My boots will not—
   LIGHT. In heaven's name! You flipped, you say?
And what about the damage!
   SERVANT.   Nothing serious.
My master sprained his hand a little bit.
The shaft broke off.
   ADAM.   I wish his neck had broken!
   LIGHT. What, sprained his hand! Oh, God! And has the smith
                            come yet?
   SERVANT. To mend the shaft, yes.
   LIGHT.   What?
   ADAM.   You mean the doctor.
   LIGHT. What?
   SERVANT.   For the shaft?
   ADAM.   Oh, bosh! To wrap his hand.
   SERVANT. Your servant, sir.—I think these chaps are mad. [*Exit.*]
   LIGHT. I meant the smith.
   ADAM.   You give yourself away.
   LIGHT. How so?
   ADAM.   You're ill at ease.
   LIGHT.   Say what!
      [*The* FIRST MAID *enters.*]
   ADAM.   Hey, Lisa!
What's that you've got?
   FIRST MAID.   Why, Brunswick sausage, Judge.
   ADAM. No, those are court sources.
   LIGHT.   Who's ill at ease!
   ADAM. They should be brought back to the registry;
File under "B."
   FIRST MAID.   The sausage, sir?
   ADAM. The sausage! Bosh! These sources here.
   LIGHT. 'Twas a misunderstanding.
   SECOND MAID. [*Enters.*]   Judge, your wig,
It isn't in the bookcase there.
   ADAM. Why not?
   SECOND MAID.   Because you—
   ADAM.   Well?
   SECOND MAID.   Why, at eleven—

Last night—
    ADAM.   Well? Will you speak?
    SECOND MAID.   You came without
Your wig into the house, you will recall.
    ADAM. What, I, without my wig?
    SECOND MAID.   Indeed you did.
And here is Lisa, who will testify the same.
The other one is at the wig shop in Utrecht.
    ADAM. You say—?
    FIRST MAID.   Yes, on my honor, Judge Adam!
You were bald-headed, sir, when you returned;
You said that you had fallen, don't you know?
I had to wash the blood stains off your head.
    ADAM. Impertinent thing!
    FIRST MAID.   As I'm an honest girl.
    ADAM. Shut up, I say, there is no truth in it.
    LIGHT. What, yesterday you got that wound?
    ADAM.   Today.
The wound today and yesterday the wig.
I wore it, powdered white, upon my head,
And with my hat I took it off, I swear,
By error when I stepped into the house.
No telling what it was she may have washed.
—Go to the devil, that's where you belong!
Go to the registry! [*Exit* FIRST MAID.] You, Greta, go
And ask the sexton if he'll lend me his;
Tell him the cat, the dirty pig, gave birth
This morning in my wig! All filthied up
It lay beneath my bed, I now recall.
    LIGHT. The cat? Say what? Are you—
    ADAM.   True as I live.
Five kittens, black and yellow; one is white.
The black ones, I shall drown them in the river Vecht.
What can one do? Would you like one to keep?
    LIGHT. What, in your wig?
    ADAM.   The devil take that wig!
I hung it up, as usual,
Upon a chair, before I went to bed,
But in the night I hit the chair, it fell—
    LIGHT. The cat then took it in her jaws—
    ADAM.   My word—
    LIGHT. And carried it beneath the bed to bear her young.

ADAM. Her jaws? No—
LIGHT.   No? How else?
ADAM.   The cat? Oh, bosh!
LIGHT. No? Was it you, perhaps?
ADAM.   My jaws! I think—
I kicked it underneath the bed today,
On seeing it.
LIGHT.   All right, that's good.
ADAM.   These wretched beasts!
They copulate and have their litters where they will.
SECOND MAID. [*Giggling.*] Then shall I go?
ADAM.   Yes, do, and say hello for me
To cousin Bombazine, the sexton's wife.
I'll send the wig undamaged back to her
This very day—to him you need not say a thing.
You understand?
SECOND MAID. I'll carry out your wish. [*Exit.*]

SCENE 3

ADAM. I foresee nothing good today, friend Light.
LIGHT. Why so?
ADAM.   My life is all askew,
And is this not a court day, too?
LIGHT.   It is.
The plaintiffs are already at the door.
ADAM. —I dreamt a plaintiff had laid hold of me
And dragged me to the judge's seat; and I,
I sat there notwithstanding on the bench,
And scolded, skinned, roughed up myself,
And sentenced my own neck into the irons.
LIGHT. What? You condemned yourself?
ADAM.   As I'm an honest man.
We two then grew to one, and took to flight,
And had to spend the night among the pines.
LIGHT. Well? And the dream, you think—?
ADAM.   The devil take it.
If not the dream, some deviltry,
I don't know what, is in the works for me!
LIGHT. Oh baseless fear! Just heed established rules
As long as the inspector's visiting.

And hand out from your bench impartial justice,
In order that your dream of judge dismissed
Does not become an actuality.

SCENE 4

Circuit Judge WALTER *enters.*
WALTER. God save you, Justice Adam.
ADAM.   Welcome to you!
You're welcome, worthy sir, here in our Huysum!
Who could, oh righteous God, who could have thought
That we should have so joyous a visit?
No dream as late as eight o'clock this morning
Might have aspired to such happiness.
    WALTER. I come without much notice, that I know, and must
Upon this journey, in the service of the state,
Be satisfied if my good hosts discharge
Me in the end with less-than-fond good-byes.
Meanwhile, as far as our relations go,
My wish is to be kind, right from the start.
The high tribunal of our land at Utrecht
Seeks to improve administration of the law
In country parts, where it appears in many ways
To operate defectively;
Abuses may expect a stern rebuke.
But my concern upon this trip is not
Yet to be stern; I'm to observe, not penalize,
And though I find that things are not as they should be,
I shall be glad if they are bearable.
    ADAM. In truth, such noble thinking must be praised.
Your Honor will at times, I have no doubt,
Find fault with our time-honored legal ways;
And though they're valid in these Netherlands
And have been since the time of Charles the Fifth,
When can't the mind create something that's new?
The world, our proverb says, grows wiser all the time,
And all men read, I know, Sam Pufendorf;
But Huysum is a small part of the world,
Which cannot hope for more, nor less, than just
Its proper share of universal wisdom.
Give kind instruction to us in the ways of law,
And be assured, Your Grace, you will have scarce

So much as turned your back to go,
When our judicial system shall
Content you to the uttermost.
Should you, though, find our court today as you
Would wish, upon my soul, 'twould be a miracle,
Since it but vaguely guesses what you want.
    WALTER. It either lacks in regulations or
There are too many, which we then shall have to sift.
    ADAM. Yes, through a mighty sieve. Much chaff! Much chaff!
    WALTER. And you're the Clerk of Court?
    LIGHT.   I am Clerk Light,
At service of Your Honor. It is now
Nine years that I have been here in this court.
    ADAM. [*Brings a chair.*] Be seated.
    WALTER.   Never mind.
    ADAM.   You've come from Holla, though.
    WALTER. Just seven miles or less—how is that known to you?
    ADAM. What, how? Your Honor's man—
    LIGHT.   A peasant told us so—
He's just now come to town from Holla.
    WALTER. A peasant?
    ADAM.   That's right.
    WALTER.   Yes, well in Holla
A quite unhappy incident took place,
Which has disturbed for me the cheerful mood
That should attend us when we're duty-bound.
No doubt you have had news of this affair?
    ADAM. And is it true, Your Honor? That Judge Pfaul,
On suffering arrest in his own house,
Surrendered to the folly of despair
And tried to hang himself?
    WALTER.   And made the evil worse.
What only seemed disorder and confusion,
Now looks as if it is embezzlement,
Which Holland's law, you know, no longer tolerates.—
How many different funds have you?
    ADAM.   We've five, sir.
    WALTER. What, five, you say? I thought—And money in them?
'Twas my belief you had but four—
    ADAM.   Your pardon!
Recall the fund for flooding of the Rhine?
    WALTER. The fund for flooding of the Rhine!
But now the Rhine is free of floods,

And so collections are not being made.
—Tell me, is this the day for holding court?
ADAM. You mean—?
WALTER.   What?
LIGHT.   Yes, the first day of the week.
WALTER. So then that little crowd I saw just now
Outside your door, were they—?
ADAM.   They probably—
LIGHT. They are the plaintiffs who've already gathered to
Present their case.
WALTER.   Good. That's just fine with me.
I ask that you admit these people now.
I will attend your session; thus I'll see
How justice is dispensed here in Huysum.
We'll do the registry, we'll check the several funds,
Right afterwards, when we are finished here.
ADAM. As you command.—Hey, bailiff! Hanfriede!

SCENE 5

The SECOND MAID *enters.*
SECOND MAID. The sexton's wife sends greetings, Judge Adam;
Glad as she'd be to lend the wig—
ADAM.   What? No?
SECOND MAID. She says they're having morning prayers today;
The sexton has one wig upon his head,
The other one she finds unfit to use,
And to the wig shop it must go this very day.
ADAM. Oh hell!
SECOND MAID.   As soon as the sexton comes back,
She'll send his wig to you at once.
ADAM. Upon my honor, please Your Grace—
WALTER.   What is it?
ADAM. An accident, most curséd, has deprived
Me of both wigs I own. And now a third,
That I had hoped to borrow, fails me too:
Bald-headed I shall have to hold my court.
WALTER. Bald-headed!
ADAM.   Yes, as God is good! And though
Without my wig's help I'll be quite
Hard-pressed to keep hold of my dignity—
Or must I try out on the farm,

And ask my tenant there—?
WALTER.   Out on the farm!
Is there no other person in the place—?
ADAM. No, for a fact—
WALTER.   The minister, perhaps.
ADAM. The minister? He—
WALTER.   Or the schoolmaster.
ADAM. Since tithes were done away with, sir,
Which in my office I have helped achieve,
I can no longer count on help from them.
   WALTER. Well, Village Judge? Well? What about your court
                                          today?
You want to wait until your hair grows out?
   ADAM. If you permit, I'll send out to the farm.
   WALTER. How far is that from here?
   ADAM.   Oh, I would say
Not half an hour.
   WALTER.   What, half an hour to wait?
And yet it's past the time for court to start.
Get on with it! For I must reach Huzzah today.
   ADAM. Get on with it! Well—
   WALTER.   Just put powder on your head!
In Satan's name, where did you leave your wigs?
—Come, do as best you can. I am in haste.
   ADAM. You, too?
   BAILIFF. [Enters.] The bailiff's here.
   ADAM. [To WALTER.]   Can I meanwhile
Provide you with a tasty bite to eat,
Some Brunswick sausage and perhaps a glass of beer—
   WALTER. No thanks.
   ADAM.   No trouble!
   WALTER.   Thanks, I said, I've had some food.
You go and use the time; I need it, too,
To jot some things down in my little book.
   ADAM. Well, if you so command—Come, Greta!
   WALTER. You've had a nasty injury, Judge Adam.
What, did you fall?
   ADAM.   A truly murderous fall
I took this morning, getting out of bed:
You see, Your Honor, 'twas a wretched crash
Into the room—I thought, into my grave.
   WALTER. I'm sorry for it.—There won't be

Aftereffects, I trust.
ADAM.   I think not, sir.
Nor shall I be impeded in my duty's course.—
Your leave!
  WALTER. Go, go!
  ADAM. [*To the* BAILIFF.] Call in the plaintiffs—march! [ADAM,
the MAID, *and the* BAILIFF *go out.*]

                    SCENE 6

FRAU MARTHA, EVE, VEIT, *and* RUPRECHT *enter.*—WALTER *and*
LIGHT *in the background.*
  MARTHA. Oh pitcher-smashing rabble that you are!
You'll pay for this, you shall!
  VEIT.   Just you be still,
Frau Martha! All that shall be settled here.
  MARTHA. Oh surely. Settled. Look at him. Smart talker.
This pitcher here, my broken one, all settled.
Who'll settle for me my unsettled jug?
Here 'twill be settled—that my jug shall stay
Unsettled. And for such a settlement
I would not give up these unsettled pieces here.
  VEIT. If you can demonstrate your right, I've said
I will replace it.
  MARTHA.   You'll replace my jug.
If I can demonstrate my right, you will replace.
You place that jug somewhere, just try it once;
Just place it there upon the shelf! Re-place!
This jug that has no leg on which to stand,
On which to lie or sit, you would re-place!
  VEIT. You heard me! Why the stir? Can one do more?
If one of us it was that broke the jug,
We'll make amends.
  MARTHA.   You'll make amends!
You might as well go take your place among dumb beasts.
You think that justice is a potter?
Well, if the mighty judges came and tied
An apron on and took the pieces to the kiln,
They might do something to that jug,
But mend it they would not. Nonsense, you'll make amends!
  RUPRECHT. Ignore her, father. Heed my words. That witch!
It's not the broken pitcher gets her sore,
It is the wedding that's been broken up,

And now by force she thinks it can be patched.
But I will put my foot down here and now:
I will be damned if e'er I wed the slut.
    MARTHA. Conceited ass! I patch the wedding up!
That wedding isn't worth the patching-wire,
Nor is it worth a single fragment of the jug.
And if the wedding stood here all agleam,
As yesterday my jug stood on the shelf,
I'd take it by the handle in an instant
And, yelling, smash it on its silly head;
But these are fragments I'd not care to patch!
I patch them!
    EVE.   Ruprecht!
    RUPRECHT.   Go, you—!
    EVE.   Dearest Ruprecht!
    RUPRECHT. Out of my sight!
    EVE.   Oh listen, I implore you.
    RUPRECHT. You treacherous—! I won't say what.
    EVE. Oh, let me whisper just a word—
    RUPRECHT.   No, nothing!
    EVE. —You go to join your regiment soon, Ruprecht:
Who knows, when once you take up arms,
If e'er I'll see you in this life again.
It's war, remember, war to which you go:
Will you then part from me with such a grudge?
    RUPRECHT. Grudge? No, may God forbid, that's not my will.
God grant you so much happiness as He
Can spare. But if I should return from war
A healthy man, with body strong as steel,
And live in Huysum to be eighty years,
Then to my dying day I'd say: you slut!
You'll swear you're that, you know, before the court.
    MARTHA. [*To* EVE.] Away! What did I tell you? Will you let
                                      yourself
Continue to be vilified? The corporal,
That is your man, the worthy Woodenleg,
Who bore his staff there in the army,
And not this gaping fool, who'll turn his back and get
The staff laid on. Today we could have all in one:
Engagement and a wedding with that Woodenleg;
Were there a christening, too, I wouldn't mind;
My burial I'd even put up with,
When first I've trampled underfoot this coxcomb's pride,

Which swelled enough to smash my pitchers.

EVE.   Mother!
What is it with this jug! Let me go see in town
If there's a skillful handicraftsman there
To glue the pieces to your satisfaction.
But if the jug is done for, then you take my bank,
My savings bank, and buy yourself another one.
Who would, just for a jug of earthenware,
And even if it is as old as Herod's time,
Make such a fuss, cause such unhappiness?

MARTHA. You show how much you know. How would you like
To put your neck inside the stocks, and in the church
Do public penance when this Sunday comes?
Your good repute was in this very jug,
And was destroyed with it in sight of all,
If not in God's eyes and in mine and yours.
The judge will be my handicraftsman, and he'll be
The executioner, too, who with his whip and chain
Will drive the rabble to the stake, where they
Will burn our honor back to spotless white
And so put back the glaze upon this jug.

SCENE 7

ADAM *enters in his robes, but without a wig.*
ADAM. [*Aside.*] It's Evie! Look! And that well-built young
                                                      scamp,
That Ruprecht! What the deuce! The whole caboodle!
—They won't accuse me to my very face, will they?

EVE. Oh, dearest mother, come now, I beseech you.
Let us be gone from this unhappy room!

ADAM. Say, clerk! What have these people on their mind?

LIGHT. How should I know? A pitcher has been broken, I
Did hear. The rest is noise that can't be understood.

ADAM. A pitcher! Hm! Well!—Er, who broke the pitcher?

LIGHT. Who broke the pitcher!

ADAM.   Yes, I'd like to know.

LIGHT. Good gosh, sit down: no doubt you will be told.

ADAM. [*Furtively.*] Evie!

EVE. [*Likewise.*]   Go 'way.

ADAM.   One word.

EVE.   I will not hear a thing.

ADAM. What *is* all this?

EVE.   I tell you, go away.

ADAM. Evie! I beg you! What does all this mean?

EVE. If you don't stop—! I tell you, let me be.

ADAM. [*To* LIGHT.] No, friend, now listen, this I cannot take.
My injured shin is making me feel sick;
You take the case, I want to go to bed.

LIGHT. To bed—? You want—? I think you've lost your mind.

ADAM. To hell with this. I have to go and vomit now.

LIGHT. I think you're really mad. You just came in—
All right, then. Tell Judge Walter your intent.
He may consent.—What in the world is wrong?

ADAM. [*Again to* EVE.] Evie! I beg of you! In heaven's name!
What is this case you bring?

EVE.   You'll soon find out.

ADAM. Is it about the jug there that your mother holds,
Which I so much as—

EVE.   Yes, it's just that broken jug.

ADAM. And that is all?

EVE.   That's all.

ADAM.   There's nothing else? You're sure?

EVE. I tell you, go away. Leave me in peace.

ADAM. Look here, by God, be wise, I caution you.

EVE. Oh, impudence!

ADAM.   In the certificate
The name in full is written, Ruprecht Tümpel.
I have it in my pocket, filled out and complete;
You hear it crackle, Evie? This you can,
Upon my word, next year come back and get,
In clothes that are cut out for mourning,
When you have heard: your Ruprecht in Batavia
Has croaked—I don't know of what fever,
It could be yellow, it could be scarlet;
Or maybe something suspicious will cause his death.

WALTER. Don't talk so with the parties, Justice Adam,
Before the session! Here, sit down and question them.

ADAM. What does he say?—What does Your Grace command?

WALTER. What I command?—I told you quite distinctly:
Before the session do not speak in secret with
The parties and in words of double meaning, too.
This is your seat and it befits your office;
An open hearing is what I expect.

ADAM. [*To himself.*] Oh, curses! I can't quite recall what
                                          happened—!

—I heard a crash just as I took my leave—

LIGHT. [*Prodding him.*] Well, Judge! Are you—

ADAM.   I? On my honor, no!
I'd left my honor carefully outside.

—And then it must have been an ox that hit—

LIGHT. What?

ADAM.   What?

LIGHT.   I asked—!

ADAM.   You asked if I—?

LIGHT. If you are deaf, that's what I asked.
His Honor yonder called to you just now.

ADAM. I thought—! Who calls?

LIGHT.   The court inspector there.

ADAM. [*To himself.*] Oh, hell! Confound it all! Two ways there
                                                                                are,
My soul, no more: it's either bend or break.

—At once! At once! At once! What would Your Grace?
Shall I begin the process now?

WALTER. It's strange you're so distracted, Judge. What's wrong
                                                                        with you?

ADAM.—My word! Forgive me, please. A guinea hen of mine,
Bought off a man who sailed from India,
Has got the pip, and I don't know the cure;
I merely asked the girl for her advice.
I am a fool, you see, in things like this,
And I think of my chicks as my own children.

WALTER. Here. Sit. Now call the plaintiff and examine him.
You, Mr. Clerk, you keep a record of what's said.

ADAM. And does Your Honor wish the hearing held
According to the set formalities,
Or as is customary in Huysum?

WALTER. According to the law's formalities,
As customary in Huysum, not otherwise.

ADAM. Good, good. I shall contrive to serve you well.
All ready, Mr. Clerk?

LIGHT.   I'm at your service.

ADAM.—Well, Justice, take your fated course!
The plaintiff may step forward.

MARTHA.   Right here, Village Judge!

ADAM. Who are you?

MARTHA.   Who—?

ADAM.   You.

MARTHA.   Who I—?
ADAM.   Who you are!
Your name and standing, home address, and so forth.
MARTHA. I think you're jesting, Judge.
ADAM.   I jesting? Bosh!
I'm sitting here in Justice' name, Frau Martha,
And Justice has to know just who you are.
LIGHT. [*In subdued voice*.] Oh, drop this line of questioning—it's
                                                        strange.
MARTHA. You look into my window every Sunday morn
When you go to your farm.
WALTER.   You know the woman, then?
ADAM. She lives around the corner, please Your Grace,
Just where the footpath goes right through the hedges;
A steward's widow, now a midwife here.
An honest woman, and in good repute.
WALTER. If you're so well informed about her, Judge,
Then questions such as those you've asked are not required.
Just put her name down in the record book
And write beside it: well known to the Court.
ADAM. Ah, ha: you shun too much formality.
Clerk, do exactly as His Grace commands.
WALTER. Now ask about the subject of complaint.
ADAM. Oh, now I should—?
WALTER.   Yes, find the matter out!
ADAM. That, please your Grace, concerns a jug.
WALTER. What? How do you already know!
ADAM. A jug. A jug, no more. Put down a jug,
And write beside it: well known to the Court.
LIGHT. What, on the basis of a random guess
You want me, Judge, to—?
ADAM.   If I bid you, on my soul,
Then write it. Is it not a jug, Frau Martha?
MARTHA. Why yes, this jug—
ADAM.   You see.
MARTHA.   This broken jug—
ADAM. Pedantic scrupulosity.
LIGHT.   I have to ask—
ADAM. And then who broke the jug? No doubt that rascal—?
MARTHA. Yes, he, that rascal there—
ADAM. [*Aside*.]   That's all I need.
RUPRECHT. That is not true, Your Honor!

ADAM. [*Aside*.]   On your guard, old man!
RUPRECHT. She's lying in her throat—
ADAM.   Be silent, dolt!
You'll find your own throat soon enough in chains.
—Put down a jug, then, Clerk, as I have said,
Together with the name of him who broke it.
This matter will be cleared up right away.
     WALTER. Why, Judge! What violent procedure.
     ADAM. How so?
     LIGHT.   Will you not formally—?
     ADAM.   Not I!
Your honor doesn't like formalities.
     WALTER. Judge Adam, if you do not know
The way to run a proper trial,
This is no time or place to teach you that.
If you've no other means to deal out justice,
Then step aside: perhaps your Clerk can do the job.
     ADAM. Pardon! I followed custom here in Huysum;
For thus Your Grace commanded me to act.
     WALTER. What, I—?
     ADAM.   Upon my word!
     WALTER.   I ordered you
To mete out justice here as law prescribes;
And laws in Huysum, so I thought, must be
As elsewhere in these Netherlands.
     ADAM. Not so, Your Honor, no, I must submit.
With your permission, here in Huysum we possess
Peculiar statutes of our own,
Not written down, I must confess, and yet
Tradition has transmitted them to us.
And from this code, I'm bold enough to hope,
I've not diverged today a single whit.
However, in your other code, as it
Is practiced through the land, I am at home.
If you want proof, then so command!
I can dispense the law in such a way.
     WALTER. You put a bad construction on my words.
So be it. Now begin the case again.—
     ADAM. Yes sir, your Honor! Mark, you shall be well content.
—Frau Martha Rull! Present now your complaint.
     MARTHA. You know the cause of my complaint: this jug;
Yet grant me time so that, before I tell
What happened to the jug, I may describe

What once it was to me.
    ADAM.   You have the floor.
    MARTHA. You see this jug here, worthy gentlemen?
You see this jug?
    ADAM.   Oh yes, indeed, we see it.
    MARTHA. No, all you see, beg pardon, are the pieces;
The fairest of all jugs is smashed to bits.
Right here upon this gap, where now there's not a thing,
The states of the United Netherlands
Were handed over to the Spanish Philip.
Here in his robes stood Emperor Charles the Fifth:
Of him all you see standing is his legs.
Here knelt King Philip and received the crown:
All but his backside is now gone,
And even that has taken quite a blow.
Two cousins there were weeping—queens they were,
The Queen of France and she of Hungary—
Tears streaming from their eyes; and if you see
The one still raise her handkerchief in hand,
It is to weep at her own fate on this doomed jug.
Here in the retinue is Philibert,
In whose own place the Emperor received a hit,
And leans upon his sword; now he must fall
As well as Maximilian: scoundrel, he!
The swords beneath them have been smashed away.
Here in the center, with his holy miter on,
Stood the Archbishop of Arras:
But every bit of him the devil got;
Only his spirit casts its presence now.
Here in the back the bodyguards stood 'round,
Pressed close together with their halberds and their spears.
And here stood houses, see, on Brussels' market square:
A curious head peeps out of this one window,
But what he sees now, I don't know.
    ADAM. Frau Martha! Let's forget the shattered treaty,
Since it does not pertain. The shattered jug
Is what concerns us here, and not
The provinces that were transferred
Where yonder gaps are visible right now.
    MARTHA. Not so! The beauty of the jug does too pertain!—
This jug was seized as spoils by Childerich,
The kettle mender, when our Lord of Orange
Attacked Briel by surprise with all his water rats.

A Spaniard there had filled the jug with wine
And had it at his lips when Childerich
Came from behind and struck the Spaniard down,
Took up the jug and drained it, then went on.
    ADAM. A worthy water rat.
    MARTHA.   The jug then came
Into the hands of Fearofgod, the grave digger;
He drank but thrice from it, the sober man,
And even then the wine was mixed with water.
The first time was when he at sixty years
Took for himself a youthful wife; the second time
Was three years after that when, happily,
She made of this old man a father;
And after she had borne him fifteen more,
He drank a third and last time when she died.
    ADAM. Good. That's not bad at all.
    MARTHA.   And now the jug went to
Zachaeus, tailor in the town of Tirlemont,
Who told my blessed husband with his very lips
What I am now about to tell to you.
One time when French were plundering, he cast
The jug with his belongings out the window,
Jumped after them, and broke his neck, the clumsy fool,
And yet this earthen jug, this jug of clay,
Fell square upon its base and was unharmed.
    ADAM. Come to the point, Frau Martha! To the point!
    MARTHA. Then by the time the fire broke out in sixty-six,
My husband owned it, may God rest his soul—
    ADAM. The devil! Woman, won't you ever finish?
    MARTHA. —If I've no leave to tell my tale, Judge Adam,
Then I am useless here, and I will go
And seek another court to hear me out.
    WALTER. Yes, you should speak, but not of things
Remote from your complaint. If you tell us
That yonder jug was dear to you, we know
As much as we require to judge the case.
    MARTHA. How much you may require to judge the case,
I do not know and will not now inquire;
But I know this, that to prefer complaint,
I must have leave to tell you what I have to say.
    WALTER. All right. Have done. What happened to the jug?
What happened to your pitcher in the fire
Of sixty-six? Will you please tell us that?

MARTHA. Why, by your leave, good gentlemen, nothing at all.
No, nothing harmed the jug in sixty-six.
The jug stayed in one place all through the flames,
And from the ashes of our house I drew it out
Next morning, highly glazed, as bright
As if 'twas pulled fresh from the potter's kiln.
　　WALTER. O.K. We know your pitcher now. We know
What happened to the jug, and what did not.
What else is there to say?
　　MARTHA.　　　　　　Well, look, this jug,
Worth just as much when broken as one that's
Fit for a lady's mouth, and good enough, when whole,
To wet the lips of her, our noble Regent,
This jug, you worthy judges, both of you,
This jug was broken by that rascal there.
　　ADAM. Who?
　　MARTHA.　　He, that Ruprecht there.
　　RUPRECHT.　　　　　　　　That is a lie,
Your Honor.
　　ADAM.　　Silence, till we question you.
Before this day is done you'll have your turn.
—Have you recorded this, Clerk Light?
　　LIGHT.　　　　　　　　　Oh, yes.
　　ADAM. Relate the details of what happened, please,
Frau Martha.
　　MARTHA.　'Twas eleven yesterday—
　　ADAM.　　　　　　　What time?
　　MARTHA. Eleven.
　　ADAM.　　　In the morning!
　　MARTHA.　　　　　Pardon, evening—
I was in bed, about to douse the light,
When noisy words from men, quite a tumult,
Within the distant chamber of my daughter,
As if the foe were breaking in, gave me alarm.
I hurried down the stairs and, running, found
The bedroom door had been burst in by force;
Abusive speeches raged against my ears, and when
I then shined light upon the scene in front of me,
What did I find, Your Honor, do you think?
I found this jug in pieces on the floor;
In every corner lay a piece of it.
My daughter wrung her hands, and he, that lout,
He stormed like mad there in the middle of the room.

ADAM. By thunder!

MARTHA.   What?

ADAM.   Go on, Frau Martha!

MARTHA.   Yes!—
I felt as if ten extra arms grew out
Of my just rage, each one equipped
With claws just like those that a vulture has.
I challenged him to tell me by what right
He came there late at night, and in a fury
Was smashing up the pitchers of the house:
And he, the answer that he gave, just guess!
Such impudence! Such bold rascality!
I'll see him on the wheel, or else myself,
I'll never sleep in peace again.
He said it was another man that knocked
The pitcher off the shelf—another man,
Would you believe, who barely had escaped
From out the room, out of his grasp—
And, oh, he heaped abuse upon my daughter there!

ADAM. Oh, artful stratagems!—And then?

MARTHA.   Upon his words
My eyes shot questions at the girl; she stood
Just like a corpse, so white, and I said, "Eve!"—
Then she sat down. "Was it another man?"
I asked. And "Joseph, Mary," she cried out,
"What are you thinking, Mother?"—"Speak! Who was it?"
"Who else," she said—and who else could it be?
And then she swore to me that it was he who broke
The jug.

EVE.   What did I swear to you? What have I sworn?
I did not swear a thing, not one.

MARTHA.   Eve!

EVE.   No! You lie.—

RUPRECHT. You hear that.

ADAM.   Curséd dog, now hold your tongue,
Unless you want this fist to stop your mouth.
You'll get your chance, but later on.

MARTHA. You didn't say—?

EVE.   No, Mother! That is false.
I will admit it cuts me to the heart
That I must now declare this publicly:
I took no oath at all, swore nothing, not one thing.

ADAM. Now children, have some sense.

LIGHT.   This is quite strange.
MARTHA. You didn't tell me, Eve, that you were sure?
You didn't call on Joseph and on Mary, too?
EVE. I didn't tell you with an oath!
It wasn't sworn. This I do swear,
And now I call to witness Joseph and Mary.
ADAM. Oh, people! Oh, Frau Martha! What behavior!
How you intimidate this poor young thing!
Now when this maiden here has recollected,
Has calmly called to mind just what took place
—I say, what *took* place in her room, and what,
Unless she speaks right out, can *still* take place—
You watch, she'll testify just as before,
No matter whether with an oath or not.
Let Joseph go unnamed, and Mary too.
WALTER. No, no, Judge Adam, no! Why, who would give
Such dubious instruction to the litigants?
MARTHA. If she can tell me to my very face,
Without a bit of shame, the wretched slut,
That anyone but Ruprecht was the man,
For all I care she can—I won't say what.
But I, I do assure you now, Your Honor
—And even if I cannot guarantee she swore—
That she named Ruprecht yesterday, and *I'll* swear that,
With Joseph and with Mary as my witnesses.
ADAM. And furthermore the maiden wants—
WALTER.   Your Honor!
ADAM. Your Grace?—What is it?—Don't you, Evie dear?
MARTHA. Now out with it! Did you not tell me so?
Did you not tell me, yesterday, this thing?
EVE. Well, who denies I said it—
ADAM.   There you are.
RUPRECHT. The harlot!
ADAM.   Write that down.
VEIT. [*To* ADAM.]   Fie, shame on you.
WALTER. Of your behavior here in court, Judge Adam,
I don't know what to think. If you yourself
Had smashed Frau Martha's jug, you hardly could
More zealously attempt to shift suspicion from
Yourself to this young man, than you are doing.—
You're putting no more in the record, Clerk,
Than just this girl's admission, I should hope,
Of yesterday's confession: write down nothing yet

As fact.—Is it the maiden's turn to testify?

ADAM. Upon my soul, I think it is her turn,
Although I may be wrong, Your Grace.
Whom else should I now question? The accused?
My word, I'm glad to be instructed.

WALTER. Why, how dispassionate!—Yes, question the accused.
Proceed to question and be done with it;
Yes, question him, I beg of you:
This is the last case you will ever try.

ADAM. The last one! What!—By all means! The accused!
For where indeed, Judge Adam, were your thoughts?
Of, curses on that chicken with the pip!
Had it but died in India of the plague!
Instead that noodle dumpling, it sticks in my mind.

WALTER. What sticks? What sort of dumpling—?

ADAM.   Noodle dumpling,
Which, by your leave, I am to give the hen.
If she won't swallow down the pill with it,
My soul, I don't know how the thing will end.

WALTER. Confound it, do your duty, I tell you!

ADAM. Accused, step forward.

RUPRECHT.   Here I am, Your Honor.
Ruprecht, the son of Veit, the Huysum cottager.

ADAM. Well, did you hear the charge before this court
Preferred just now against you by Frau Martha?

RUPRECHT. Indeed, Your Honor, yes.

ADAM.   And will you dare
To bring up anything to contradict her, eh?
Will you confess, or will you be so bold,
So Godforsaken a young man,
As to deny the charge that she has made?

RUPRECHT. You ask what I can say in contradiction here,
Your Honor? Well, I say, with your permission, sir,
That she has uttered not a word of truth!

ADAM. You do? And you expect to prove it, too?

RUPRECHT. Oh, yes.

ADAM.   Frau Martha, you, my worthy friend,
Don't worry, everything will turn out fine.

WALTER. What has Frau Martha, Judge, to do with you?

ADAM. What she—? My Lord! Shall I as Christian soul—?

WALTER. [*To* RUPRECHT.] Say what you have to say in your
                                                   defense.—

Clerk, do you know how to conduct a trial?

ADAM. What's this!

LIGHT.   Do I—why, if Your Grace would please—

ADAM. [*To* RUPRECHT.] Why stare like that? What have you to
                                                    bring up?
Does not this ass stand there just like an ox?
What have you to bring up?

RUPRECHT.   What have I to bring up?

WALTER. Yes, you, you're now to tell us just what happened.

RUPRECHT. Upon my soul, I am to have my say.

WALTER. In truth, Judge, methods like yours aren't to be borne.

RUPRECHT. It may have been at ten o'clock last night—
A January night as warm as one
In May—that I said to my father, "Dad,
I think I'll go and talk with Eve a bit."
For you must know, I planned to marry her;
A sturdy wench she is: at harvest time
I saw how quick and sure her hands, and how
She made hay fly, as if 'twas hunted through the air.
So I said, "Will you?" And she answered, "Oh,
How you do cackle!" Later she said, "Yes."

ADAM. Stick to the subject. Cackle! What!
I asked her, "Will you?" And she answered, "Yes."

RUPRECHT. She did in faith.

WALTER.   Get on with it! Get on!

RUPRECHT.   Well then—
I said, "You hear me, Father? Let me go.
We'll have a little chat outside the window."
"All right," says he, "you run; but you'll remain outside?"
"Upon my soul," says I, "I swear I will."
"Then go," says he, "and be back at eleven."

ADAM. Says he, says you, and cackle to no end.
How soon will you have had your say?

RUPRECHT.   And so
I says, "A deal," and put my cap atop my head
And leave; and go to cross the bridge but must instead
Walk through the village, since the brook is swollen.
Along the way I think, by thunder, Ruprecht, damn!
By now the gate to Martha's yard is shut:
For only up to ten does my Eve leave
It open. If I am not there by ten,
I won't be going there at all.

ADAM. Disreputable doings, these.

WALTER.   And then?

RUPRECHT. And then—as I come nearer through the linden trees
At Martha's, where the rows are closely arched
And somber, just like Utrecht's grand cathedral,
I hear the creaking of the garden gate.
Well, hey! Then Eve is out there still, says I,
And happily send out my eyes to search the place
From where my ears had brought me news of her—
And scold my eyes when they come back to me
A blank, and on the spot I send them out
A second time, to take a better look,
And rail at them as villainous defamers,
As vile inciters, nasty slanderers,
And send them out a third time, and I think,
Because I've made them do their duty thus,
In anger they will tear themselves from out my head,
And ask for transfer to another man:
It's Eve herself, I know her by her bodice,
And someone else is with her there.
    ADAM. What? Someone else? And who, you smartypants?
    RUPRECHT. Who? Well, upon my soul, you have me there—
    ADAM.   You see!
And till he has been named, I guess, he can't be blamed.
    WALTER. Go on! Complete your tale! Judge, leave him be!
Why do you interrupt so much, Judge Adam?
    RUPRECHT. I cannot swear it by the Sacrament:
It was pitch-dark, and in the dark all cats are black.
But you must know that Lebrecht—he's the cobbler
Whom lately they declared unfit for service—
Has long since been upon Eve's trail.
Last fall I said to her, "Now listen, Eve,
That rascal comes too near your house,
Which I don't like a single bit;
Tell him that you're no banquet for his palate,
Or else, my word, I'll toss him out the gate."
She said, "Don't pester me," and told him something
Inconsequential, something neither here nor there.
So I went to her house and threw the scoundrel out.
    ADAM. So, Lebrecht is his name?
    RUPRECHT.   Yes, Lebrecht.
    ADAM.   Good.
That is a name. We'll get this straightened out.
—You've got that in your record, Mr. Clerk?
    LIGHT. Oh, yes, and all the other things, Your Honor.

ADAM. Speak further, Ruprecht, go ahead, my son.
RUPRECHT.   Well now,
Since I was seeing these two outside at
Eleven—I would always leave
At ten—all hope was not yet lost.
Thinks I, hold on there, Ruprecht, you've got time;
As yet you haven't grown a set of horns.—
But you must carefully inspect your brow
To see if horny bumps are sprouting there.
I squeeze in gently through the garden gate
And hide myself behind a bush of evergreen.
And there I hear some whispering,
A little teasing back and forth,
A tug from this side, then from that.
Upon my soul, I thought I'd—
EVE.   Villain, you!
How shamefully you acted!
MARTHA.   Why, you scoundrel!
My teeth I'll show you yet, when once we are alone!
Just wait! You don't know yet quite where
I keep my claws! But you shall learn!
RUPRECHT. A quarter hour this thing went on; thinks I,
What's going on? This is no wedding day.
Before I could complete the thought, whish! They
Were in the house, without a visit to
The priest.
EVE.   Now, Mother, let things happen as they will—
ADAM. Be silent now, I counsel you, or lightning
Will strike you down, you uninvited chatterbox!
Wait till I call you up to testify.
WALTER. By God, this is so very strange.
RUPRECHT. And now my temperature is rising, Judge,
My blood is boiling. Give me air!
A button bursts upon my vest: air, now!
I open up my vest: air now, I say!
And then I run, and push and kick and thunder,
Because I find her chamber door is bolted shut.
I brace myself, and knock the door right in.
ADAM. You devil!
RUPRECHT.   As it's crashing in,
The jug there tumbles from the mantlepiece,
And whish! A man goes jumping out the window:
I see his coat tails flying as he leaps.

ADAM. And that was Lebrecht?

RUPRECHT.   Why, who else, Your Honor?
There stands the girl, I push her to one side,
Rush to the window, and I find
The fellow hanging by the posts that hold
The trellis where the vines go climbing upward to
The roof. And since I hold the handle in my hand,
Which came off when I pounded in the door, I land
Him quite a shot with steel across his pate:
For that, Your Honor, still was in my reach.

ADAM. It was a handle?

RUPRECHT.   What?

ADAM.   Was it a—

RUPRECHT.   Yes,
The handle to the door.

ADAM.   That's why.

LIGHT. Perhaps you thought it was a sword?

ADAM. A sword? I thought—how so?

RUPRECHT.   A sword!

LIGHT.   Oh yes,
In this case one can easily mishear.
And I think that the handle to a door
Has much in common with a sword.

ADAM. I think—

LIGHT.   In faith, both have a shaft, your Honor.

ADAM. A shaft!

RUPRECHT.   A shaft! But that was not the case.
You see, it was the handle's other end.

ADAM. The handle's other end it was!

LIGHT. Aha!

RUPRECHT.   And this old handle had a knob
Of lead, quite like a sword hilt, I must say.

ADAM. Yes, like a sword hilt.

LIGHT.   Good. Just like a hilt.
Some nasty kind of weapon, certainly,
It must have been. That much we know.

WALTER. Stick to the point, good sirs, I beg! The point!

ADAM. Let's stop this foolishness, Clerk Light! Proceed, you!

RUPRECHT. The fellow falls, and I'm about to turn away,
When in the dark I see him start to struggle up.
Thinks I, what, still alive? I mount the window sill
To get down there and stop the rascal short.
But now, good sirs, as I am crouched to leap,
A handful of coarse sand comes flying up

Like hail and strikes me squarely in the eyes:
And man and night and world and window sill
On which I stand—so help me God,
Before I know what's going on—
Get jumbled up in one big blinding sack.
 ADAM. How terrible! Just think! And who did that?
 RUPRECHT. Who did it? Lebrecht.
 ADAM.   Scoundrel!
 RUPRECHT.   Yes, upon
My word. If it in fact was he.
 ADAM.   Who else?
 RUPRECHT. As if a stream of hail had cast
Me down ten fathoms from a mountain slope,
So did I tumble down into the room:
I thought I'd certainly break through the floor.
I didn't break my neck, that's true, nor did I break
My back or hips or other bones, but now
I could no longer lay hands on the culprit.
I then sat up and wiped sand from my eyes.
She comes, and "Oh, dear God!" she cries, and "Ruprecht!
What's happened to you?" 'Pon my soul,
I raised my foot, and good thing that it was
I couldn't see where I was kicking.
 ADAM. The sand did that?
 RUPRECHT.   The sand did, yes.
 ADAM. Hot damn! A hit!
        When I got up again,
I thought I'd not profane these fists of mine.
I railed at her instead and called her filthy slut,
And thought that this was good enough for her.
But then I cried and couldn't say a word.
For when Frau Martha came into the room
And raised the lamp, so that I saw the girl
All trembling there before me, pitiful,
She who had always been so brave and free,
I could but say unto myself,
No, blindness would not be so bad.
And I'd have gladly given up my eyes
As marbles, which some child could then play with.
 EVE. The villain, he's not worth it—
 ADAM.   Hold your tongue!
 RUPRECHT. The rest you know yourself.
 ADAM.   What do you mean, the rest?
 RUPRECHT. Oh well, Frau Martha came along and fumed,

And neighbor Ralf came in, and neighbor Hinz,
And cousin Sue and cousin Lisbeth came,
And men and maids and dogs and cats walked in:
It was a spectacle, and then Frau Martha asked
The maiden here who was it broke the jug,
And she, she said, you know, that it was me.
My word, good sirs, she's not so wrong at that.
The jug that she got water in, I once broke that.
And it is true: because of me
The cobbler's head now has a hole.—
 ADAM. Frau Martha! What is your reply to this?
Speak up!
 MARTHA. What I would answer in reply? I'd say
This speech comes sneaking in just like a weasel,
And throttles truth as if it were a cackling hen.
All friends of right should take a club in hand
And put to death this monster of the night.
 ADAM. Then you must put your statement to the proof.
 MARTHA. Quite willingly. Here is my witness.—Speak!
 ADAM. Your daughter? No, Frau Martha.
 WALTER.   No? Why not?
 ADAM. As witness here, Your Grace? Does not the law
Code state—is it in section four or five?—
That when pitchers or such—how should I know?—
Have been by young louts smashed to bits,
Then daughters may not for their mothers testify?
 WALTER. Within your head lie knowledge and stupidity
Close by, together kneaded as a dough of sorts;
With every slice you give me some of each.
The maiden cannot testify just yet;
She has to make a declaration first.
If, and for whom, she can and will bear witness,
We won't know that until she has declared.
 ADAM. Aha, declare. Good. That's in section six.
But what she says is not to be believed.
 WALTER. Come forward, child.
 ADAM.   Hey, Lisa!—[*To* WALTER.] By your leave!
My tongue is drying up—Margreta, you!

SCENE 8

A MAIDSERVANT *enters.*
ADAM. A glass of water!

MAID.   Right away!
ADAM.   Can I get you—?
WALTER. No thanks.
ADAM.   Moselle? Or Rhine wine? What you will.
[WALTER *bows; the* MAID *brings water and withdraws.*]

SCENE 9

ADAM. —If I may be so bold to speak, Your Grace,
This case is ready for a settlement.
   WALTER. A settlement? That is not clear to me.
Judicious folk do in the end find settlements;
But how you hope to settle matters *now,*
Before the case has even been untangled,
I must confess I'd like to hear you say.
How will you manage that, pray tell?
Have you a judgment ready-made?
   ADAM.   Upon my soul!
If I, because the law forsakes me now,
Must take philosophy to be my aid,
Then it was—Lebrecht—
   WALTER.   Who?
   ADAM.   Or Ruprecht—
   WALTER.   Who?
   ADAM. 'Twas Lebrecht, yes, that broke the jug.
   WALTER. Who was it then? That Lebrecht or this Ruprecht?
I see your judgment blindly grope about,
Just like five fingers in a sack of peas.
   ADAM. With your permission, sir, I'd like—
   WALTER. Be still, I tell you!
   ADAM.   As you wish.
I swear that it would please me well,
If both of them had been the guilty ones.
   WALTER. Ask her, and you'll find out.
   ADAM.   Most willingly.
But I'll be damned if you get something out of her.
—[*To* LIGHT.] You have the record book in readiness?
   LIGHT. Quite.
   ADAM.   Good.
   LIGHT.   I now begin a special page,
Eager to see what will be written down on it.
   ADAM. A special page? That's good.
   WALTER.   Now speak, my child.

ADAM. Speak, Evie, mark you, speak up, maiden Eve!
Give God, my darling, mark you, give to God,
Upon my soul, and to the world a bit of truth.
Think that you're at the judgment seat of God,
And that you must not with retractions vex
Your judge, and must not babble silly words that are
Beside the point. Oh pshaw! You have good sense.
A judge, you know, will always be a judge,
And we need judges every day.
Say then that it was Lebrecht: very good;
Or say that it was Ruprecht: also good!
Say either one, and I'm no honest man
If things don't turn out just as you would like.
But if you try to blab about another man,
A third perhaps, and mention foolish names:
Then, child, look out, that's all I have to say.
In Huysum, damn it, no one will believe you,
And no one, either, in the Netherlands;
You know that whitewashed walls don't testify,
And this third man will manage to defend himself:
And then your Ruprecht will catch hell!
      WALTER. I wish you would desist from all such talk.
Mere prattle, neither this nor that.
      ADAM. Your Honor does not follow me?
      WALTER.   Get on with it!
Too long you have been speaking from the bench.
      ADAM. My word! I am no learned man, Your Grace.
Although I seem to be obscure to you,
A circuit judge who comes from Utrecht,
Among these folks perhaps it's not the same:
The maiden knows, I'll venture, what I want.
      MARTHA. What *is* all this? Come, out with it, and talk!
      EVE. Oh, dearest Mother!
      MARTHA.   You—! I'm warning you!
      RUPRECHT. Upon my soul, it's hard, Frau Martha, to speak out,
When conscience holds a person by the throat.
      ADAM. Keep still now, smarty, hold your tongue.
      MARTHA.   Who was it, then?
      EVE. Oh Jesus!
      MARTHA. [*Pointing to* RUPRECHT.] Wasn't it that common fool
                                        right there?
"Oh Jesus!" she says like a pious whore.
Was it Lord Jesus?

ADAM.   Senseless words, Frau Martha!
What sort of talk—! Just leave the girl in peace, can't you?
You scare the whore—the child—you muttonhead!
That gets us nowhere. She'll soon recollect.
    RUPRECHT. Oh, sure she will.
    ADAM.   You lout, now shut your mouth.
    RUPRECHT. The cobbler's name will pop up in her head.
    ADAM. You Satan! Call the bailiff! Hey, Hanfriede!
    RUPRECHT. All right. I'll say no more, Judge, let it go.
She'll do your will and hit upon my name.
    MARTHA. Now listen, make no scenes here, I declare.
For I have come to nine-and-forty years
In honor, and I'd like to make it fifty soon.
The third of February is my day of birth;
Today's the first. Now hurry up. Who was it, Eve?
    ADAM. I call that good! Good work, Frau Martha Rull!
    MARTHA. Her father said before he died, "Now Martha,
You get the girl a proper man as spouse;
And if she should turn out to be a debauchee,
Then give the digger of my grave an extra coin
And have him lay me on my back again,
For I'll have turned right over in my grave."
    ADAM. That, too, is pretty good.
    MARTHA.   If you would honor
Your father and your mother now, Evie,
The way the fourth commandment bids, then say:
"Into my room I let my Ruprecht, my
Intended husband come," you hear? "But it
Was not the cobbler or somebody else."
    RUPRECHT. I grieve for her. Forget about the jug, I beg;
I'll take it into Utrecht for repairs. That jug—
I only wish 'twas really me who smashed it up.
    EVE. Ignoble words from you! O fie, for shame
That you don't say: all right, I broke the jug!
Fie, Ruprecht, fie! Oh, shame on you, that you
Cannot have faith in me and what I did.
Did not I give my hand and answer, "Yes,"
That time you asked me, "Eve, will you have me?"
Do you suppose you're not the cobbler's match?
And even if you'd seen me through the keyhole there
With Lebrecht, drinking from the jug,
You should have thought: my Eve is good and true,
And to her credit all will be explained,

If not in this life, then beyond the grave.
And when we rise again there'll still be time.
    RUPRECHT. Upon my soul, Eve, that would take too long for me.
What I can put my hands on now,
That's where I like to place my faith.
    EVE. Suppose it had been that Lebrecht,
Then why—may I have died eternal death
Had I not told you to your face alone,
But why before the neighbors, servants, and the maids?—
Supposing that I had some reason to conceal
The truth, then tell me, Ruprecht, speak, why shouldn't I,
Relying on your trust, say it was you?
Why shouldn't I do that? Why not, I say?
    RUPRECHT. Then speak my name, confound it all, I'll go along,
If that's your way to dodge the pillory.
    EVE. Oh, you atrocious man! Ungrateful creep!
Well worth, that I should dodge the pillory! Well worth,
That with the single word "Ruprecht" I clear my name
And put the blame for all of this on you.
    WALTER. Well—? And this single word—? Don't waste our time.
It was not Ruprecht then?
    EVE.   No, sir, Your Grace,
Since that's the way he wants it, I can see.
'Twas only for his sake I hid the truth:
This earthen pitcher Ruprecht did not break;
He says he didn't, and you may now take his word.
    MARTHA. What, Eve! Not Ruprecht?
    EVE.   No, dear Mother, no!
If I said "Ruprecht" yesterday, I lied.
    MARTHA. My girl, I'll break your every bone!
    EVE. Do as you will.
    WALTER. [*Threatening.*] Frau Martha!
    ADAM.   Bailiff! Hey!
Take hold of her and throw her out, the curséd hag!
[*To* MARTHA.] Why did it have to be just none but Ruprecht?
And did you hold the light for him, I wonder?
The maiden, I should think, must know the facts:
I am a rogue if it was not Lebrecht.
    MARTHA. Now was it he perhaps? Was it Lebrecht?
    ADAM. Speak, Evie darling, was it not Lebrecht?
    EVE. You shameless man! You miserable sneak!
How can you say that Lebrecht was—
    WALTER.   Young woman, please!

What impudence! Is that the due respect
You pay the judge upon the bench?

    EVE. Good Lord! This judge you mean! He well deserves
To stand as sinner here before the court—
He that could better tell who broke the jug! [*Turning to Judge*
    ADAM.]
Did you not send Lebrecht to town yourself,
To Utrecht yesterday, to take to the
Commission there the list of names,
From which they'll choose recruits? How can you say
That Lebrecht broke the jug, when you
Know well that he had gone to Utrecht?

    ADAM. Well then, who else? If he was not the one, oh hell—
Not Ruprecht and not Lebrecht—What to do?

    RUPRECHT. Upon my soul, Judge Adam, let me tell you this,
The girl is not so wrong in what she says,
For I myself ran into Lebrecht yesterday
As he was bound for Utrecht; eight A.M. it was,
And if he got no ride upon a cart,
Bowlegged as that fellow is, it's sure
He did not hobble back by ten at night.
It may quite well have been another man.

    ADAM. What's that? Bowlegged! Fathead, you! That chap
Can shake a leg as well as any man.
Let me not be a man with two good feet
If any shepherd dog of average size
Would not be forced to trot to keep abreast of him.

    WALTER. [*To* EVE.] Now tell us just what happened.

    ADAM.   By Your Honor's leave!
For such a task the girl would hardly serve.

    WALTER. Not serve? Not serve for this? Why not, I ask?

    ADAM. She's stupid. You see that. A good but stupid child.
Quite young yet, scarce confirmed; she's still ashamed
To see a beard a mile away. Such girls
Will let themselves be used at night, but then
By day deny it to their judge's face.

    WALTER. You're so considerate, Judge Adam, I must say,
And very temperate in all that touches her.

    ADAM. To tell the honest truth, Judge Walter, sir,
Her father always was a friend of mine.
And if Your Grace will be so kind today,
Then let us do no more than just our duty here
And let his little daughter go.

WALTER. I feel a great desire in me, Judge,
To probe this matter to its very heart.—
Be bold, my child; tell us who broke the jug.
You stand before no person presently,
Who could not well forgive an erring step.
    EVE. Most worthy Lord, and dear and gracious sir,
Do not insist that I should tell you all,
And don't take it amiss that I refuse.
It's Heaven's wondrous dispensation, sir,
That seals my lips in this uncommon case.
That Ruprecht didn't touch the jug I will
Affirm, and I will swear to it,
If you demand, before the altar of the church.
But that which happened yesterday is mine,
With every detail that belongs to it,
And Mother cannot claim the total cloth
Because one thread, that may be hers to claim,
Just happens to run through the tangled web.
I cannot here report who broke the jug,
For secrets that are not my property,
That are quite foreign to the jug, I'd have to bare.
Some time or other I'll confide in her,
But this tribunal here is not the place
Where she may claim the right to ask me this.
    ADAM. No, not by rights. Upon my honor, no.
The girl knows when to use the reins.
If she will take her oath before this court,
The mother's charge against Ruprecht is null and void:
To this there can be no objection made.
    WALTER. Frau Martha, what is your reply to this?
    MARTHA. If I do not at once say something full of weight,
Your Grace, then do believe, I beg of you,
It is because a stroke has dulled my speech.
It has been known to happen that a desperate man,
To elevate his name before the world,
Committed perjury before a court; but that
A lying oath could be performed upon
The altar of a church, in order to
Achieve the pillory, that is
A thing the world has never seen.
Had any other man but Ruprecht, sir,
Been proven to have sneaked into her room,
If such a thing were even possible, Your Grace,

You understand, I would be gone from here by now.
It's home I'd be, where I would place
Just one piece from her dowry, it could be a chair,
Outside her door and say: "Go 'way, my child,
The world is wide, you'll pay no rental there;
And part of your inheritance is your long hair,
On which, when you feel ready, you can hang yourself."
    WALTER. Calm down, calm down, Frau Martha.
    MARTHA.   Inasmuch
As I can furnish proof in other ways
Than through her who refuses to do so,
And am convinced for sure that it was Ruprecht, he,
And no one else who broke the jug, this eagerness
Of his to make a flat denial here
Creates a foul suspicion in my mind.
For last night hides, I think, another crime
Besides simply the smashing of the jug.
For I must tell you, honored sir, that Ruprecht's been
Conscripted, and it won't be long till he's supposed
To swear his fealty to the flag at Utrecht.
The younger lads, I hear, have been deserting.
Suppose that Ruprecht said to Eve last night:
"What think you, Evie? Come. The world is large.
To chests and drawers you have the keys, you know—"
And she, suppose that she had balked a bit:
Why then, by accident, when I walked in on them—
With rage at work on his part, love on hers—
The whole thing could have happened as it did.
    RUPRECHT. You carrion! To say such things as that!
To chests and drawers—
    WALTER.   Be still!
    EVE.   What, he desert!
    WALTER. Stick to the point! We're speaking of the jug.—
Bring on the proof that it was broken by Ruprecht.
    MARTHA. All right, Your Grace. I will first prove
That Ruprecht broke my jug, and then
I want to have a look around my house.—
You see, I will produce a tongue to testify
For me, which will refute each word that he has said;
I would have led in witnesses in groups,
If I'd so much as dreamed this girl of mine
Would not employ her tongue in my behalf.
But if you'll call Frau Bridget into court—

That's Ruprecht's aunt—then she will serve my needs,
Since she'll contest the central point in all of this.
For she, at half past ten there in the garden—
Mark that: before the pitcher had been broken—
She came upon him crossing words with Eve;
And how the fable that he has constructed,
Is split in two thereby from head to foot,
And by a single tongue, I leave that inference
To your own wits, you worthy judges.
    RUPRECHT. Who saw me—?
    VEIT.   Sister Briggy?
    RUPRECHT.   Me with Eve? Outside?
    MARTHA. Saw him with Eve, outside, at half past ten,
Before he went in by surprise, as he pretends,
To break her chamber door down at eleven:
Exchanging words, now petting her,
Now pulling on her arm, as if
To try to talk her into something.
    ADAM. [*Aside.*] My Lord! The devil's on my side.
    WALTER. Bring in this woman.
    RUPRECHT.   Gentlemen, I beg of you:
No word of that is true; it isn't possible.
    ADAM. Just wait, you villain!—Bailiff! Hey! Hanfriede!—
When someone's in a hurry, pitchers break.—
You, Clerk, please go and bring Frau Bridget here!
    VEIT. You curséd knave, now listen, what is this you've done?
I'll break your bones in two.
    RUPRECHT.   You will? And why?
    VEIT. Why did you hide the fact that you
Were flirting with that maiden in the yard
At half past ten? Why did you hide that fact?
    RUPRECHT. You ask me why? Good heavens, Dad! Because
It isn't true. If that is what Aunt Bridget says,
Then I'll be hanged. And so should she be, too,
And by the legs, for all I care.
    VEIT. But if that is her testimony, you
Had better stay away from me!
You and this tidy maiden Eve right here,
Whatever tale you tell this court, the same
Stick tars you both. For there is still
Some shameful secret left, of which the girl
Has knowledge but conceals out of regard for you.

RUPRECHT. A secret! What?

VEIT.   Why were you packing up last night?
Come now, why did you pack your things?

RUPRECHT.   My things?

VEIT. Your trousers, yes, and coats and underwear;
You made a bundle that a traveler might
Throw on his back.

RUPRECHT.   Because I'm going to Utrecht!
I have to join my regiment! For heaven's sake—!
You think that I would—?

VEIT.   To Utrecht? Indeed, Utrecht!
You've been in haste to get to Utrecht, eh?
Two days ago you didn't even know
If you would leave in five days or in six.

        WALTER. Do you, sir, have something to tell the court?

        VEIT. —Your Grace, I do not want right now
To maintain anything. I was
At home when yonder jug got broken,
And of an undertaking other than
His packing of some clothes, I had
Not yet observed a thing, when I think back,
That threw suspicion on my son—that is the truth.
I came here quite convinced he had no blame,
And my intent, when once this trial was done,
Was to break off his coming marriage to this Eve
And to get back for him the silver chain
And little medal he had given her
Last autumn, when they got engaged. If there was talk
Of flight, however, and attempts were made
To work some treason on this aging head,
That is as new to me, sir, as to you:
In that case, may the devil break my Ruprecht's neck.

        WALTER. Please have Frau Bridget brought to court,
                                             Judge Adam.

        ADAM. —Will not Your Honor find himself worn out
By this long case? It's dragging on and on.
You know you still have my accounts to see,
And then the records, too.—What is the time?

        LIGHT. The clock just struck half past.

        ADAM.   Past ten!

        LIGHT. No, past eleven, Judge.

        WALTER.   It matters not.

ADAM. [*To* LIGHT.] I think the time's gone crazy. Either that
Or you have. I'm no honest man, if you are right. [*He looks at the
clock.*]
Well, what's your will?
    WALTER.   I think we should—
    ADAM. Conclude the hearing? Good, agreed!
    WALTER. Excuse me, please! I think we should go on.
    ADAM. You think we should—fine, just as well. Or we could
                                    meet,
Upon my word, tomorrow morning at nine sharp
To end the case to your complete contentment.
    WALTER. You know my wishes, Judge.
    ADAM.   As you command.
Clerk Light, send out the bailiff; bid him bring
Frau Bridget straight before the court.
    WALTER. I beg you, Clerk, to save my precious time,
Please go yourself and bring the woman here.

SCENE 10

The same without Clerk LIGHT. *Later:* MAIDSERVANTS.
    ADAM. [*Rising.*] Meanwhile one might, if one were so inclined,
Get up and stretch one's legs a bit—
    WALTER.   Hm? Oh. [*Pause.*]
I'd like to ask—
    ADAM.   Will you permit
The parties here, until Frau Bridget comes—?
    WALTER. What's that? The parties?
    ADAM.   Yes, outside, if you—
    WALTER. [*Aside.*]
Oh, hell! What next? [*Aloud.*] Judge Adam, would you then
Give me a glass of wine to pass the time?
    ADAM. With all my heart I will. Hey, Greta!
You make me very happy, sir.—Margreta!
    MAID. [*Enters.*] I'm here.
    ADAM. [*To* WALTER.]   What is your choice?—You may go
                                        out,
The rest of you.—French?—Out there in the waiting room.
—Or Rhine wine?
    WALTER.   Wine from our own Rhine.
    ADAM. Good.—Out, you people, till I call you back.
    WALTER. Where to?
    ADAM.   Go get the sealed wine, Greta.—

What? To the waiting room.—Here. Someone, take the key.
  WALTER. Hm. Wait.
  ADAM.   Go! March, I say!—Go, Greta!
Bring butter, freshly molded cheese from Limburg,
And some of that smoked Pomeranian goose.
  WALTER. Please wait a moment! Do not make so great
A fuss here, Judge, I beg of you.
  ADAM.   You folks, you get
The devil out of here! [*To the* MAID.] Do as I said.
  WALTER. You're sending out the parties, Judge?
  ADAM.   Your Grace?
  WALTER. I asked—
  ADAM.   They will withdraw, if you permit.
But only till Frau Bridget comes.
Or is your will perhaps—?
  WALTER.   Hm! As you like.
I wonder if it's worth the trouble, though.
You think that it will take so long
To find her in the village?
  ADAM.   Wood day is today,
Your Honor, and the women hereabouts
Are mostly in the woods, to gather kindling there.
It might well be—
  RUPRECHT.   No, Auntie is at home.
  WALTER. At home. So let's not send the parties out.
  RUPRECHT. She'll be right here.
  WALTER.   She'll be right here, he says.
Bring on the wine.
  ADAM. [*Aside.*] Oh, damn!
  WALTER.   Go 'head.
But serve no food, I beg, except
A slice of bread without the butter. Give me salt.
  ADAM. [*Aside.*] I need two seconds with Evie alone—
[*Aloud.*] What, bread with salt? No butter! Nonsense.
  WALTER.   No it's not.
  ADAM. At least a piece of Limburg cheese. For cheese
Prepares the tongue so it can taste the wine.
  WALTER. All right. A piece of cheese, but nothing more.
  ADAM. [*To the* MAID.] Then go. And lay a cloth of damask,
                                  white.
Quite plain, all this, but still it's good. [*Exit* MAID.]
That is the benefit we bachelors get,
Though much maligned we often are:

That what the others, poor and sorrowful,
Must daily share with wife and hungry kids,
We can enjoy with friends at proper moments, to
Our heart's content.

WALTER.   I'd like to ask—
How did you ever get that wound, Your Honor?
A nasty hole, indeed, there in your head!

ADAM. —I fell.

WALTER.   You fell. Hm. Well! When? Just last night?

ADAM. No, pardon me, this morning; it was half past five,
As I was getting out of bed.

WALTER. And over what?

ADAM.   Why, please Your Grace,
To tell the truth, I fell over myself.
I crashed down on the stove head first,
And till this hour I don't know why I did.

WALTER. Crashed backward?

ADAM.   How? Crashed backward—

WALTER.   Or crashed forward?
You have two wounds, one front and one in back.

ADAM. Crashed forward, then crashed backward—Greta! [*The
two* MAIDS *come in with wine, etc. They set the table and go out
again.*]

WALTER.   What?

ADAM. First this way and then that. First on the iron edge,
Which knocked my forehead in, then right away
I fell down backwards on the floor,
And thus I smashed my head there in the back. [*He pours wine.*]
Please have some wine.

WALTER. [*Takes the glass.*] Now if you had a wife,
Then I could credit most peculiar things,
Judge Adam.

ADAM.   How is that?

WALTER.   Yes, by my faith,
I see you scraped and scratched on every side.

ADAM. [*Laughs.*] My God, no! Women's nails did not do that.

WALTER.   No doubt.
That also is a benefit of bachelorhood.

ADAM. [*Keeps laughing.*]
These scrapes and scratches come from silkworm branches set
Up there to dry beside the stove, right where I had
My fall.—Here's to your health! [*They drink.*]

WALTER.   And just today

You had to lose your wig so strangely, too!
That would at least have covered up your wounds.

ADAM. You're right. It seems misfortune comes in twos.
Here—from this fat cheese now—can I—?

WALTER.   A little piece.
From Limburg?

ADAM.   Straight from Limburg, gracious sir.

WALTER. —But how the devil, tell me, did that happen?

ADAM. What?

WALTER.   Why, that you have lost your wig.

ADAM.   I'll tell you how.
Last night I sat and read a legal case,
And since I had mislaid my glasses, I
Kept moving closer to the lighted candlewick
The more I got into the case, until at last
My wig caught fire. At first I thought that flames
From Heaven had reached down to strike my sinful head,
Pull off the wig, and cast it far from me;
And 'fore I could untie the ribbon at my neck,
My wig was burning just like Sodom and
Gomorrha. I could barely save the three hairs you
See now.

WALTER.   Too bad! You say your other one's in town?

ADAM. Yes, at the wig shop in Utrecht.
—Now let's enjoy our wine and cheese.

WALTER. Wait, not so fast, I beg of you, Judge Adam.

ADAM. Oh pshaw! Time rushes on. Another glass for you. [*He
pours wine.*]

WALTER. [*Indicating* RUPRECHT.]
Now if that fellow there did tell the truth
The first time that he spoke, then Lebrecht must
Himself have had a nasty fall.

ADAM. Upon my honor, yes. [*He drinks.*]

WALTER.   So if this case
Is left unsolved here, as I fear 'twill be,
You will be able to detect the culprit by
His wounds when he appears about your town. [*He drinks.*]
Niersteiner?

ADAM.   What?

WALTER.   Or first-rate Oppenheimer?

ADAM. Nierstein. Hey, hey! You know your wines. From
                                        Nierstein, sir,
As if I'd gone to fetch it back myself.

WALTER. I tried it at the winery three years ago. [ADAM *pours wine again.*]

—How high, then, is your window?—You! Frau Martha!

MARTHA. My window?

WALTER.   Yes, the window of the room
In which your daughter sleeps.

MARTHA.   The room itself is just
One story high, atop the cellar down below;
The window's but nine feet above the ground. And yet
The whole arrangement, well-devised though it may be,
Is very awkward, sir, for leaping out.
For two feet from the wall there is a vine
That sends its thorny branches twining through
A trellis up the length of the entire wall;
The window frame itself is lined with vines.
A sturdy boar, though armed with heavy tusks,
Would have no easy task to break through all of this.

ADAM. No boar was caught in there. [*He fills his glass.*]

WALTER.   You think not, eh?

ADAM.   Oh pshaw! [*He drinks.*]

WALTER. [*To* RUPRECHT.] Where did you hit the sinner? On the
                                        head?

ADAM. [*Reaching for* WALTER's *glass.*]
Here.

WALTER. Stop.

ADAM.   Give here.

WALTER.   It's still half full.

ADAM.   I'll fill it up.

WALTER. You heard me.

ADAM.   Raise the number that
You'll drink by half.

WALTER.   I beg you, please.

ADAM. No chance! We heed Pythagorean rules. [*He fills*
WALTER's *glass.*]

WALTER. [*To* RUPRECHT.] How often did you hit the sinner's
                                        head?

ADAM. One is the Lord; dark chaos, that
Is number two; and three's the universe.
At least three glasses, that's my style.
For with the third glass you have suns to drink,
And with the rest you have the firmament.

WALTER. How often did you hit the sinner's head?
You, Ruprecht, I am asking!
    ADAM.   Will you speak?
How often did you hit the scapegoat? Out with it!
Good heavens, doesn't he himself know if—?
Don't you remember?
    RUPRECHT.   With the handle to the door?
    ADAM. Well, how should I know?
    WALTER.   Yes, when you reached out and struck
Him through the window.
    RUPRECHT.   Twice, good sirs.
    ADAM. The rascal! So he knows! [*He drinks.*]
    WALTER.   Two times!
With two such mighty blows you could
Have killed him, you know that—?
    RUPRECHT.   Oh, if I had,
I'd have him here right now. And that would suit me well.
If he lay dead before me, I could say,
That's him, good sirs, I haven't lied to you.
    ADAM. Yes, dead! That I believe. But now—[*He pours wine.*]
    WALTER. You couldn't recognize him in the dark?
    RUPRECHT. Not in the least, Your Grace. What chance of that?
    ADAM. Why didn't you just open up your eyes!
—Touch glasses!
    RUPRECHT.   Open up my eyes! I had
Them opened wide. That Satan filled them full of sand.
    ADAM. [*To himself.*]
Yes, sand! Those staring eyes, why did you open them
So wide?—Here. [*Gesturing with his glass toward* WALTER.]
                    To our best belovéd circuit judge!
Let's touch!
    WALTER. —I toast what's right and good and true,
Judge Adam! [*They drink.*]
    ADAM.   Well then, let us finish this, if you
Don't mind. [*He pours wine.*]
    WALTER. You sometimes visit at Frau Martha's place,
No doubt, Judge Adam. Tell me, if you please,
Who else but Ruprecht comes and goes around that house.
    ADAM. I'm not so often there, sir, by your leave.
I cannot tell you who goes in and out.
    WALTER. What? Don't you go there frequently to see
The widow of your late lamented friend?

ADAM. Indeed I don't, I'm seldom there.

WALTER.   Frau Martha!
Have you destroyed your friendship with Judge Adam?
He says he doesn't often call on you.

MARTHA. Destroyed, Your Grace? Hm! Not exactly that.
I think he still does call himself my friend.
But that I see him often in my house,
Of that, I'd say, I can't exactly boast.
It's nine weeks now since he was last inside,
And then 'twas just as he was passing by.

WALTER. How's that?

MARTHA.   What do you ask?

WALTER.   Nine weeks ago—?

MARTHA.   Yes, nine,
On Thursday 'twill be ten. He asked me for some seeds,
For pink carnations and for primulas.

WALTER. And Sundays, when he goes out to his farm—?

MARTHA. Yes, he peeps through my window then
And says good day to me and to my Eve;
But after that he just continues on his way.

WALTER. [*Aside.*] Hm! Have I, then, misjudged the man—?
                    [*He drinks; to* ADAM.] I thought,
Since you from time to time employ the girl
To help out in your house, in gratitude
You'd call upon her mother now and then.

ADAM. Why's that, Your Grace?

WALTER.   Why's that? You said yourself,
The maiden here had nursed your chicks to health
When they fell sick on you. And didn't she
Today give you advice about a hen of yours?

MARTHA. Yes, to be sure, Your Grace, she has done all of that.
Two days ago he sent a guinea hen to her,
So sick that it was close to death. Last year
She cured one of the pip for him, and this one too
She'll save by feeding it her noodle dumpling:
But he has never come to show his thanks.

WALTER. [*Confused.*]—Pour out some wine, Judge Adam, if you
                                                will.
Fill up my glass. We'll drink another round.

ADAM. I'm at your service, sir. This makes me happy. Here. [*He
pours wine.*]

WALTER. Here's to your health.—[*To* MARTHA.] Judge Adam, I
                                          should think,

Will sooner or else later come to show his thanks.
 MARTHA. You think so? I myself have doubts.
If I had Nierstein wine, such as you drink,
And as my late lamented husband kept
From time to time down in the cellar of
Our house, and served it to the village judge,
Then matters would be different. But now,
Poor widow that I am, I've not a thing
Within my house to lure him inside it.
 WALTER. So much the better.

SCENE II

LIGHT, FRAU BRIDGET *with a wig in her hand, and the* MAIDS.
 LIGHT.   Right this way, Frau Bridget.
 WALTER. Is this the woman named to us, Clerk Light?
 LIGHT. This is Frau Bridget, yes, Your Grace.
 WALTER. Then let us now conclude the case.
Maids, take this out. Here. [MAIDS *go out with glasses, etc.*]
 ADAM. [*While this is going on.*] Listen, Evie, now,
You camouflage that pill the way you should
For me, and then this evening I
Will eat a carp with you to celebrate.
That rascal's got to swallow pill and all:
If it's too big to take, death may be on the way.
 WALTER. [*Catches sight of the wig.*] What sort of wig is in Frau
                                         Bridget's hand?
 LIGHT. Your Grace?
 WALTER.   I asked what sort of wig
The woman has there in her hand.
 LIGHT. Hm!
 WALTER.   What was that you said?
 LIGHT.   Beg pardon, sir.
 WALTER. Will you speak up?
 LIGHT.   If you will be so kind
To have the Judge put questions to the woman,
You will find out to whom the wig belongs,
And other things as well, I have no doubt.
 WALTER. —I do not want to know who owns the wig.
How did she get the wig? Where was it found?
 LIGHT. The woman found the wig upon the trellis
Outside Frau Martha Rull's abode. It sat,
Just like a nest, amid the twining vines,

Beneath the window where the maiden sleeps.
    MARTHA. What? By my house? My trellis?
    WALTER. [*Aside*.]   Justice Adam,
If you have something to confide to me,
I beg you, for the honor of the court,
Please be so kind and tell me now.
    ADAM.   What, *I* tell *you*—?
    WALTER. Well? Have you not—?
    ADAM.   Upon my honor—[ADAM
seizes the wig.]
    WALTER. This wig now, does it not belong to you?
    ADAM. This wig here, gentlemen, is mine indeed!
It is the very one, in heaven's name,
That I gave to this lad a week ago
To take for me to Master Meal in Utrecht.
    WALTER. To whom? Say what?
    LIGHT.   To Ruprecht?
    RUPRECHT.   Me?
    ADAM.   When you, you rogue,
Went into Utrecht just a week ago,
Did I not give this wig to you to take
And have the barber put it back in shape?
    RUPRECHT. You ask—? Well, yes. You gave me—
    ADAM.   Speak then, why
Did you, you scoundrel, not deliver it?
Why didn't you, at my express command,
Go to the barber and drop off the wig?
    RUPRECHT. Why did I not—God's lightning strike me dead! I *did*
Go to the barber shop, where I dropped off your wig.
And Master Meal, he took it—
    ADAM.   Took it, yes?
And now it's hanging there in Martha's trellis?
Hold on, you scamp! You don't escape like that.
Behind all this I smell a rank disguise,
Some mutiny or the like—Your Grace, will you
Permit me to interrogate this woman here?
    WALTER. You say you gave this wig—?
    ADAM.   Your Grace,
When yonder fellow there, on Tuesday last,
Drove into Utrecht with his father's oxen,
He came into my office and he said,
"Have you an errand to be run in town?"
"My son," says I, "if you will be so good

To take this wig and have it put back into shape"—
I didn't say to him: go now and keep
The wig, disguise yourself in it,
And leave it hanging in Frau Martha's trellis.
    BRIDGET. Good sirs, your pardon: Ruprecht here, I think,
Is not the one you want. For when last night
I went to see my cousin on her farm,
She being hard in labor, in Frau Martha's yard
I heard the girl say scolding words, but softly did
She speak, for fear and fury seemed to rob her of
Her voice. "Fie, shame on you, you awful man!
What *is* this? Go! Or I will call my mother";
She spoke as if the Spaniards were
Afoot inside the Netherlands.
Then "Eve!" I called out through the fence, "Oh, Eve!
What is it? What's the matter?" All was still.
"Well? Answer me!"—"Yes, aunt, what do you want?"—
"What's going on?" I asked—"What do you mean?"—
"Is Ruprecht there?"—"Oh, that; it's Ruprecht, yes.
Just go your ways."—Save your own hide, I said then to
Myself. These youngsters love as others scold and fight.
    MARTHA. And so—?
    RUPRECHT.   And so—?
    WALTER.   Hush! Let the woman finish.
    BRIDGET. As I was coming back home from the farm,
About the hour of midnight, and was just
Beneath the linden trees near Martha's garden gate,
A fellow whisks right past me, bald of pate;
He has one foot that is a horse's hoof,
And as he runs on by, there is a stink
Of sulphur, smoke, and pitch, all mixed with hair.
I speak a hasty prayer to God and turn
Around in horror, and I see, upon my soul,
The bald spot swiftly disappearing, gentlemen,
Just like a ball thrown hard into the night.
    RUPRECHT. Dam—nation! What!
    MARTHA.   Frau Briggy, are you mad?
    RUPRECHT. You think it was the Devil—?
    LIGHT.   Hush!
    BRIDGET.   Upon my soul,
I know what I did see and what I smelled.
    WALTER. [*Impatient.*] I am not here to ferret out the Devil,
But if 'twas he, he cannot be accused.

If you can name us any other, fine:
But with that sinner spare us any traffic, please.
   LIGHT. I beg Your Grace, let her complete her tale.
   WALTER. What crazy folk!
   BRIDGET.   All right, as you command.
But here Clerk Light can testify for me.
   WALTER. What? You a witness?
   LIGHT.   In a manner, yes.
   WALTER. In truth, I don't know what—
   LIGHT.   I humbly beg that you
Do not disturb this woman in her tale.
That 'twas the Devil I would not maintain;
As to the horse's hoof, and shiny pate, and smell
Of smoke, however, if I do not err by far,
All that is quite correct!—Now then, proceed!
   BRIDGET. Well, when today I learned to my surprise
What had occurred at Martha Rull's, and I,
To ferret out the smasher of the jug,
Whom I'd encountered by the garden there,
Investigate the spot where out he leaped,
I find some tracks, good sirs, right in the snow—
What sort of tracks, I ask you, did I find?
The left foot fine and sharp and neatly edged,
A human foot, as regular as any such,
And to the right of it, misshapen, grossly formed,
A monstrous thing, a rounded horse's hoof.
   WALTER. [*Vexed.*] Oh, nonsense! Crazy, damnable—!
   VEIT. It isn't possible!
   BRIDGET.   Upon my faith!
Right by the trellis, where the leap was made,
Behold an area, quite large, of trampled snow,
As if a sow had rolled around in it;
And human foot and horse's hoof
And human foot and horse's hoof, go off
Right through the garden, out into the world.
   ADAM. The deuce!—You mean the rascal had the brass,
Disguised in devil's form—?
   RUPRECHT.   What! I!
   LIGHT.   Hush! Hush!
   BRIDGET. The man who searches out a badger in the woods
And finds his trail—this hunter doesn't triumph as
I did. "Hey, Mr. Clerk," says I, for at that point
I see the worthy man, sent after me by you,

"Clerk Light," says I, "give up your trial.
The pitcher smasher you'll not bring to judgment, no,
He'll find no worse a place to be than hell:
You see, here are the tracks he left."
    WALTER. [*To* LIGHT.] And then you were convinced?
    LIGHT.   Your Grace,
These tracks she has quite properly described.
    WALTER. The right one was a horse's hoof?
    LIGHT.   A human foot,
Please, sir, that looked just like a horse's hoof.
    ADAM. My word, good sirs, this seems a serious thing.
We've seen a lot of sharply written books
That won't admit that God exists;
But to my knowledge, not one atheist
Has yet shown proof that there is not a devil.
The case before us seems then to deserve
Particular consideration. So I would
Propose, before we try to formulate
A verdict, first to ask the Synod at the Hague
If our court has warrant to assume,
Beelzebub himself did smash the jug.
    WALTER. Such a proposal I'd expect from you.
What's *your* opinion, Mr. Clerk?
    LIGHT.   Your Grace
Need not consult the Synod to decide.
Complete—[*To* WALTER.] with your permission!—your report,
You there, Frau Bridget, please; the case will then
From circumstantial evidence, I hope, be clear.
    BRIDGET. "Now, Mr. Clerk," says I, "let us
Pursue these tracks a little way, and see
To where the Devil may have got away."
"All right," says he, "Frau Bridget, good idea;
Perhaps we shall not go too far astray,
If we go straight to Justice Adam's house."
    WALTER. Well? And you found—?
    BRIDGET.   Well, first of all we found
Beyond the garden, in the linden lane,
The place where, sending out his sulfur fumes,
The Devil had run into me: a curve,
As when a dog goes swerving to one side,
To dodge a cat that hisses in his face.
    WALTER.   And then?
    BRIDGET. Not far away, close by a tree, there stands

A monument that makes me start with fright.
    WALTER. A monument? What?
    BRIDGET.   What? Yes, you will be—
    ADAM. [*Aside.*] Oh damn, I've got to move my bowels.
    LIGHT.   Please pass that by.
Pass by that spot, I beg of you, Frau Bridget.
    WALTER. I want to know just where the footsteps led!
    BRIDGET. Where to? Upon my faith, directly here to you,
Exactly as Clerk Light has said.
    WALTER. To us? To here?
    BRIDGET.   Straight from the linden lane
Onto the green, and then along the fishpond, out
Across the bridge, then through the churchyard, right
To here, I say, to Justice Adam's house.
    WALTER. To Justice Adam's house?
    ADAM.   Here to my house?
    BRIDGET. That's what I said.
    RUPRECHT.   The Devil surely would
Not live here in the court?
    BRIDGET.   Faith, I don't know
If he lives in this house; but it was here,
As I'm an honest woman, he turned in:
The tracks go to the doorway at the rear.
    ADAM. Could he perhaps have gone right in—?
    BRIDGET. Yes, gone right in. Could be. That, too.
The tracks in front—
    WALTER.   Were there some tracks in front?
    LIGHT. In front, if I may speak, Your Grace, there were no
                                   tracks.
    BRIDGET. In front, of course, the tracks were brushed away.
    ADAM. Ah, brushed away. And then he went
In through the back. I am a rogue:
This fellow, mark my words, has on the law
Put something over here. I am no honest man
If nothing's rotten in the registry.
If my accounts, as now I do not doubt,
Turn out to be confused and tampered with, upon
My word, I will not take responsibility.
    WALTER. Nor I. [*Aside.*] Hm, hm! I wonder, was
It left or right? One of his feet—
Judge Adam, please! Your snuffbox!—Be so good.
    ADAM. My snuffbox?
    WALTER.   Snuffbox. Hand it here!

ADAM. [*To* LIGHT.]   You get it, Clerk.
WALTER. Why make a fuss? It's just a step away.
ADAM. No, that's all right. [*To* LIGHT.] You take it to His Grace.
WALTER. I would have uttered something in your ear.
ADAM. Perhaps we'll later have a chance—
WALTER.   All right.
[*After* LIGHT *has sat down again.*]
Tell me, is there some person in
The village here who has misshapen feet?
  LIGHT. Hm! Well, there is indeed a man in Huysum—
WALTER. Oh? Who?
  LIGHT.   Now if Your Grace will ask the Judge—
WALTER. You mean Judge Adam?
ADAM.   I have no idea.
Ten years I've been in office here in Huysum,
And to my knowledge everyone is sound of foot.
  WALTER. [*To* LIGHT.] Well? Whom have you in mind?
MARTHA.   Oh, keep your feet outside!
Why stick them underneath the table so
And make us think you left those tracks yourself?
  WALTER. Who's that? You mean Judge Adam?
ADAM.   I? Those tracks?
Am I the devil, then? Is that a horse's hoof? [*He shows his left
foot.*]
  WALTER. [*Ironically.*] Upon my word. That foot is good.
  [*Aside to* ADAM.]
Now put an end at once to these proceedings.
  ADAM. And if the Devil had a foot like this,
It's out to balls he'd go and dance his fill.
  MARTHA. I say so, too. How could our village judge—
ADAM. Oh, bosh! I!
WALTER.   Make an end at once, I say.
  BRIDGET. The only problem left, my worthy sirs,
Is, seemingly, this solemn decoration.
  ADAM. What sort of solemn—?
BRIDGET.   Here, this wig I hold!
Who ever saw the Devil wearing such a thing?
A towering structure, filled up with more grease
Than any bishop's in the pulpit of his church!
  ADAM. We rustic folks have but imperfect knowledge,
Frau Bridget, of the fashions down in hell.
They say he wears his own hair usually,
But when on earth, I am convinced,

He throws a wig upon his head, so that he then
Can mingle unobserved with people who have rank.
    WALTER. Oh villain! Worthy to be publicly
Chased from the bench in shame! What saves you here
Is nothing but the honor of the court.
Conclude the session now!
    ADAM.   I hope you don't—
    WALTER. You hope in vain. Withdraw as best you can.
    ADAM. You think that I, the Judge, I, yesterday,
Forsook my wig among Frau Martha's vines?
    WALTER. No, God forbid! For yours went up in smoke,
Like Sodom and Gomorrha, you recall.
    LIGHT. Or rather—pardon me, Your Grace!—the cat it was
That had a litter in it yesterday.
    ADAM. Good sirs, appearances condemn me, I agree:
But do not be too hasty, I beseech. At stake
For me is honor or the worst disgrace.
And if the girl won't talk, I do not see
What right you have to put the blame on me.
I sit here on the judge's bench at Huysum and
I lay this wig upon the table now:
The one who claims this wig belongs to me,
I'll summon to the highest court in Utrecht.
    LIGHT. Hm! Well, the wig will fit you, by my faith,
As if it had grown out from your own pate. [*He puts the wig on*
ADAM.]
    ADAM. A slander on my name!
    LIGHT.   It does not fit?
    ADAM. As cloak about my shoulders it
Would be too big, say nothing of my head. [*He surveys himself in
the mirror.*]
    RUPRECHT. Oh, such a whopping scoundrel!
    WALTER.   Quiet, you!
    MARTHA. Oh, such a curséd judge! I'm thunderstruck!
    WALTER. Once more, will *you* conclude the case? Shall *I*?
    ADAM. Well, what do you command?
    RUPRECHT. [*To* EVE.]   Eve, speak, is he the one?
    WALTER. [*To* RUPRECHT.] Keep still, I say.
    ADAM. [*To* RUPRECHT.]   Wait, brute, I'll get you yet.
    RUPRECHT. Oh, you damned horse's hoof!
    WALTER.   Hey, bailiff!
    VEIT. [*To* RUPRECHT.] Shut up, I say.
    RUPRECHT. [*To* ADAM.]   You wait! Today I'll get my hands

On you. Today you'll throw no sand into my eyes.
    WALTER. [*To* ADAM.] Have you not sense enough—?
    ADAM.   Well, if Your Grace
Permits, I will pronounce the sentence now.
    WALTER. Good. Do. Pronounce it.
    ADAM.   Now the case is solved,
And Ruprecht there, the scoundrel, is the guilty one.
    WALTER. That's fine. Go on.
    ADAM.   His neck goes into shackles,
And since he has most disrespectfully
Behaved toward me, his Judge, I'll throw
Him into prison, behind bars. For just
How long, I shall determine later on.
    EVE. What, Ruprecht—?
    RUPRECHT.   Me to prison?
    EVE.   And in shackles, too?
    WALTER. Don't be alarmed, my children.—Are you done?
    ADAM. He may replace the jug or he
May not: it's all the same to me.
    WALTER. All right. This session now is at an end.
And Ruprecht will appeal his case to Utrecht.
    EVE. You say he must appeal in Utrecht?
    RUPRECHT. What. I—?
    WALTER.   Confound it, yes! And till that time—
    EVE. And till that time—?
    RUPRECHT.   I have to go to jail?
    EVE. His neck in shackles? Are you judges, you?
It's he, that shameless one, who's sitting there,
He was the one—
    WALTER.   You hear me, damn it! Silence!
Till then no harm will come to him—
    EVE.   Up, Ruprecht!
Judge Adam was the man who smashed the jug!
    RUPRECHT. [*To* ADAM.] Oh, wait, you!
    MARTHA.   He?
    BRIDGET.   That man?
    EVE.   Yes, he! Up, Ruprecht!
It's he who came to your Eve's chamber yesterday!
Up! Seize him! Take him down from off that bench,
And do it any way you like.
    WALTER. [*Rises.*] Stop there! The first to violate the peace—
    EVE.   Who cares?
You have already earned the shackles, Ruprecht. Go!

Go, throw him off the judge's bench.
    ADAM. Your leave, good sirs. [*He starts out.*]
    EVE.   Now! Up!
    RUPRECHT.   Stop!
    EVE.   Quickly!
    ADAM.   What?
    RUPRECHT. Damned limping devil!
    EVE.   Got him?
    RUPRECHT.   Thunder, lightning, no!
I have his cloak, but that is all!
    WALTER. [*To* LIGHT.] Go, call the bailiff! Do it now!
    RUPRECHT. [*Strikes the cloak.*] Blam! That is one. And blam!
                         One more. And blam!
Again! Since I can't reach his crooked back.
    WALTER. [*To* RUPRECHT.] Unruly churl!—Bring order to this
                                  court!
—If you don't shut up right away,
The shackles will be yours this very day.
    VEIT. [*To* RUPRECHT.] Be quiet, you confounded rogue!

SCENE 12

    All move downstage.
    RUPRECHT.   Oh, Eve!
How shamefully I've injured you today,
God knows! And what about last night! Oh, you,
My darling girl, love of my heart!
Will you forgive me ever while you live?
    EVE. [*Casts herself at* WALTER*'s feet.*] Sir, if you do not help us,
                                we are lost!
WALTER. Why lost? How so?
    RUPRECHT. [*To* EVE.]   Good God! What's wrong?
    EVE. Oh, save my Ruprecht from conscription, sir!
For this enlistment—and it was Judge Adam who
Confided this to me in secrecy—
Goes to the Indies; and from there, you know,
Out of three soldiers only one comes back!
    WALTER. What! To the Indies! Have you lost your senses, girl?
    EVE. To Bantam, yes, Your Grace; do you want proof?
Here is the letter, with its confidential
Instructions that the army is to heed,
Just lately issued by the government:
You see, I am informed on every point.

WALTER. [*Takes the letter and reads it.*]
What monstrous guile! What base deceit!—
The letter's false!
    EVE.   False?
    WALTER.   False, upon my life!
Clerk Light, now speak: tell us if that's the order
That recently was sent to you from Utrecht.
    LIGHT. The order! What! The sinner! It's a note
That he wrote out in his own hand!—
The troops conscripted by the government are meant
For service in this country; not a soul
Would dream of shipping them to the Indies!
    EVE. No, can that really be, dear sirs?
    WALTER.   Upon my faith.
And as a guarantee of what I say:
Your Ruprecht, if that letter's genuine,
Then I will buy him free!
    EVE. [*Rises.*]   Oh, God
In heaven! How the villain lied to me!
For just with all this fearful apprehension
He tortured me, and came to me at night
To force on me a lying affidavit.
He said that his false witness of disease
Could free Ruprecht from military service;
Assuring me that this was so, he slipped,
To fill the affidavit out, into my room:
Demanding there such shameful things of me
As maiden lips would never dare to speak!
    BRIDGET. Oh, what a villainous and vile deceiver, he!
    RUPRECHT. Forget the horse's hoof, my darling girl!
And know that if a horse itself had smashed the jug,
I'd be as jealous as I am right now! [*They kiss.*]
    VEIT. And so say I! Kiss and be reconciled;
At Pentecost, if that is what you want,
We'll have the wedding!
    LIGHT. [*At the window.*]   Look at Justice Adam,
I beg of you: up hill, down dale,
He stumps through fallow winter fields
As if in rapid flight from rack and gallows both!
    WALTER. What? Is that Justice Adam?
    LIGHT.   No one else!
    SEVERAL. There, now he's got onto the road. Look, look!
See how the wig acts as a whip on his hunchback!

WALTER. Run quick, Clerk Light, and bring him back!
Keep him from making evil matters worse.
He is suspended from his office, yes,
And I appoint you, pending further notice, to
Administer the post yourself; if his
Accounts are straight, however, as I hope,
I shall not then force him to leave this place.
Go now! Do me this favor, bring him back! [*Light goes out.*]

LAST SCENE

MARTHA. I beg you, gracious sir, where shall I find
The seat of government in Utrecht?
WALTER. And why, Frau Martha?
MARTHA. [*Bridling.*]   Hm! And why? Well, shall
My jug not find some justice in the capital?
WALTER. Forgive me! To be sure. On the great square,
On Tuesdays and on Fridays, too,
The highest court holds session.
MARTHA.   Good!
In one week I'll present myself right there. [*All go out.*]

The End

Select Bibliography

Atkins, Stuart. "Some Notes to Kleist's *Der zerbrochene Krug.*" *Philological Quarterly* 22, no. 3 (July 1943): 278–83.

Blankenagel, John Carl. *The Dramas of Heinrich von Kleist: A Biographical and Critical Study.* Chapel Hill: The University of North Carolina Press, 1931.

Burckhardt, Sigurd. *The Drama of Language: Essays on Goethe and Kleist.* Baltimore: The Johns Hopkins University Press, 1970.

Calhoon, K. S. "Sacrifice and Semiotics of Power in *Der zerbrochene Krug.*" *Comparative Literature* 41, no. 3 (Summer 1989): 230–51.

Ellis, John M. *Heinrich von Kleist: Studies in the Character and Meaning of His Writings.* Chapel Hill: The University of North Carolina Press, 1979.

Flygt, Sten. "Kleist's Struggle with the Problem of Feeling." *PMLA* 43, no. 2 (June 1943): 514–36.

Furst, Norbert. "The Structure of Kleist's Plays." *The Germanic Review* 17, no. 1 (February 1942): 48–55.

Gearey, John. *Heinrich von Kleist: A Study in Tragedy and Anxiety.* Philadelphia: University of Pennsylvania Press, 1968.

Gelus, Marjorie. "Laughter and Joking in the Works of Heinrich von Kleist." *German Quarterly* 50, no. 4 (November 1977): 452–73.

Graham, Ilse A. "The Broken Pitcher: Hero of Kleist's Comedy." *Modern Language Quarterly* 16, no. 2 (June 1955): 99–113. Reprinted in Graham, *Heinrich von Kleist: Word into Flesh; A Poet's Quest for the Symbol,* 27–41. Berlin: de Gruyter, 1977.

Hamburger, Michael. "Heinrich von Kleist." In Hamburger, *Reason and Energy: Studies in German Literature,* 107–44. London: Routledge and Kegan Paul, 1957.

———. "Heinrich von Kleist: An Introduction." *Partisan Review* 22 (1955): 222–33.

Helbling, Robert E. *The Major Works of Heinrich von Kleist.* New York: New Directions, 1975.

Krumpelmann, John T. "Kleist's *Krug* and Shakespeare's *Measure for Measure.*" *The Germanic Review* 26, no. 1 (February 1951): 13–21.

———. "Shakespeare's Falstaff Dramas and Kleist's *Zerbrochener Krug.*" *Modern Language Quarterly* 12, no. 4 (December 1951): 462–72.

Lindsay, J. M. "Faulty Communication in the Works of Kleist." *German Life and Letters,* n.s. 31, no. 1 (October 1977): 57–67.

———. "Figures of Authority in the Works of Heinrich von Kleist." *Forum for Modern Language Studies* 8, no. 2 (April 1972): 107–19.

Löb, Ladislaus. *From Lessing to Hauptmann: Studies in German Drama.* London: University Tutorial Press, 1974.

Maass, Joachim. *Kleist: A Biography.* Translated by Ralph Manheim. New York: Farrar, Straus, and Giroux, 1983.

March, Richard. *Heinrich von Kleist.* New Haven: Yale University Press, 1954.

McClain, William H. "Kleist and Molière as Comic Writers." *The Germanic Review* 24, no. 1 (February 1949): 21–33.

McGlathery, James M. *Desire's Sway: The Plays and Stories of Heinrich von Kleist.* Detroit: Wayne State University Press, 1983.

Milfull, John. "Oedipus and Adam: Greek Tragedy and Christian Comedy in Kleist's *Der zerbrochene Krug.*" *German Life and Letters,* n.s. 27, no. 1 (October 1973): 7–17.

Nicholls, Roger A. "Kleist's *Der zerbrochene Krug,* Oedipus, and the Comic Tradition." *Theater Annual* 21 (1964): 23–28.

Reeve, W. C. "Ein dunkles Licht: The Court Secretary in Kleist's *Der zerbrochene Krug.*" *The Germanic Review* 58, no. 2 (Spring 1983): 58–65. Reprinted in Reeve, *In Pursuit of Power: Heinrich von Kleist's Machiavellian Protagonists,* 9–22. Toronto: University of Toronto Press, 1987.

Russ, Colin A. H. "Human Error in *Der zerbrochene Krug*: A Typological Approach." *Publications of the English Goethe Society* 41 (1971): 65–90.

Schrimpf, Hans. "Tragedy and Comedy in the Works of Heinrich von Kleist." *Monatshefte* 58, no. 3 (Fall 1966): 193–208.

Seidlin, Oskar. "What the Bell Tolls in Kleist's *Der zerbrochene Krug.*" *Deutsche Vierteljahrsschrift für Literaturwissenschaft und Geistesgeschichte* 51, no. 1 (March 1977): 78–97. Reprinted in *Wege der Worte: Festschrift für Wolfgang Fleischhauer,* edited by Donald C. Riechel, 313–31. Cologne: Böhlau, 1978.

Silberman, Marc. "The Ideology of Re-presenting the Classics: Filming *Der zerbrochene Krug* in the Third Reich." *German Quarterly* 57, no. 4 (Fall 1984):

590–602. Reprinted as "Kleist in the Third Reich: Ucicky's *The Broken Jug* (1937)" in *German Film and Literature: Adaptations and Transformations,* edited by Eric Rentschler, 87–102. New York: Methuen, 1986.

Silz, Walter. *Heinrich von Kleist: Studies in His Works and Literary Character.* Philadelphia: University of Pennsylvania Press, 1961.

———. "A Note on Kleist's Verse Style." *Modern Language Notes* 58, no. 5 (May 1943): 351–54.

Spuler, Richard C. "Fate, Chance, and the Comedy of Kleist's *Der zerbrochene Krug.*" *Proceedings of the Pacific Northwest Conference on Foreign Languages* 27, no. 1 (1976): 68–70.

Stahl, E. L. *Heinrich von Kleist's Dramas.* Oxford: Basil Blackwell, 1961. Originally published as *The Dramas of Heinrich von Kleist.* Oxford: Basil Blackwell, 1948.

Stamm, Israel S. "A Note on Kleist and Kant." In *Studies in Honor of J. A. Walz,* 31–40. Lancaster, Pa.: Lancaster Press, 1941.

Stillmark, Alexander. "Kleist's *Der zerbrochene Krug* and Gogol's *The Inspector General*: A Comparative View." *New Comparison: A Journal of Comparative and General Literary Studies* 3 (Summer 1987): 45–51.

Ulvestad, Bjarne. "A Fairy-Tale Motive in Kleist's *Der zerbrochene Krug.*" *Journal of American Folklore* 68, no. 269 (July–September 1955): 290, 312.

Ward, Mark G. "Kleist's *Der zerbrochne Krug* and Romanticism." *Orbis Litterarum* 35 (1980): 20–46.

Wilkie, Richard F. "A New Source for Kleist's *Der zerbrochne Krug.*" *The Germanic Review* 23, no. 4 (December 1948): 239–48.

Wittkowski, Wolfgang. "*Der zerbrochne Krug*: Juggling of Authorities." In *Heinrich von Kleist Studies,* edited by Alexej Ugrinsky et al., 69–79. New York: AMS, 1980.

Woe to the Liar!

A Comedy in Five Acts

by
FRANZ GRILLPARZER

Translated by
Bert Cardullo

Translated from the following edition:
Grillparzer, Franz. *Weh dem, der lügt!* In *Dramatische Werke,* edited by Reinhold Backmann, vol. 3. Wien: Bergland Verlag, 1947.

Characters

Gregory, Bishop of Chalons
Atalus, his nephew
Leon, his kitchen boy
Kattwald, Count in the Rhine Province
Edrita, his daughter
Galomir, her fiancé
Steward (Sigrid), to Gregory
Steward, to Kattwald
Servants and Maids, to Kattwald
Three Soldiers, in Kattwald's Service
A Pilgrim
A Frankish Captain and His Men
A Ferryman
His Helper
Poor People and Cripples
Choir Boys

175

Act 1

Garden of the Episcopal Palace at Dijon, bound by a wall in the rear, and with a large iron gate in the front. LEON, *the kitchen boy, and the* STEWARD *are at the gate.*

LEON. I simply have to see the Bishop, sir.
STEWARD. It's not allowed, I say, you saucy boy.
LEON. [*Drawing his kitchen knife.*]
You see? My sword is drawn. Will you give way?
Part sun from wind: en garde, my lord!
STEWARD. [*Giving ground.*]
Oh, help! Assassin!
LEON.   It was just a joke.
But I must see the Bishop, sir, I must.
STEWARD. Impossible! This hour of morning every day
He takes a little walk and meditates.
LEON. Oho, but first he'd better meditate on me
And my request; it's next on his agenda.
STEWARD. Your place is in the kitchen, go at once!
LEON. The kitchen, do you say? Just show me one!
The kitchen's where you do the cooking, and
You'll search in vain for one around this place.
Where no one cooks, there can't be any kitchen, sir.
Where there's no kitchen, there's no cook, you see.
I wished to tell the Bishop that—I *will*,
I really will, however cross you look.
For shame on stinginess forever more!
The cook was first to go. So now, thought I,
They've lots of faith in me. And I felt proud.
When I began to show my skill, however,
Then "all is much too high, costs far too much."
And I'm to cook with naught, though naught is what I cook!
Just yesterday I bought a bit of game,
As tasty as could be, the price dirt cheap,
And I was pleased to think our master,
The weak old bishop, would be cheered at this.
Let's toast the meal! Did I not have to sell it though,
To sell it to some slop house at a loss,
Because it seemed too dear, so very costly?
Now do you call that stinginess, or what?
STEWARD. I'll put you out if you're not careful, boy.
LEON. You'll put me out? Please spare yourself the chore.

I'm going. See, my apron, just for you!
And here's my knife, which gave you such a fright just now. [*He*
   throws both onto the ground.]
I throw them down to pick them up no more.
Go find another cook to fix your fasts!
You think I served your master just for pay?
Believe me, there are other, better ways
A lad like me can help himself get by.
The King has need of men, and on my word,
A sword is none too heavy for this hand!
But once I'd seen your Bishop on the street,
With snowy beard and curly hair all white,
His head weighed down by many years gone by,
And yet upheld by what I do not know,
It must be something noble or sublime;
Eyes opened wide, as though he gazed at paintings
From places far away and strange,
These paintings far too big for little frames:
When once I'd seen him passing on the street,
I heard a call from deep inside: serve him you must,
If need be as a stable boy. So I came here.
And in this house, I thought, God's peace would reign,
Though all the world had war. Well, in this place
I now must watch him stint himself on food
As though he'd vowed to starve himself to death,
And see him count each morsel that he eats.
You may observe him if you will; I won't.
   STEWARD. Why worry 'bout him so when he himself does not?
He's strong beyond his years, not true?
   LEON. Could be! But something else, and deeper, is at work.
At times, I can describe it to a tee,
At times, it's like a ghost: outside my grasp.
To me he stood for all that's fine and pure,
And now I see there's such a filthy stain
As greed, a blot so mean and ugly,
Upon the cloth of white that should be clean,
See though I must, go my own way I will.
All men for me are now set down a peg,
And that means me and you and, yes, the world,
Since I so long thought him the very best.
And this torments me so I can't go on.
In short, I quit; I can't stand any more.
   STEWARD. And you intend to tell him that?

LEON.   I do.
STEWARD. You wouldn't dare!
LEON.   Oh, I'd dare more than that.
I'll bid him wash his stain away, I'll bid
Him give me back my high regard for him,
And if he won't, then I must say good-bye.
For shame on stinginess forever more!
    STEWARD. You dare charge him with that, this pious man?
Why, don't you know the poor, the blind, the lame,
That they're the safe in which he puts his money?
    LEON. I know he gives away a lot, God bless!
But do you call it good when one gives alms
To those in need, yet takes from those who give?
Now hear! He sent for me a while ago
And from a chest so large he gave me funds,
The kitchen budget for the coming week.
Before he did this, though, he took a silver piece
And looked it up and down ten times, then kissed it,
And put it in a pouch filled full and tight
That stood back in a corner of the chest.
And now I ask you, sir! A pious man
Who kisses coins? A man who suffers hunger,
Yet has a sack piled high with cash?
By what name call you that, or such a man?
I will not be his cook. I'll tell him so myself.
    STEWARD. You foolish, crazy fellow, why don't you stay put?
Would you disturb so good a man today,
When grief is all he feels inside his soul,
As he recalls one year ago today
The sending of his nephew Atalus
To Treves as hostage for the guarantee of peace?
Now that the war has broken out anew,
The pious boy is held there by the foe,
Who cruelly say they'll hear no talk of ransom.
    LEON. The nephew of our master?
STEWARD.   Yes, it's been a year.
    LEON. Have no attempts been made to rescue him?
    STEWARD. Indeed there have; but all in vain.
Here comes the master now, and deep in thought.
Do step aside, young man. Don't trouble him.
    LEON. He writes.
STEWARD.   What words he'll preach in church this week.
    LEON. How pale he is!

STEWARD.   He's sad of heart, that's why.
LEON. But I must speak with him, no matter what.
STEWARD. You'll come with me! [*Taking hold of him.*]
LEON.   I'll get away from you! [*Both exit.*]

The BISHOP *enters, a notebook in hand, in which he writes from time to time.*

GREGORY. A simple yes or no will do in such a case.
Because of all the evil human nature knows,
Of all that's wrong or bad or foul,
The false word is the worst, the lie hurts most.
If man were true, he'd find he's good as well;
For how could sin survive on earth
If no one told a lie or would deceive?
From man to other men on up to God
No sin there'd be to plague the world.
The wicked man perforce would have to say
When he was all alone: "I am a knave."
And who could long endure his own contempt?
All these are lies by any other name:
First vanity, then pride, false modesty,
Fake generosity or superficial strength,
And shallow love, ideals pretending to be high.
Good ends that say they justify bad means—
Each one just covers up what's really bad inside
And actively gets in the way
When conscience bids man face the looking glass.
But worst of all, the *conscious* lies! Who'd think
Them possible if they did not exist?
Would you, you men, destroy your maker's world?
Why say you something isn't when it is?
And that it is, when it has never been?
Why, you attack existence at its core!
And what about compassion, friendship, love,
Those bonds that tie one life unto the next,
What holds them fast if not your words of truth?
The truth is all of Nature, cyclical:
The wolf is true that howls ere he devours,
The thunder true that sounds before the storm,
The flame is true that warns you as it burns,
The flooded stream whose rushing torrent roars—
They're true because they are, to be is to be true.
What are you when you tell your brother lies,

Deceive your friend, and cheat those closest you?
You're not a beast, for beasts are true;
No dragon or a wolf, no hemlock or a stone.
You are a devil: he alone tells lies,
And you're a devil when you do the same.
Just tell the truth, then, my beloved brothers,
A simple yes or no will do the job.

My pride itself returns to punish me.
For had I told the truth in answer to the King,
Who lately asked what I might need,
If I had just requested ransom for my child,
He'd now be free, at peace would be my heart.
Since I was angry, though, and with good cause,
I said, "I need no wealth of yours, good sir.
Such wealth belongs to those who also rob your land.
You don't know whom I mean? Your sycophants."
And then he turned away from me in rage.
The consequence: my Atalus still lies in chains. [*He sits down on
    a grassy bank, exhausted.*]
    LEON. [*Entering from the side.*]
It took some work to get away from that old man.
And there my master sits—with head all bare!
He doesn't eat, and now he breathes spring air
That's raw and chill. As empty as his stomach is,
He'll catch his death of cold. My word to God,
Were I to stay on here, I'd buy a cap
And put it where he'd find it—on this path.
His head he then could cover; certainly
He'd never get one for himself.
For shame on stinginess forever more!
He doesn't see me. Speak I must or else
Old Sigrid, he'll be back, and then no chance.—
My reverend master!
    GREGORY.   Atalus, you call?
    LEON. It's me, sir.
    GREGORY.   Who are you?
    LEON.   Why, Leon, sir,
The kitchen boy; or possibly, God willing,
I'm Leon, cook to you, the Bishop.
    GREGORY. [*Strongly.*]
Indeed, God willing, that you'd better say.
For if He isn't, dead you'll lie and nil you'll be.
    LEON. You frighten me!

GREGORY.   What do you want?

LEON.   Sir, I—

GREGORY. Where is your knife, and where's your apron, cook?
And whose are those that lie here in the dirt?

LEON. The knife is mine, and that's my apron, sir.

GREGORY. Why on the ground?

LEON.   In anger, sir, I threw
Them down.

GREGORY. You laid them down in anger, boy,
So pick them up in meekness once again.

LEON.   But, sir—

GREGORY. If that's too hard, I'll do it for you, then. [*He bends
down.*]

LEON. [*Running up to him.*]
But reverend master, no! You can't do that! [*He picks up the knife
and apron.*]

GREGORY. Now put them on and look the way you should.
I like a man to show me what he does.
As you just stood before me then,
In essence out of uniform,
You could as well have been an idle rogue,
A man who takes the road to nowhere and no good.
I know, though, from your apron, you're my cook,
And you know, too. And now, my son, please speak.

LEON. I hardly know what I had planned to say.
You make me quite confused.

GREGORY.   Not by design.
Think back, my friend. Perhaps you have complaints?
My guess is yes because you threw your apron down.

LEON. You're right, that's it, I have complaints.
And you're the one I have complaints about.

GREGORY. I am? Is that the case? I'll tell you something, friend.
I make complaints about myself, and every day.

LEON. I don't mean that kind, sir, oh, no. And yet I do.
But I complain as cook, and not as Leon,
As cook for you, and as your servant, sir.
Because you hate your own self, I must say.

GREGORY. The charge is grave, indeed, it is!
To hate oneself is worse than love of self.
For one should only hate what's evil through and through;
And frankly, friend, I don't believe I am.

LEON. What words you utter! Evil through and through, sir,
                                                        you?
You're wholly good, completely so,

With one and only one exception.
    GREGORY. And this is that I hate myself?
    LEON. That you're so stingy with yourself; that you deny
Yourself what others get so much of from your hand.
I can't stand by, your cook, and witness that.
For when the Judgment Day arrives, it's you
Who, as is right, will have to answer for your soul
And I who'll have to answer for your body.
And so I speak here from my office as your cook.
Now look, a man must eat, as everybody knows;
And what he eats affects his very being.
Eat fast-day fare and watch your mind grow weak,
Eat beef and you'll feel strong and brave.
Drink wine and you'll be merry and loquacious,
Drink water and you add too much to just enough.
You're not much good if you don't eat, dear sir.
I know that for myself and that is why I speak.
My stomach, if it's empty, I am slow and dense.
But after breakfast, wit and sense return
And I'll take on the world if so you wish.
You see?
    GREGORY.   You've eaten once today already, no?
    LEON. Oh, yes.
    GREGORY.   God knows that's why you talk so well.
    LEON. Talk well or badly, sir, the truth is what I speak.
That venison I bought just yesterday,
You made me take and sell it back,
A piece of meat like none you've ever seen.
    GREGORY. It cost too much for me, my friend.
    LEON.   Too much?
For such a man as you? Oh, please! There's no such thing.
Besides, it would have cost you next to nil.
Yes, almost nothing. Like to have it later, sir?
I have it once again and now it's free.
You see, truth is some pious folk
Have made a gift of it to you.
A gift, that's so.
    GREGORY.   You lie to me?
    LEON.   Er—what?!
    GREGORY. Thou shalt not lie!
    LEON.   Well, but—
    GREGORY.   The impudence!
    LEON. Oh, if I lied, to good end did I do so.

GREGORY. You think you know, weak soul, of means and ends?
The One above His own way in such matters wends.
It's speak the truth you should, brash boy!
    LEON. Well, then, that meat, good sir, I have to say—
I should have paid for it myself right from the start.
Why so much fuss? I won't transgress again.
And on my life, I'd never once have thought
That such a lie, a white one, was a sin.
    GREGORY. Please leave!
    LEON.   Farewell, I say!
[*He goes but comes right back.*]
                              But one more word.
Now don't be angry, speak I must in truth.
A man so pure, the smallest lie that's told
Resourcefully, provokes him—hold your wrath!
I'm not about to say that lying's right,
I only mean—that such a man as you—so cheap!
I ask you, what does money have
That makes you love it so?
    GREGORY.   What makes you think I do?
    LEON. With your permission, gracious sir,
I saw you kiss a silver piece
And put it in a sack filled full and tight,
The one that stands back in the corner of your safe.
You're stinting yourself here, so you can save up there?
You call that right? You see, we're even now.
    GREGORY. So that was it?
    LEON.   Yes, that. I'm not the only one
Who thinks it wrong of you to save in such a way.
It hurts me, faithful servant that I am,
To say that others think it wrong as well.
    GREGORY. I see I have an obligation, then:
To vindicate myself in all of this.
A shepherd has to set a good example
And never give vexation to his flock.
Sit down and hear how I defend myself.
    LEON. Sir, really—
    GREGORY.   Seat yourself, I say!
    LEON.   All right, then here.
[*He sits down on the ground in front of the* BISHOP.]
    GREGORY. It bothers you to see me put by savings
And kiss the coins for which I've pinched and scraped?

Perhaps you will forgive me if you listen.
A year or more ago when peace was struck,
As long we'd hoped, with those barbarians
Across the Rhine, both sides took hostages,
In mutual and justified mistrust.
My nephew, Atalus, my only sister's son,
Was one among a number of poor boys
Who, torn away from hearth and home,
Supposedly would guarantee the fragile peace.
He'd hardly reached the place where he'd be held,
The Province of the Rhine, so far away from Treves,
Where coarseness that we clothe in politesse,
In primal nakedness makes beasts of men—
He'd hardly reached this place when war broke out anew,
Incited by a breach of faith.
Each side takes out its wrath on hostages,
On innocent young men, for what it says
Is perfidy committed by the foe.
My Atalus is cruelly trapped in bondage now
And must perform slave labor for his captors.
    LEON. Oh, no! My God!
    GREGORY.   I've interceded for his ransom;
His captors, though, demand a hundred pounds
In good hard Frankish currency,
And I don't have that much.
    LEON.   You must be joking, sir.
The Langres congregation pays three hundred pounds
And more in tithes to its presiding bishop.
    GREGORY. We get that here as well, my boy,
But it belongs to poor folk, not to me.
The people gave to me that I in turn might give.
It's steward of the funds I am, not owner.
A bishop has a right, however, just
Like other men, to clothing, food, and life's
Necessities. And what he saves from what
He spends on them is his, perhaps.
Perhaps; and perhaps not. I dared to think it true.
As often as I save a silver coin
From those I call my share, I put it by,
As you observed. Sometimes I like to kiss it,
Which you reproached me with, for it's the ransom
For Atalus, my nephew who's a son to me.
    LEON. [*He jumps to his feet.*]

And you have plenty in the sack?
GREGORY.   Almost ten pounds.
LEON. And he's to cost a hundred? Pardon, sir,
You'll have to save for quite some time
If that's the mark you have to reach.
Meanwhile they'll plague the poor young man to death.
GREGORY. I fear you're right.
LEON.   Your way will never work.
We must devise a different plan, my master.
If I just had ten lads like me, by Satan!—
By God, I meant to say—I'd set him free.
And so I can, too, I alone.
If only I were there where he's confined!
What will you give me, sir, I ask—
Oh, I'm just talking now: I want no pay—
What will you give me, sir, if I can set him free?
If only I were there, I'd lie him out of jail.
GREGORY. To him who lies comes woe!
LEON.   You may be right,
But, sir, with your permission, please:
They'll never give him up for love of God.
And so there's nothing we can do but speak the truth,
And he'll stay where he is. Forgive me and
May God be with you evermore!
I meant no harm. [*He goes.*]
GREGORY.   O God, the Father of us all,
Into Thy hands I now commend my Atalus!
LEON. [*Coming back.*]
Forgive me, sir. I spoke too hastily.
One hardly knows how one should talk to you.
I had a little plan about worked out,
You see, to trick those devilish fools
Who hold your nephew there in that barbaric land.
And I could even set him free if all goes well.
But at the same time always tell the truth?
GREGORY. Thou shalt not bear false witness, no,
So spake the Lord thy God amid the thunderclaps.
LEON. But think a bit—
GREGORY.   Thou shalt not lie!
LEON. And if your nephew lost his life because of this?
GREGORY. So be it, then, and I would follow him.
LEON. Oh, how lamentable! What have you done?
Now I'm imprisoned, too; tormented, beaten,

Can never rest, or eat, or drink, or sleep again,
As long as Atalus, that frail
Young gentleman, is kept from you.
He's held near Treves, you said; that's right?
　　GREGORY. Quite so.
　　LEON.　　　　　　　What if someone went to the enemy
And gave himself in place of Atalus?
　　GREGORY. The sons of noblemen must serve as hostages;
Leon can barely answer for himself,
How then is he to answer for another?
　　LEON. Hm, yes, I see.—And what if Atalus
Perceived the chance to flee from his captivity?
　　GREGORY. Then he could do it without sin, for war
Negates all hostages as guarantees of peace,
And no one has the right to keep
Them prisoner for a single moment more.
Except, how could a youth so gently bred,
Perhaps too gently, make his way alone
Through ravaged plains, defying foes,
Privation, misery?—my nephew never could.
　　LEON. But if a strapping lad stood by his side,
And brought him back to you alive and well?
Release me from your service, sir!
　　GREGORY.　　　　　　　What's on your mind?
　　LEON. I'm going there, to Treves.
　　GREGORY.　　　　　　　You are?
　　LEON. I'll get your nephew, Atalus.
　　GREGORY. You think this is a time for jokes?
　　LEON.　　　　　　　　　A time for what?!
I do not joke; and neither should you joke with me.
I'm deadly serious: I'll bring you back your son.
　　GREGORY. And if you tried, if this you undertook,
To slip into the house where he is held,
Deceive the enemy, play tricks on this our foe,
Abuse the trust men place in other men,
And free my Atalus with lies,
I'd turn him out when he got here,
I'd send him back to new captivity;
I'd curse him, too, I'd curse you both.
　　LEON. Agreed. I'll follow your conditions, sir. But look,
If I'm to have no help from some deceit,
Where do I get my help?
　　GREGORY. [*Mightily.*] From God!

He's mine, He's yours, He's everyone's.
   LEON. [*Falling to his knees.*]
Oh my, sir!
   GREGORY. What?
   LEON.   A bolt of lightning!
   GREGORY.   Where?
   LEON. Or so it seemed to me, at least.
   GREGORY. The Holy Spirit shined inside your heart,
The Evil Spirit fell before his flash.
Whatever at this moment seems correct to you,
That do! And to thine own self and to God be true.
Thou shalt not lie!
   LEON. [*Who has risen.*]
                   You give to me your blessing?
   GREGORY. You do what your God bids you; trust in Him!
Do put your trust in Him as I have not,
Poor, wretched sinner that I am.
                  Here, take this key;
It opens up the sack you saw inside my safe. [*He takes the key
from his garment and goes to give it to* LEON, *but then hands it
to the* STEWARD, *who has come up beside him. The* STEWARD
departs with the key.]
Ten pounds are in the sack, the ransom for my nephew,
Which I have saved, have stolen from the starving,
With hope that gold would do what only our God can.
Distribute some of it among the poor,
And with the rest of it please aid the sick.
Such savings aren't for a bishop to amass.
A shepherd must provide for members of his flock;
The profit in this is the Lord's. Farewell, my son!
The vintner calls the tender of his vine.
The bell has tolled; my flock awaits its bread and wine. [*He exits.*
   LEON *stands very still. A* PILGRIM *approaches.*]
   PILGRIM. [*Putting out his hand.*] A coin for this poor pilgrim.
   LEON.   What? And who are you?
   PILGRIM. A poor man on a pilgrimage
From Campostella, far from home.
   LEON.   Where is this place?
   PILGRIM. The Province of the Rhine, dear sir.
   LEON. The Province of the Rhine?
   PILGRIM.   It's back of Treves.
   LEON. Of Treves, you say?
   PILGRIM   And seven miles from here.

LEON. To Treves?—Good Heavens!—Won't you take me with
                                                you, friend?
PILGRIM. If rough roads and bad food don't bother you. [*The*
    STEWARD *has come with the sack of money.* LEON *takes it from
    him.*]
    LEON. Bad food? You see this purse?!—But wait!
My master, the good man, he meant it for the poor,
So to the poor it goes. My friend, here's some for you,
Since you're poor, after all! [POOR PEOPLE *and* CRIPPLES, *who had
    gathered at the iron gate, have been entering little by little.*]
                                        The rest belongs to you.
I'm marching off with God as my protection. [*He divides the
    money among them.*]
He will complete what through Him has begun. [*To the* PILGRIM,
    who follows the money with his eyes.]
You have your share. Now on to Treves, along with God! [*He pulls
    him away, and the curtain falls.*]

Act 2

Inner courtyard of KATTWALD'*s residence. On the right side there
is a mud wall with a large gate. On the left, halfway down, is a
kind of arbor of boards that serves as a front kitchen; its con-
tinuation is masked by the wings. At the back of the stage,
extending to midstage, and surrounded by a moat, is the great
hall of the house, whose windows look toward the audience.
Linkage is created by a wooden bridge that runs parallel to the
stage from the door situated on one side of the great hall and
then turns downstage on an incline. The* PILGRIM *and* LEON *come
in.*

PILGRIM. Just look, my promise has been kept:
We're at the house of Kattwald, Rhenish Count.
This wall here closes off the inner court,
And that great hall is where he greets his guests.
Invited guests, that is; for uninvited guests
Receive rough treatment at his hands.
I say this to you in advance, so you'll beware.
    LEON. I will be careful, thanks. So this is it:
The place where Kattwald, Rhenish Count,
Keeps Atalus a prisoner.
    PILGRIM. The whole trip long you've been so full of cheer,

But now you're serious.
    LEON.   I get that way
From time to time. You're on to something, though:
The cheerful heart alone achieves its goals.
So Leon, be yourself: be Leon first.
Keep this in mind as well: "Thou shalt not lie."—
At least the Bishop wants it so. [*Shrugging his shoulders.*]
We'll have to see.—Now, friend, a few more words with you.
    PILGRIM. Hard as it is for me to say,
I'd like a word more with you, too.
I've led you here to Kattwald's house
And in so doing, I have strayed far from my path.
I must retrace my steps back to this path
For several miles, and my supplies are spent.
    LEON.   Too true.
I wished to talk about just that.
    PILGRIM.   Indeed.
When we began this journey, you yourself
Assured me of—
    LEON.   A rich reward.
    PILGRIM. And now—
    LEON.   I don't exactly look to you
Like one who'd give too much of a reward?
    PILGRIM. Well, if you want to know the truth, I fear—
    LEON.   Don't fear!
You want the cash or its equivalent,
It's all the same to you, not so?
    PILGRIM. Oh, yes.
    LEON.   Now I don't have the cash on hand, it's true;
But merchandise I own, my friend, yes, merchandise.
    PILGRIM. And is it light enough to lift?
    LEON. If you can lift a man about our weight.
In short, a slave is what I have for you!
    PILGRIM. And where might he be, then, I ask?
    LEON. Right here.
    PILGRIM. [*Looking around.*]
                         Right where? We're all alone, you see.
    LEON. That means, the slave is either me or you.
    PILGRIM. [*Drawing back.*]
Well, I'm a free man, that I know.
    LEON. Then what must be the logical conclusion?
If there are two of us, and one's a slave,
And it's not you, then it can be no one but me.

PILGRIM. Your jest is crude.
LEON.   The jest, as crude as it
May be, refined enough it is
For people who are somewhat crude.
In short, my friend, I make myself a slave to you
On one condition: that you sell me off
And to this house right here. The money will be yours;
It's your reward, the one I promised you. [*He walks toward the
     house.*]
Hey, you there in the house! Come out!
PILGRIM.   Be quiet now!
Let's listen for an answer to your call.
     LEON. Nobody home?
     KATTWALD. [*From inside the house.*]
                                        Who? What? Be gone, I say!
     LEON. We can't make out your answer, you inside.
Let's get a look at you!
     KATTWALD. [*Appearing on the bridge.*]
                                   What's this supposed to mean?
     PILGRIM. He looks to me to be a little mad.
     KATTWALD. [*Coming down to them.*]
Who let you get this far?
     LEON.   Who let us get this far?!
We let ourselves. We didn't even think to ask.
Now who are you?
     KATTWALD.   The nerve! It's who are *you?*
     LEON. And who are *you?*
     KATTWALD.   Get moving now, you two!
Count Kattwald's who I am.
     LEON.   You're Kattwald? Just the man:
The one my master wants to sell me to.
     KATTWALD. To me?
     LEON.   It's basically ridiculous, yes, sir!
A handsome lad of good Franconian stock,
Brought up at court, his manners just impeccable,
To sell him into such a savage den,
Half barn, half open to the air. How terrible!
It's been decided, though, and it must be.
     KATTWALD. You know I could call out my men
Who'd give you and your master just what you—
     LEON. [*To the* PILGRIM.]
You see? He can't control himself.
There's no way this can work, I fear.

Please sell me to some humans, not to him.
  KATTWALD. Who is this crazy youth?
  PILGRIM.   Well, sir—
  LEON.   Permit me, Count!
I am his slave, a gift to him from friends.
And now he wants to sell me, that is all.
  KATTWALD. Sell you? No work that you could do
Would pay for all the food you'd eat.
  LEON. That shows how much you know! Why, I supply much of
My food myself, and that of others, too. [*To the* PILGRIM.]
Explain to him just who I am
And what abilities I have.
  PILGRIM. He is a cook, renowned throughout his field.
  KATTWALD. So you know how to cook?
  LEON. [*To the* PILGRIM.]   Did you hear that?!
[*To* KATTWALD.] Yes, cook, sir. But I only cook
For Frankish palates: they know how to taste a sauce;
They note the seasoning you've used and the fine spice.
They lean their heads back just like this, they raise
Their eyes to Heaven, close their mouths halfway,
And lustily suck air between their teeth,
In order to enjoy the aftertaste
As long as possible in rapture and delight.
  KATTWALD. Oh, I can do that, too, you know.
  LEON. A roast browned to perfection makes their faces flush;
They pale before a roast if it's too rare.
  KATTWALD. Brown, brown, I like it better brown.
  LEON. But, sir, if it's too brown—
  KATTWALD.   No, medium's just right.
  LEON. They choose the lean and tender saddle of the deer.
The rest they throw to dogs.
  KATTWALD.   Oh, but the shank—
  LEON. They throw to dogs, I say. But why this talk?
You people eat because you must:
The Franks alone know how to eat.
  KATTWALD. I also like to eat, especially good things.
[*To the* PILGRIM.] So what's he worth to you, that fellow there?
  LEON. Oh, in the end I'm really not for you.
  KATTWALD. I'll treat you well: according to
Your wishes and according to your will.
  LEON. It's through his art an artist lives and moves.
  KATTWALD. Oh, you be as artistic as

You please: the more the better, yes.
I've wanted a Franconian cook for oh so long;
They talk a lot of wonders such cooks work.
[*To the* PILGRIM.] Now what's the price for him? And right away,
On this, my daughter's wedding day, you'll get
A chance to show what you can do.
There won't be any lack of guests
To treasure to the full what you prepare.
[*To the* PILGRIM.] Now what's your price?
    LEON.   But only if you promise
To treat me like a housemate and an artist,
Not like the other servants.
    KATTWALD.   Yes, of course.
    LEON. You must as well refrain from all rough ways
In what you say and do.
    KATTWALD.   What am I, then, a bear?
[*To the* PILGRIM.] Now what's the price for him?
    LEON.   But only if—
    KATTWALD. Why, damn it all! What's going on?
[*To the* PILGRIM.] What is your price for him? I ask again.
Can you not talk, or don't you want to talk?
    PILGRIM. Why, sir—
    KATTWALD.   Well, what?
    PILGRIM.   It is—
    KATTWALD.   How much?
    PILGRIM.   I thought—
    KATTWALD. If you don't name the price for me at once,
I'll set my dogs on you and you'll be gone.
You think I am your fool?
    PILGRIM. [*To* LEON.]   If speak I must—
    LEON. By all means, speak.
    PILGRIM.   Then twenty pounds, I think.
    KATTWALD. Edrita! Twenty pounds from my old safe!
    LEON. What's wrong with you? Just twenty pounds? For shame!
An artist like me calls for more.
    KATTWALD. What has all this to do with you?
    LEON. I will not do it, no. [*To the* PILGRIM.] I'll go with you.
    KATTWALD. Stay put.
    LEON.   No, not for twenty. Make it thirty pounds!
    KATTWALD. A slave who wants to set the price on his own head!
    LEON. Not under thirty pounds.
    KATTWALD. [*To the* PILGRIM.]   We've made our deal.
    LEON. But I won't have it.

KATTWALD.   Oh, we'll force you to accept.
LEON. You'll force me? You? If you don't pay the thirty,
I'll run away from you first chance I get.
KATTWALD. Just try it!
LEON.   I'll jump from the highest point.
KATTWALD. We'll tie you up.
LEON.   I'll oversalt your soup.
KATTWALD. Hold on, you rash young man!—I'll go to twenty-
                                                   five.
To twenty-five and—
LEON.   Thirty, sir, no less.
My honor is at stake.
KATTWALD.   O.K., O.K.!
You'll get the thirty pounds you want.
[*To the* PILGRIM.] Now go into my house and have them pay you
                                                   off.
I can't take any more of this: I'll die of rage.
PILGRIM. So should I then—?
LEON.   Go in and get your money!
PILGRIM. But you will stay?
LEON.   I'm staying here, with God.
PILGRIM. May He protect you, if He understands your ways.
[*He exits.*]
KATTWALD. [*Who has seated himself.*] Now you belong to me,
                              so I can pay you back
For all your impudence, your saucy words.
LEON. If that's your wish, act fast; for, as I said,
I'll run away.
KATTWALD. [*Leaping to his feet.*] You what?!—And yet, such
                                                   talk
Is foolish. Look, you can't get out of here.
You make me laugh. Know what befell a lad
Who lately tried to flee this place? A hostage from
Across the Rhine?
LEON.   Oh, sir!
KATTWALD.   We quickly caught the youth,
And—
LEON.   And?
KATTWALD.   We tied him to a strong tree trunk;
His chest became a target for our arrows.
LEON. Was he a Frank? This hostage was a Frank?
KATTWALD. That's right. The nephew—
LEON.   Nephew?

KATTWALD.   Of one Klotar, King's
High Chamberlain.

LEON. [*Breathing a sigh of relief.*] Forgive me all my impudence!
Two words are all I have: thank God!

KATTWALD. So you're a smart one, after all,
And you won't try to get away.
You see, I'm sure of that, say what you will.
You'll find that in the end this place is good for you,
For cheerful people know where their advantage lies;
It's gloomy folk whom one can never please.
I might allow that saucy tone of yours as well
When we're alone. In front of other people, though,
My boy—

LEON.   Shoo, shoo!

KATTWALD. [*Startled.*] What's up?

LEON.   A weasel just ran by
Right into the henhouse.

KATTWALD.   A plague on you!
I've had enough. The whip must be your teacher—

LEON. [*He sings.*]

> The cook, if he is whipped,
> Will surely get revenge.
> The whip will have to cook:
> The cook must convalesce.

KATTWALD. Don't sing! [LEON *whistles the previous tune.*]
                              And don't you whistle, either.

LEON. What else is there to do, then?

KATTWALD.   Talk.

LEON. All right: Your threats I pay no heed.
Torment me you can do; torment you back I will.
You let me starve, I'll let you do the same.
Your stomach: it is subject to my will;
From now on it's my humble slave.
We stand as equals face to face.
Hence if you wish it, let's make peace.
I'll stay with you as long as I'm content;
I'll be your cook as long as I see fit.
When I'm no longer happy here,
I'll take my leave, and all your rage and threats
Won't keep me here or bring me back again.
If you agree with all of this, then let's shake hands.

KATTWALD. Shake hands with you?! You must be kidding me.

LEON. You're back to your old tone again.—Hey, guards!
Come here and tie me up! Bring stakes and ropes,
Or from this place I'll fast be gone
Before I've been here very long.
Hey guards! Ho!
    KATTWALD.   Just be still, you crazy lad!
I'll shake your hand if you'll remain—
    LEON. And leave if—
    KATTWALD.   If you can, and if you *wish*.
I add this part and know well what I say.
If you cook all my food the way I like,
Then surely you'll be most content in Kattwald's house.
And now take up your duties: give me evidence
Of culinary art.
    LEON.   The kitchen, where is it?
    KATTWALD. Right there.
    LEON.   That little doghouse? God forbid!
It has no room, no style, few implements.
    KATTWALD. I know, I know! Make do for now;
I'll see what I can do. So what's for lunch today?
    LEON. Today, for lunch? [*Contemptuously eyeing him.*]
                     Roast venison, let's say.
    KATTWALD. That's fine.
    LEON.   And what about a stew?—But no.
    KATTWALD. [*Eagerly.*] Why not?
    LEON.   You first must learn to eat,
Must step by step refine your taste,
Until you're worthy of the riches of my art.
We'll stick with roast today; to top it off—
We'll see.
    KATTWALD.   Oh, yes, do see!
    LEON. [*Calling out.*]   Now I need wood,
And lard and flour and spice. Just gather up
Whatever you can find throughout the house.
Hey, servants, maids, there's work that must be done! [*Enter
    SERVANTS and MAIDS.*]
You, sweep the floor! You, fetch some wood!
You call those pots and pans?! You have no sharper knives?
The meat may pass, but ugh, what dried up beets! [*He hurls them
    out of sight.*]
The pepper's flat. [*He scatters it on the floor.*]
            What are you doing, nibbling on
That food? You oaf, go on, get out! [*He chases him out of the

kitchen with a kick of his boot.]
                                        Confounded help!
          [*He takes an apron from one of them and puts it on.*]
My work's cut out for me with all these beasts about.
     EDRITA. [*Entering.*] What's all this noise I hear?
     KATTWALD.   Hush! Our new cook's at work.
     EDRITA. The one for whom you paid so much—
     KATTWALD.   The very one.
Be still! Or he'll show even both of us the door.
     EDRITA. But who permits this cook to kick up such a row?
     KATTWALD. Oh, heavens! He's an artist, child!
A great man who, like all such men, is off his head.
You must endure their ways to get them to create.
I'll steal away; you stay right here and see
What you can learn. But please don't bother him.
You hear me? Not a word! We meet
At noon in our great hall for lunch. [*He exits.* LEON *busies himself
     in the kitchen.* EDRITA *stands at a distance and watches him.*]
     LEON. [*He sings.*]
                         My wine, I like it dry,
                         A good man must be spry.
[*Speaking.*] Pfooey on wine that's sweet! The devil take such drink!
     EDRITA. A handsome lad, but saucy, it appears.
I'll watch him just a little more.
     LEON. [*He sings.*]
                         The horseman rides, ho, ho!
                         She calls from up above, hey, hey!
                         But he just smiles, ha, ha!
                         "You're there?" she says.
[*Speaking.*] Well, but of course. Where else was I supposed to be?
     EDRITA. Can it be true, he doesn't notice me?
Or does he just pretend? Well, I will go and speak
To him. Hello, my friend!
     LEON. [*Without looking up.*]   Hello to you.
Oh, I can bear some friends like you!
     EDRITA. What are you doing there?
     LEON. [*He continues preparing the meat without looking up.*]
                                        I'm splitting wood, you see.
EDRITA. [*Drawing back.*] Now that was very rude of you.
     LEON. [*He sings.*]
                         If you have eyes and use them not,
                         If you have ears and seal them tight,
                         You don't deserve your eyes and ears.

EDRITA. I saw what you were doing well enough;
I also saw you ruin the piece of meat
You meant to trim. And that was why I questioned you.
Just look: you're cutting off the choicest parts. See here? [*She
    points with her finger, putting it close to the chopping block.
    LEON brings the knife down with greater strength, and she pulls
    her finger back with a cry.*]
My God, the lad's a brute! Watch out!
I'll say no more, though this time he
May double the amount of meat he's wasted.
    LEON. No use! It's only when you're home
That work's a joy. Here it becomes
Hard labor. Down with you and off with you! [*He puts his knife
    down and takes off his apron.*]
They'll have to see to their own meals today.
I want to take a little walk.—Yes, there,
It's there: the road to open spaces. Let me see!
    EDRITA. You'll get the worst of that, you uncouth man!
The moment you walk through the gate, the guards
Will grab you, lead you back, and beat you all the while.
    LEON. I get it, yes! You're worried I might catch a cold.
The open air is bad for health. Quite so!
In that case let us have a chat, just you and I.
[*To himself.*] So fine a girl! Now then, my lovely child,
Can I get close to you without much risk?
    EDRITA. What do you mean by that?
    LEON.   Well, this: you meet
A creature from a species never seen before,
You try to learn if it will pinch or sting,
Or scratch or bite you. Caution wills, at very least,
That one behave in such a way.
    EDRITA. You think we're animals?
    LEON.   Oh, not at all!
You are stouthearted folk. But, pardon me,
From beast to human being there are many steps
To climb!
    EDRITA. How mean you are!
    LEON.   Look here, my girl,
I like you. That you can be taught, I don't despair.
    EDRITA. Do you know who I am besides?
    LEON.   Of course. A girl.
    EDRITA. And daughter of Count Kattwald, your good master!
    LEON. But oh, dear girl, you've not much there.

A Frankish peasant would not change his place
With Kattwald's king. For, just between ourselves,
The more a man's a human being, so
Much more the man does he become. [*He casts a glance at his
    surroundings.*]
This place reminds me somewhat of a trough.
But you are beautiful, and beauty was and is,
Like academic headdress to a scholar,
A woman's patent of nobility. [*He starts to put his arm around
    her.*]

EDRITA.   Don't dare!
The Franks are praised for their good breeding,
But you're degenerate and low.
What did you see in me? What did I say or do,
To make you think you had the right to put
Your hands on me. And even if—

LEON. My child, is that a little teardrop in your eye?
Now listen! Turn your pretty face toward me.
I beg forgiveness! Are you satisfied?

EDRITA. I am, yes. I don't like to hold a grudge.
Besides, I should have taken less offense.
Indeed, I would have put a damper on
Your bold approach much earlier,
Had I not liked you from the very start.
The Franks are so much talked about,
Their manners and devotion to the arts.
The first one I run into, though,
He's very boorish and he's coarse.

LEON. Forgive me, please, once more. I won't do that again.
We've come to know each other's ways;
From this day on we'll let no quarrel intervene
And make us sad.

EDRITA.   From this day on?
How many days is that to you?
My fiancé is here; and in that hall
Tomorrow they're to give my hand to him.
Then two days later, three at most,
We'll leave for his far piece of land.

LEON. So you're a bride-to-be? That doesn't make
Me happy, I must say. Who is the groom?
What is his name and what's he do?

EDRITA. I simply call him this: my stupid Galomir.

LEON. Your *stupid* Galomir? Oh, my!

EDRITA.   That's right!
But he's our nearest relative,
And so to him must go my hand.
      LEON.   Yes, certainly!
As for his lack of brains, my dear,
You'll find that stupid men make better husbands.
      EDRITA. I thought that would be true.
      LEON.   They'll put
Up with whatever you devise.
      EDRITA. And they don't have to have their way in everything.
And yet, you know, sometimes—not always, to be sure—
A girl in fact enjoys a clever chat.
      LEON. Each time you get the urge to have a clever chat,
Go out into the woods and tell it to the trees.
You'll be relieved, and then you can come home.
Because what's good for you, for others just won't work;
Besides, what many women in a husband want,
Is in abundance everywhere.
      EDRITA. I don't grasp what you say entirely,
But I will keep it in my mind. Although,
I must confess, I like an answer when I talk.
      LEON. You get one, sooner than you thought! But now
Let us use up what daylight we have left.
Please lead me out into the fields, show me around.
And also I would like, as my job here demands,
To search for vegetables, and herbs and spices, too.
O Atalus!
      EDRITA. What did you say?
      LEON. Just Atalus.
      EDRITA.   Is that another herb?
      LEON. It may well be.
      EDRITA.   And one that nourishes?
      LEON. It nourishes my heart and mind.
But I don't want to start with a deception.
A friend's the one who owns the name,
A friend whom I am looking for.
You smile?
      EDRITA. I do. I know an Atalus,
The one who's here with us.
      LEON.   A Frank?
      EDRITA.   Yes, from the Rhine.
      LEON. The nephew of—?
      EDRITA.   I don't know any more,

Except that he is here as hostage of our Count.
He's quite a dull young man, therefore
An easy one to tease. If you
Will promise to be good and most agreeable,
And not to try by any chance to flee—
    LEON. Concerned about me, eh?
    EDRITA.   Just think of all
The money that my father paid for you
A little while ago.
    LEON. [*To himself.*]   A stingy girl
She is, like every member of her sex!
    EDRITA. But surely you must know, escape's impossible.
I'll take the basket, then; you follow me.
    LEON. Someone approaches there.
    EDRITA.   So what? Whoever!
    GALOMIR. [*He becomes visible on the bridge.*]   Hey!
    EDRITA. Why do you bother me, oh stupid Galomir? [GALOMIR
clumps back across the bridge and into the house.]
Oh, go tell Father, do. That doesn't worry me
A bit. Let's go, before they stop us: follow me,
Be quick. I'll show the garden and this area
To you. And then I'll show our Atalus, who may
Be just the one you seek, who knows? At least he is
A countryman of yours. The sight of him
Will make up for the sight of us.
Now don't pretend! It's true! So if you want to, come! [*She goes
toward the gate.*]
    LEON. All this is going faster than I thought or hoped.
It seems that Heaven shortens my work here.
I'm grateful for the help.—I'm coming, look and see! [*He follows*
EDRITA. *Both exit.*]

Small area, surrounded by trees. Enter KATTWALD'*s* STEWARD,
preceded by ATALUS.

    STEWARD. You have been idling once again, as usual.
The horses graze right over there; right here is where
You stay. If one of them gets lost and you
Can't find him, you'd best lose yourself.
    ATALUS. [*He sits down on the ground, downstage right. The*
STEWARD *exits. After he leaves,* ATALUS *speaks.*]
Do go away, you surly peasant. Him and all

Like him—I wish I could destroy them with one glance! [*He
    whittles at some wood.*]
When once I get this good thick piece of wood hewn down,
Let one of them get close to me. Such curséd folk!
I'm made to wear this shirt, so coarse it irritates
My skin, and bread and greens are all I get to eat.
If only I were back home with my uncle!
He doesn't think of me, however, and
He gets on well, while I must waste
Away among this heathen tribe. [*Enter* EDRITA *and* LEON.]
    EDRITA. [*As she picks.*]
See, here's some sage, and here's some parsley, too.
And there's your countryman, look, Atalus.
He mutters to himself and wields a club,
And means to kill us all with it.
Good day to you, my noble gentleman!
That angers him.—Wait here a little bit.
I want to check the steward's little garden;
Fine mint grows there along the fence.
I'll grab you some and bring it back. [*She puts down the basket.*]
Stay put meanwhile.
    LEON.   I will.
    EDRITA.   I'll soon return. [*She exits.*]
    LEON. [*He sits down on the ground, downstage left, and spreads
    out the contents of the basket.*]
There's cabbage here and kale—Hey, Atalus!
    ATALUS. [*Looking up into the trees.*]
Who calls for me?
    LEON.   And carrots there—
Your uncle sent me.
    ATALUS.   Who? My uncle!
    LEON. Stay where you are! Don't say a word.
No one must notice us.
    ATALUS. [*Standing up.*]   You spoke about
My uncle.
    LEON.   Sit back down! Be quiet!
    ATALUS.   He himself—
    LEON. If you don't sit still, I will leave. [*He stands up and moves
    toward the back of the stage.*]
    ATALUS. [*Sitting down again.*]
Another one who's just like all the rest!
They tease me and have lots of fun at my expense.

I'll take that from that pretty girl,
But from these rude young fellows?—By God, no! [*He pounds the earth with his club.*]
I wish one blow would be enough for all of them.
> LEON. [*Coming toward the front of the stage again and sitting down.*]
I'll say it once more, Atalus: keep still
And hear my words. Your uncle sent me here
To rescue you.
> ATALUS.   And how will you begin,
I'd like to know?
> LEON.   With help from God I will succeed.
Already I've gained entrance to this place:
As the new cook.
> ATALUS.   That's really something! Now you're sure
To set me free!
> LEON.   I say that any means
Is good if it can help achieve the end.
The master of the house is well-disposed toward me:
I'll ask that you be made assistant-to-the-cook.
> ATALUS. Assistant in the kitchen? Me?
> LEON.   That's right!
> ATALUS. You'll have to look for someone else aside from me.
> LEON. And if you can escape no other way? What then?
> ATALUS. Much better to be captive here, or anywhere,
Than so to stain my family's name. [*The* STEWARD *passes by at the rear of the stage, keeping an eye on them.*]
> LEON. [*Rummaging in the basket.*] Here's celery and those are
                              parsnips there.
This onion burns my eyes. That watercress
Is not enough: we need much more. [*The* STEWARD *exits.*]
If this concerned just you and you alone,
I'd stop right now my work to set you free.
Your uncle, though, wants me to try; therefore, young sir,
I think you'll have to do it.
> ATALUS.   Have to! I?
> LEON. Yes, sir! If you refuse the job,
I'll pick you up and take you to it.
> ATALUS.   You just try,
You surly peasant!
> EDRITA. [*Entering.*] Here's some more.
Will this, then, be enough for you? [*She shakes vegetables out of her apron and into the basket.*]

And did you speak with your compatriot?
A strange young man, don't you agree?

ATALUS. [*Getting up.*] If you would talk to me, I'd fast reply.
The one you're talking to, he's foolish and lowborn.

EDRITA. He's smarter, I should say, than you.

ATALUS.   Oh, really, now?
You don't do well to treat me with such scorn.
If some day I go home, who knows?
I might decide that you should come along.

EDRITA. You'd even go so far as offering
Your hand to me?

ATALUS.   Perhaps.

EDRITA.   My, my!

ATALUS. Provided that our ruler, the good King,
Will grant your house a Frankish coat of arms and crest.

EDRITA. And then you think—?

ATALUS.   And then, oh, yes!

EDRITA.   Oh, no!
I like this lad right here, for he is lighthearted
And gay; you're just depressing, though, and troublesome.

LEON. I want him in my kitchen.

ATALUS.   So you're back to that?

LEON. To help me with the cooking.

EDRITA.   He's too clumsy to
Do that.

LEON. But even so, he is a Frank
And for this reason can be taught.

ATALUS. But I won't do such work, I tell you once again.
I watch the horses in the end because I must,
Because also a horse is such
A noble and courageous beast.
But work in someone's kitchen? Better that
I lose my life right here, torn limb from limb. [*He has grabbed his
club. Enter* KATTWALD *and* GALOMIR.]

KATTWALD. A fight is breaking out! [GALOMIR *then points to the
group with a violent gesture.*]

KATTWALD.   Yes, I have eyes, you know.
What are you doing here?

EDRITA.   We searched for potherbs and
The like. This fellow knows them all by sight.
He spotted them; I did the gathering.

LEON. I also thought to get myself an assistant;
This countryman of mine is perfect for the job.

Except that he won't do it.

ATALUS.   No.

KATTWALD.   A simple no?
You just won't do it, eh? And you give as
Your single reason: no? But I tell you, if in
My name he bids you follow him, you will comply
Without a no; or else my men might use
You to discover if the iron head
Is fast attached to every axe and spear.

    EDRITA. Now you stand there and don't know what to do,
And yet you must obey. I knew this would occur.

    KATTWALD. [*To* ATALUS.] Mark well: if he should bid you follow
him
In *my* name, you must go without complaint.
But just now you can still remain outside.
[*To* LEON.] My friend, you snoop around this place too much for
me;
You pry about, I've noticed, everywhere you can.
You doubtless seek a comrade for your flight.

    LEON. You guessed it, sir! The going's easier for two.

    KATTWALD. Well now you've seen my playful side,
When I can give and take a snappy word.
But if I put my hand up to my mouth
And shout my battle cry, why then, good friend,
Your blood's the price.

    EDRITA.   You there, that's true.

    LEON.   I have no doubt.
The blood's also the price by me: from chickens, ducks,
And quail, which do not bite and meekly acquiesce. [*He begins to
toss the vegetables out of the basket.*]

    KATTWALD. [*Promptly.*] What are you doing, man?

    LEON.   What's all this stuff
For anyway? Nobody's here to take it to
The kitchen.

    KATTWALD. *You're* the one who'll take it there.

    LEON.   Oh, is
That so? Since when have I been in your service as
A porter?

    EDRITA. Let me—

    LEON.   Take the trouble in my place?

    KATTWALD. Am I myself supposed—?

LEON.   Who does it's all the same
To me.
KATTWALD. [*Looking around.*]
                          It's clear the only thing that will help here
Is a good stick.
ATALUS. [*Leaning on his club, pleased with what is happening.*]
                          All hell will break loose now!
He's far too insolent, that boy.
KATTWALD. [*To* ATALUS.] Too insolent? And you're too stupid,
                                    you numbskull!
With capable young men, one pardons certain things;
With those who are inept, however, pardons don't
Occur: for anything they do draws down one's wrath.
You take that basket now and help the cook.
If he complains, this cook, he should be mindful of
My heavy hand. We'll doubtless find a master for
Him, too. You dare to contradict?!
EDRITA. He didn't even say a word.
KATTWALD. Well then, let's go! Get started!
                                    [*To* GALOMIR.]
                                    Make them run!
[*As* GALOMIR *overzealously starts to draw his sword.*]
Hey, hold it! I don't want my cook run through
And roasted to a crisp! Just use your hands on him.
LEON. [*To* EDRITA.] While they comport themselves in such a
                                    charming way,
Let us get out of here. All right?
EDRITA.   Suits me!
LEON. Whoever runs the best shall get—well, what?
EDRITA. Why, nothing! [*They run away hand in hand.*]
KATTWALD.   Wow! Can they run! My,
They surely got to know each other fast.
What do you think of that, poor Galomir?
GALOMIR. Me?
KATTWALD.   Yes, I know: you hardly think at all.
Cheer up, though, son! In only one more day or two
She'll be your wife and you will move away. [*Pointing to* ATALUS.]
Perhaps then you will take this fellow here with you.
And if the other fellow makes meantime
Too much a nuisance of himself,
We'll do to him as he does to the hens

And let him have the axe. For now, be patient.
We need him, after all, to cook this evening's feast.
[*To* ATALUS.] You there, get going! Let us make our way toward
                                                    home.
The guests may have arrived by now. [*Starting to go, then
   stopping.*]
My mouth is watering for tasty morsels! [ATALUS, *carrying the
   basket in his left hand and his club over his right shoulder,
   leads the way reluctantly, and the other two follow.*]

The curtain falls.

Act 3

Outer courtyard of KATTWALD'*s house, as in Act 2. The great hall is
   illuminated and guests can be seen sitting at a long table.* LEON
   is busy in the foreground; ATALUS *sits on a stone in front of the
   kitchen and plays with his club.*

LEON. [*Handing a large roast to a* SERVANT.] Just take this up
                                          and say that it's
The last. When it is gone, they'll have
To satisfy their appetites on wine. [*The* SERVANT *crosses the
   bridge into the hall.*]
LEON. [*After he observes* ATALUS *for a while.*]
Well, have you thought about it?
   ATALUS.   About what?
   LEON. About all that I said to you.
   ATALUS. What did you say to me?
   LEON.   So help me, this
Is more than I can take. So pay attention, please.
You know why I have made you my assistant,
And that old werewolf must have his suspicions now.
I heard him say that when his daughter moves
Away, he wants to send you with
Her, far into the countryside.
   ATALUS. Oh, that would be just fine with me.
   LEON.   It would? Indeed!
   ATALUS. She's quite a pretty girl.
   LEON.   I noticed that myself.
   ATALUS. She likes me, too.
   LEON.   I didn't notice that.

ATALUS. And has liked me for a long time.

LEON. But it appeared to me as though she laughed at you.

ATALUS. [*Rising.*] My uncle settled on a studious life for me;
As a result, I've not mixed much with women and
Know only little of their ways.
But if she teases you, she likes you, so they say.

LEON. But teasing and derision, sir, they're different things.

ATALUS. I know that; still I think she likes me.

LEON.   O.K., great!
But if you go with your belovéd, who does love
You so, far off into the countryside,
What then, sir, of your uncle's wish and our escape?

ATALUS. You're right on that.

LEON.   Then hear what else I have to say.
[*Shouting and the noise of clinking glasses are heard from the
    hall. He looks toward the rear, in the direction of the hall.*]
Go on, go on! That fits in with my plan.
At first my scheme looked to a distant day;
I thought we'd have to wait for weeks in order to
Escape. But if they separate the two
Of us, all hope will fade away.
And opportunity's a fickle paramour
Who won't return a second time
If she has found the door was locked the first time 'round.
I hope that now the foreign dishes,
Which I have spiced and peppered all the more,
Will, like the summer heat, cause them to drink much wine.
I hope from this to see the revelers
So overcome—the servants imitating their
Good masters faithfully as well—[*Pointing to the large gate.*]
You see the key there in that lock?
If they forget to take it out tonight,
The way is clear—Be still! Move farther off!
[*They separate from each other. A* SERVANT *with a cumbersome
    walk enters, humming a song off-key to himself. He goes to the
    gate, locks it, and takes the key out.* LEON *makes a movement
    toward him, but steps back again at once. The* SERVANT *goes
    across the drawbridge into the house.*]

ATALUS. [*Laughing.*] Ha, ha! That plan did not come off.

LEON.   You're glad of it?

ATALUS. Only because you think that you're so smart.

LEON. Whether I am or not, the next step that I take

Will show. I'll get the key again, my word on it.
For I've found out that key is placed each night
In Kattwald's chamber, at the head of his big bed.
If wine and sleep will do their job, then I
Will go and grab it from its hanging place. [*Renewed noise in the hall.*]
Hear that? But it's already weaker: they are tired.
What can be done this day you don't put off until
The next; a helper like this feast is seldom had.
Besides, the roads I traveled here I still
Recall in part; in part I will rely on signs
I left that further time will scatter and destroy.
And so it's now or never for my plan.
When morning comes and they awaken late,
God willing, we'll have quite a lead on them. [*The lights in the hall are extinguished one after the other.*]
Look there! It's getting dark up in the hall;
Soon wine and sleep will have performed their task.
In case they learn before daybreak of our escape,
There's still another thing to do.
You see that bridge, as crude as all else here
And badly built, its piles propped up by wooden stakes
Alone? A man need only shovel out the mud
Around one pile to have the bridge come crashing down
The moment someone walks on it: the first to aim
At chasing us will wind up in the slimy moat.
That makes us safe from those inside the house;
The servants, well, they'd sooner race
To pull this fellow from the moat
Instead of racing after us.
Before they can restore the bridge, we'll be long gone.
So we've two things that we must do:
Since we are two, that's one for each.
While one of us sneaks in the house to fetch the key,
The other will dig loose a pile's supports,
As I've described. And we already have
The tools for that right here at hand.
    ATALUS. I'll break into the house.
    LEON.   Oh, really? You, indeed!
    ATALUS. If I just had a sword, I'd get that key.
    LEON. If I had one, I'd get it, too!—What rubbish! If
And but, the proverb goes, don't get things done.
I won't dispute your other gifts,

But I'm the slyer of us two, dear sir.
I'll slip into the house while you,
To your delight, dig up the mud.
    ATALUS. And so the hardest work must always fall to me?
    LEON. You call such work the hardest? Come, now, man!
    ATALUS. [*Kicking the pick and shovel aside.*] I will not touch
                                         such lowly tools.
I'm better born than you, therefore
The bolder deed is mine. To me
You must entrust it. I'll break in the house.
    LEON. What if someone confronts you in the passageway?
    ATALUS. I'll seize him by the throat—
    LEON.   And he will cry for help.
You fight the lions, sir; leave it to me
To catch the birds. We'd better do as I have said.
Your uncle put his trust in me
And I must take responsibility.
Hence my good sense must govern our pursuits. Or else
I'll send you back to mind those grazing horses,
Where you can chew on your displeasure
While I make use of my quick feet to run away
From here. In that case, what they paid for me will have
Been squared by services that I have rendered them.
Your uncle waits impatiently
For your homecoming. Can you hear his voice?
It seems his prayers are borne along to us
On evening winds; they shield us, keep us safe,
And angels with broad wings will flock
Around the two of us wherever we may go.
I have a mind to coax you as one does a child.
Believe me: digging is a noble occupation;
Whatever greatness you achieve or you promote,
The man who digs your grave will triumph over all
Your triumphs, labors, splendors, and ambitions. Here
Then, is your shovel: bear it like a sword.
And here's your pick—not yet, however, not just now.
    EDRITA. [*She appears on the bridge.*]
You're still awake?
    LEON.   We are.
    EDRITA.   Then go to sleep.
    LEON. We will.
    EDRITA.   You've had your fill of talk by now?
    LEON. No man is full as long as he's still hungry.

EDRITA. If you're amused by all your talk, then fine.
For me it's time to go to bed.
    LEON. Will you most likely lock the door up there?
    EDRITA. That is my father's nighttime chore;
He makes the rounds himself before he goes to bed.
But this night, I would say, he won't be doing it.
He's guzzled too much wine, and now
He lies flat on his back, asleep. It's his concern,
Not mine. I only do what I've
Been told to do, no more. Am I not right?
    LEON. Yes, that's what everyone should do.
    EDRITA.   Then go to sleep:
At night that is for tired men a welcome duty.
And dreams awaken just as soon as we're asleep.
Will you be dreaming?
    LEON.   How should I know?
    EDRITA.   *I* know.
I'm almost sleeping now. Good night!
    LEON.   Sleep well.
    EDRITA.   I will. [*She goes
into the house.*]
    LEON. [*After he has watched her leave.*] Now get to work, God
                         at your side. Here are
The tools, but ply them gently lest the night
Prick up its ears. Above all else use caution. [*He leads him toward
    the rear of the stage.*]
Just climb down in the moat. See, here's the way.
Dig in your heels there where the grass leads down,
And you will safely reach the bottom. It's not deep:
If all else fails, you can jump in. [ATALUS *has climbed down into
    the moat.*]
You made it. Very good! Now for the tools. [*He hands them to
    him.*]
Dig up that pile there on the right.
It looks the least entrenched and least secured.
The ground is soft: this job will be a piece of cake. [*Coming
    toward the front of the stage.*]
And now I must prepare for *my* job in the house. [*Feeling at his
    throat.*]
My head is still on straight? Yes, it's in place.
I wouldn't bet, though, on its staying there for long.
If I have gotten them so used to the extremes
In rudeness and in impudence

That they can't tell when I am serious
And when I jest, or when I am
Insulting them and when I beg their pardon—
But courage, man: your life is not in danger yet. [*Singing
    somewhat loudly.*]
"And once upon a time—" Oh, yes, I must be still.
And then, if in the end this really does succeed
And he, the good old gentleman—On guard!
Prepare to charge! Shield up! March double time! [*He hurries up
    the bridge, looking down into the moat.*]
That's right, my mole, you burrow down into that ground!
But don't dig all of those supports loose yet,
Or else I may be caught by my own trap when I
Come back. [*A loud sound is heard below.*]
                  Slow down! Too loud!—I must be quiet, too.
                     [*He goes into the house.*]

ATALUS. [*From below, in the moat.*]
Leon! [*He appears.*]
              So he's already gone!
How insolent that fellow is!
He leaves me here to slave while he—Just wait and see!
He'll pay me back with interest in due time. [*He disappears
    again.*]

SCENE CHANGE

*A room without much depth. In the rear wall, a large arched
opening; next to it on the left, a smaller, door-shaped one. Both
are closed with curtains. Near the smaller opening, in the side
wall, is a door. After a pause,* LEON *peeks through the curtain of
the smaller opening.*

LEON. [*In a hushed voice.*] Here is the room, if I'm correct,
And there the place where our old werewolf rests.
Is he asleep? [*He sets one foot into the room and stamps it down
    somewhat hard, after which he immediately draws back and
    disappears. After a little while he appears again.*]
                He sleeps.—So far, so good!
And yet, conditions could be even better.
The key hangs at the head of his big bed.
But though he lies deep in both wine and sleep,
A bird of prey still keeps one eye pried open,
When it itself is being preyed upon.—It's now
Or never! One quick grab and I'll have done the job.

If he wakes up, an artful lie will help.
But wait! The Bishop has forbidden that,
Although to do so is quite foolish, silly,
Ridiculous. How is a man supposed to deal
With deviltry if not through such
Invention?—Well, no matter! Try I must! [*He has drawn near the
     larger curtain, behind which* KATTWALD *sleeps.*]
If only I could get the key on my first try! [*Listening.*]
I hear him breathing—snoring is the word, I think.
If he's so coarse, then why am I so civilized? [*He goes behind the
     larger curtain.* EDRITA *appears from the curtain behind the
     smaller opening, her finger on her lips. Listening, she advances
     a few steps.*]
     KATTWALD's VOICE. [*Behind the larger curtain.*]
Hey, what! That key there—
     LEON. [*Also behind the larger curtain.*] Hear me out.
     KATTWALD. That key, I say, give it to me! Where is my sword?
I'll cut you in one hundred thousand bits.
     LEON. Just listen!
     KATTWALD.   *You* listen, declares my sword.
[*At the first exchange of words above,* EDRITA *turns toward the
     side door on the left and quickly takes the key out of the lock.
     Then she steps with it behind the curtain of the smaller
     opening.*]
     LEON. [*Emerging.*] Now God protect us all! Come out, you
                                                  traitor!
[*He throws the key in the area of the smaller opening.*]
     KATTWALD. [*Following him with drawn sword.*]
Go forth, my sword! Where is the brazen thief?
     LEON. [*Glancing toward the key.*]
Perhaps I still can snatch it up as I go out.
     KATTWALD. Where is the key, where?
     LEON.   I don't have it.
     KATTWALD. You took it.
     LEON.   Yes, I did.
     KATTWALD.   Where is it, then?
     LEON. I threw it on the floor.
     KATTWALD. [*Drawing back his sword for the thrust.*]
                                             Well, pick it up.
     LEON. I'll have to look for it. [*He searches on the opposite side
of the room.*]
     KATTWALD.   You'll have to *what?!*
     LEON. [*Searching on the floor.*] It isn't here.
     KATTWALD.   But I don't want to know
                                                  where it

Is not. I'm asking where it is.

LEON. [*Standing up.*] I ask that, too, sir.

KATTWALD.   Search, I say!

LEON. [*Bending down again.*]

O.K., I'm searching.

KATTWALD.   Tricky slave!

Is this the same mad daring and brash prankishness
With which you sold yourself into—?

LEON.   Please lift your foot.

KATTWALD. What for?

LEON. [*Raising his foot for him.*] And here—we do not find it,
                                            either.

KATTWALD.   Damn

It all! So now you're making fun of me, to boot!

LEON. One has to make a thorough search, you know. [EDRITA
*has meanwhile stepped in softly, picked the key up from the
floor, put the other one in its place, and quietly left the room.*]

KATTWALD. All right! I'm counting up to three. And if by three
The master key is not here in my hand,
I'll put my sword right in between your meaty ribs.
So. One!

LEON. Now listen!

KATTWALD.   Two!

LEON.   You wouldn't do—?

KATTWALD. [*Drawing back his sword to strike.*] And—

LEON. [*Crying out.*]

Of course! [*Coolly pointing to the other side of the room.*]
            We haven't yet looked over there! [*Picking up the key.*]
And here in fact we find the prize, right on the floor.

KATTWALD. High time, I'd say. You came quite close.

LEON. But this key's lighter; either that
Or I can't tell because my hand still shakes.

KATTWALD. Now put it back where it belongs.

LEON. It *is* a different key.

KATTWALD.   Go hang it up, I say!

[*He has violently pulled the curtain back; a bed and the footstool
next to it are visible.*]

LEON. [*Bending down over the floor.*]

We must search for the other one.

KATTWALD.   By God,

You're making fun of me again!
You put that key back in its place!

LEON. But what if it's not the right one?

KATTWALD. It *is* the right one—just because you say it's not!

LEON. I almost think so, too. There's not

Another key around here on the floor. [*Going to the head of the bed.*]

So I'll hang up this one. [*He does so.*]

KATTWALD.   Where is it? Show your hands!

LEON. Here are the both of them: they're empty.

KATTWALD. [*The old man feels* LEON's *hands.*]   Good.

LEON. And there's the key.

KATTWALD. [*Reaching up to feel with his hands, he loses his balance and winds up sitting on the bed.*] O.K., it's there.

LEON. Lie back now and just sleep it off.

KATTWALD. Eh? What was that?

LEON.   I said to sleep it off: you're drunk,

You know.

KATTWALD. I'll let you off this time.

LEON. Because you need a cook tomorrow.

But I'll toss poison into all the sauces that

I fix for you.

KATTWALD. I'll make you test them first before

I eat.

LEON.   Why, thanks for telling me. Now I'll forgo

The use of poison, and my friend and I will eat

Up everything. He is far more important to

Our land than all your seedy guests and kindred are

To theirs.

KATTWALD. [*He starts to get up, but* LEON *quickly shoves the stool at his feet and he sinks back down.*]

                     Damnation.

LEON.   Easy. You'll need quicker feet

For that. Tomorrow you can pass all this off to

A dream and say it never was. And now, good night. [*He goes out the smaller opening.*]

KATTWALD. [*Still sitting.*] You can't be cross with such a fellow

                                             in the end.

He comes right out and says just what he means.

And he's a lot of fun as well.

If I were in his place, I'd do as he has done.

The key is back where it belongs and— [*His head drops down, then he immediately starts up.*]   Hey there, lad!

Yes, he is gone. I'll go to sleep again.

That wine has really gone straight to my head. [*Half lying down,*

*he frees the curtain with the tip of his sword; the curtain falls
into place and hides the bed from view.*]

SCENE CHANGE

Outer courtyard of the house, as at the beginning of the act.

LEON. [*Standing on the bridge.*] Hey, Atalus!—I have to think
                                                that's he's asleep.
[*Coming down.*]
So what if he is sleeping?! All his digging can't
Do us a bit of good, since we still lack
The key that would enable our escape. [*Listening.*]
He's digging! Oh, that I could set so little store
By him! And he completes the small amount of work
That he was asked to do, while I
Have failed at the great task I set myself. [*Speaking toward the
    rear of the stage.*]
Enough!—But first before I do another thing,
I'll check to see if the two halves
Of that big gate so tightly fit, that rage,
My rage at my incompetence, can't— [*He has drawn near the
    gate; suddenly stepping back.*]
Oh, gracious Heaven! Do my eyes deceive?
Does night play tricks?—A key is in the gate!
Keep digging, Atalus!—It isn't possible!
How did the key get here, when just now up inside
The house—yet there it glitters, ogling me. [*Running up to the
    gate.*]
I have to touch you, test to see if—[*Grabbing the key and with it
    locking and unlocking the gate.*] It's the one!
And freedom blows right in, as air does through the Alps. [*With
    folded hands.*]
Does Heaven thus make manifest its will?
Do angels stand about and keep us safe?
    EDRITA. [*Who had earlier become visible; stepping forward.*]
You're wrong. No angel lends his help where man
Sets to his work with falseness and deceit.
    LEON. With falseness and deceit?
    EDRITA.   You wish to flee from here.
    LEON. I never hid that wish.
    EDRITA.   Oh, yes you did!

So that is why you think you're honest? Is it?
Although in fact you always spoke the truth, [*Laying her hand on
    her heart.*]
I feel in here you have deceived me.
So put no hope in God by all you do:
I was the one who brought the key to you.
You want to run away?
    LEON.   I do.
    EDRITA.   All right. Now why?
    LEON. You dare to ask me why a slave wants to be free?
    EDRITA. You had it good with us.
    LEON.   There's something I've left out.
I gave a promise to the pious man I serve,
So pious that when I think of his parting words
And of the words your childlike lips have just
Now spoken, I must drop my eyes in shame.
I promised I would bring his own nephew—
That Atalus right over there—to him.
Oh, if you only knew this saintly, worthy man!
    EDRITA. Your people's holy men are not unknown to me.
For Christian missionaries travel through our land
From time to time in hopes of winning kindred souls
For their Lord's flock. And for their work
They often suffer torture and then death.
They teach there's but a single God, and it is true [*Touching his
    hand.*]
That what the heart clings to in its abundant faith
Is only and forever one divinity.
Oh, have no fear, if you remain,
That I will torture you with tenderness.
I'm not the way that many people are:
"Oh, that is beautiful! I have to have it." Or,
"That is so fine and it will soon belong to me."
I can take joy in all that's fine and beautiful,
As one enjoys the sun's warm rays,
Which no one owns but just belong to everyone.
Besides, I am no longer my own person, free
To do just what I please and when, although to think
About who owns me makes me shudder.
You'll get on well if you stay here with us.
My father's only harsh when he is angry;
That other man—I can't, no, *won't* endure it!

Remain with us! See what tomorrow brings,
See what the coming year will hold.

    LEON. But what then happens to my friend if I stay here?

    EDRITA. Let him escape all by himself.

    LEON. You know what kind he is, how lost and helpless he
Will be. He'd doubtless fall a prey to his
Pursuers. After I have helped to get
Him home, though, then—

    EDRITA.   Be careful now!
You were about to say: then I'll return.
You won't come back once you have left this place.

    LEON. [*Taking hold of her hand.*]
Edrita!

    EDRITA. Never mind my hand!
If you can do without me, I
Can do without you, too. And now
On to more pressing matters. Where's your friend?

    LEON. He's digging over there under the bridge.

    EDRITA. He's digging?

    LEON.   Shoveling out the earth around one pile,
So that the bridge will tumble down
The first time someone steps on it.

    EDRITA. [*Laughing.*] And your pursuer falls down in the moat?
Well that is good!—There stands the gate, unlocked.
And yet—just look how cunning and
Deceit come home to roost.

    LEON.   How's that?

    EDRITA. You think that your escape is guaranteed.
But guards move all about outside, swift-footed men
With orders to kill everyone who does not know
The word that must be given if you want to pass
At night. The word is "Arbogast." Take note!

    LEON.   I have!

    EDRITA. A ferryman, indebted and beholden to
My father, lives there by the river bank.
You trick him into thinking, only if the truth
Permits you to, that you are traveling
By order of my father. And say "Arbogast":
He'll then take you right over to the other side. [*A loud sound is
    heard from the moat.*]
What's that now?

    LEON. [*Hurrying over to where* ATALUS *works.*]
                      Hang it all! Why do you make such noise?

ATALUS. [*Climbing up out of the moat.*]
That was my shovel knocking up against the pile;
The job is done.
    LEON.   You had to make so loud a thud?
    ATALUS. [*Going up to* EDRITA.]
And here's the girl as well.
    EDRITA. [*To* LEON.]
                      Protect me from this man!
And now you have your friend, so dear to you,
Who will repay your faithfulness with love.—
[*To* ATALUS.] Ha, ha! Oh my, you're quite a sight!
All wet and covered head to toe with mud. [*Touching him with her
    finger.*]
                                  Poor sir!
    ATALUS. He made me do that work!
    EDRITA.   You both had best
Get going now, for even if my father's fast
Asleep, suspicion might well cause
Him to wake earlier than usual. [*She goes to the gate to open it;
    * LEON *opens it for her.*]
The road runs straight at first, then it divides.
Go left and you'll make faster time on your way home.
But you should choose the path that's on the right; it leads
Through woods, and as our men chase after you by horse,
You will quite easily get through
What blocks their way and holds them up.
Now put the key from outside in the gate,
And as you leave, just turn the lock and throw
The key away. Another barrier
Will thus look your pursuers in the face. [LEON *does what she
    says.*]
    EDRITA. [*To* ATALUS.] If they catch up with you, then grab a
                                   stick
And fight with fierceness, like a lion, for your friend.
    ATALUS. I'll look out for myself, that's all.
    EDITA. [*To* LEON.]   You hear? Fine words!
Get moving now! There's no time to delay.
And since you're partners in a robbery,
Like thieves slip out of here.
    KATTWALD. [*Who, with* GALOMIR, *appears at a window of the
    hall.*]   Look, there they are!
    EDRITA. Be quick! [LEON *and* ATALUS *run away, leaving the
    gate open.*]

KATTWALD. [*To* GALOMIR.] You follow them! And run!

EDRITA. Now I'm the one who'll bear the full brunt of this
storm.

[GALOMIR *has come out of the door and stepped onto the
    bridge. It wobbles and finally collapses, sending him tumbling
    into the moat.*]

EDRITA. [*Moving upstage.*] Ha, ha, ha, ha! You stupid Galomir!
Those two were very sly to set that up.

KATTWALD. [*At the window, getting ready to throw a spear.*]
You wicked child! I lay the blame for this on you!

EDRITA. Oh no, oh no! They'll kill me if I stay!
And those lads left the gate wide open, too.
I'll lock the gate on my way out,
And not come back until his wrath subsides. [*She hurries through
    the gate, which she closes behind her and locks.*]

KATTWALD. [*At the window, with his hands in his hair.*]
Let lightning strike! A plague on them! Give me their heads!
Can no one hear me? Servants! People! Anyone!
I can't just stand here, choking on my rage!
I must go after them myself.

*As he makes a vain attempt to climb down from the window, the
    curtain falls.*

Act 4

*Wooded area with a thick undergrowth. Downstage left, a large tree
    with a moss covering. Upstage left, thick bushes and masses of
    rock that together form a cave-like hiding place. It is daytime.
    Enter* LEON *and* ATALUS.

LEON. This is the path we take.

ATALUS.   No, that one there!

LEON. No, this one here!

ATALUS.   It's that one there.
The girl told me herself.

LEON.   Oh, she told you?

ATALUS. Yes, me. And she was most concerned
Because I was soaked through, and touched my arm.

LEON. Well, you can live in sweet delusion if you want.
But this one is the path to take.

ATALUS.   I won't go on.
Must we do everything as you alone see fit?

Besides, I'm tired. [*He sits down on a stone to the right.*]

ATALUS. If they do that, oh, then it's bad for you. And as
For me, my uncle will send ransom, I assume.

LEON. What if they catch up with us?

LEON. He'll ransom you? Because he can't and won't
Be able to, is just the reason I came here.

ATALUS. You say he won't? That's very mean of him.

LEON. You speak against this pious man, your uncle who
Does not have any faults but one?
It's not that he is miserly, as I once thought.
No, it's that he was so consumed with higher things,
He didn't educate you better for the world.
Because he loves you is the reason that he sent
Me here. And were it not for him,
I'd long ago have left you in the lurch.

ATALUS. That would have been just fine with me!
We don't exactly get along, you know.

LEON. You'd still be minding horses but for me!

ATALUS. So what? I liked it there and also had
My fill of food. [*Standing up.*] Now then, since you believe that
                                                    you're
So very clever, what's our path
And way, our goal and destination?
Have you considered all that we will need on such
A trip? What good is it that we're out here and free,
If we must perish horribly for want of food?
The forest must go on for miles on end,
And sooner will we find a starving beast
To eat us up than something we can eat.

LEON. Have trust in God, who has brought us this far.
He will relieve our hunger with His bread,
As He did give us freedom from imprisonment.
And now—

EDRITA. [*Her voice from offstage.*] Leon!

LEON. Someone is coming. Let's get out
Of here, and fast!

ATALUS. But listen first.

EDRITA. [*Her voice is closer.*] Leon!

ATALUS. It is the girl who calls.

LEON. That may well be,
But here there are just us and enemies.
And she can hardly be alone.

ATALUS. She is.

I see her.

LEON.   Well then, we will stay
And talk away our precious time.

ATALUS. No doubt she'll think of something new to aid our
                                                    cause.
But go ahead and leave if that is what you wish.
I'll wait for her.

LEON.   What am I to do now
But raise my hands toward heaven helplessly?!
When this proves to be a mistake, though, don't blame me.

EDRITA. [*She enters.*] Why, here you are! And it's a good thing, too.

ATALUS. Hello to you, I say!

EDRITA. [*To* LEON.]   What makes you turn from me?
Are you afraid I will delay your flight?
It's just the opposite: delay is what you must
Do now.

ATALUS. You see?

EDRITA.   What should he see?

ATALUS. I wished to stop awhile; he pushed to go.

EDRITA. Then he was right and you were wrong, because
You did not know what only I can know.
My father's men went down the other path by horse.
So far, so good. But this path here,
It joins the other one at forest's edge;
And since, of course, there is no horse that can't catch up
With you, it would be bad if you got to
The junction sooner than the men on horse.
If you stay back of them, however, you'll be safe.

LEON. But one more thing, for Heaven's sake: How did
You find us here?

EDRITA.   Who, I? Oh, I see what you mean!
You've done well up to now with one exception.

ATALUS. Why, he does well in everything!

EDRITA.   Yes, everything
But this. You two were barely gone
When they attempted to kill me;
My father had his spear raised in his hand.
I ran away a little stretch into the woods,
Intending to return at break of day.
But when the daylight came, I saw the clear
Footprints that you had left in the soft grounds.
I thought to myself then: their footsteps will
Betray them; so I walked along

The grassy border of the road
Where I knew my steps wouldn't show,
And covered up your tracks with sand and earth.
Then I walked on and on, and here I am.
Now that I'm here, I won't return again.
    LEON. What do you mean?
    ATALUS.   Yes, yes! Stay here with us!
    EDRITA. Consider for yourself. If finally
My father goes back home and hasn't caught
You two—which may your God forbid!—then he'll
Beat me and throw me down into the dungeon,
Where I once lay just as my mother did.
And next he'll make me wed that Galomir.
I will not have him, though; I tell you now, I won't!
Do take me with you; I can be of use some more:
I know the roads and all the hidden bypaths here.
And you are not as safe in back of them as you
Would think. They've brought along the dogs; I heard their

                                                      sounds.

The moment that they get your scent, they will
Come barking after you ahead of those men that
They serve. But since they know me, they'll be still,
And if I pet them, they will lie down on their paws.
I wish to go to your own master and
His uncle, where I'll listen carefully
To holy teachings about God and right
And duty that he surely knows. And if
My father wants me, he should come there, too,
And learn with me, no matter if he's gray and old.
It's sure to do him good: like all
Our people, he's far too uncivilized.
    LEON. I won't permit it, though!
    EDRITA.   Why not, Leon?
    LEON. I gave a promise to my pious master
And said that nothing terrible or wrongful would
Occur while I was on this mission,
One that necessity alone excuses.
Now that I have deprived the master of his slave,
I will not further rob the father of
His daughter, in the process adding to
The curse already on our head.
    EDRITA. Just listen, please!
    LEON.   It shall not, must not, cannot be.
    ATALUS. He's not all there.

EDRITA.   Oh, more of him is there than you
Would think. He is a man whose sense of right is cut
And dry. This sense of right would not consent exactly to
The cheating of a foe or telling lies to him.
But by his putting on a mode of conduct that
Is frank and plain, this man inspires trust,
Creates some expectations, which his own
True word then loudly contradicts.
His sense of right permits him to do this, you see,
And he does execute it thoroughly.
[*To* ATALUS.] So let me come with *you,* please.
ATALUS.   But of course,
Quite happily.
LEON.   I won't permit it, no.
EDRITA. We aren't asking you. Since we are two
Of the three people present, our decision rules.
LEON. Then from this moment we must go our separate ways.
EDRITA. That's fine with us! We'll make our way without your
                                                    help.
I know all of the roads up to the river,
And Atalus knows them from that point on.
ATALUS. I don't know them.
EDRITA.   Oh, well, in any case
We won't be far from your homeland,
And people there will guide us safely to our goal.
LEON. Good luck to you!
ATALUS.   You see? He always has
Something to say.
EDRITA.   We finally will step
Before your uncle and we'll say,
"Your servant Leon's done us wrong.
But we made our own way all by ourselves
As best we could."
                        [*To* LEON] You look so sad.
LEON. My spirits did run high, but now
They don't; they've been transferred to you.
EDRITA. You see? You simply have to be
Agreeable and eager, too, or else
Necessity will make decisions for you and
You will not get the thanks you could have had. [*The sound of a
horn at a distance.*]
LEON. Give ear to that! You're trembling, you who were so
                                                    brave.
EDRITA. If I am trembling now, it is for you.

ATALUS. Let's go!

LEON.   I'm staying.

EDRITA.   Let us stop
This foolishness, which just torments.
That is no troop of men; it is one man
Who calls out to his comrades with his horn
Because he's lost. He'll march right by, since he's alone
And more than one is needed to catch two.
I know a hiding place that's over there in back
Of us, where shrubbery grows thickly and
Will shelter us from sight. We'll wait behind these shrubs
Until his steps recede. Perhaps you can sneak up
And overpower him. For now let's just
Take cover, but we'll go the long way 'round, so that
Our steps won't leave a straight and easy trail for him.

*She leads them noiselessly on the tips of their toes up to the trees
on the right, then quickly back into the bushes on the left and the
cave they form with the masses of rock. Short pause, then enter*
GALOMIR *from the left. He has a spear on his left shoulder, a
sword at his side, and a horn hanging on a cord from his neck; he
is bending over looking for footprints in the earth.*

GALOMIR. There, there!—Hey, hey! The little one—Oh! Over
                                                   there!
[*Pursuing the trail with his finger.*]
Wait, wait!—I'm lost! Nobody there!
Where? Oh, too far.—Ugh!—Hot! [*Feeling his legs.*] And tired!—
                                                   Here to sit.—
Ah, shade there! Tree. Now rest, man, rest! Then further. [*He sits
   down on a mound.*]
Hot helmet! [*He takes his helmet off and lays it down beside him.*]
                                        One more time call out.
                  [*He shouts through his hands.*] Hello!
[*He listens a moment, then turns toward the rear of the stage.*]
Oh, no one hears! Why have a horn?
To blow on!—Tangled up, all tangled up.
[*He leans his spear against the tree down left and untangles the
   cord that holds his horn.*]
Ah, free! Now to my lips! [*He puts the horn to his lips.*]
   EDRITA. [*She has appeared during the previous business, and
   with a gesture bidding* LEON *and* ATALUS *be quiet, she now
   steps forward.*]
                           Don't blow that horn!

GALOMIR. [*Catching sight of her.*]
Oh, oh!
    EDRITA. It's me! What now?
    GALOMIR.   Er, catch, catch you! [*He grabs at her.*]
    EDRITA. Why do you need to catch what is already yours?
If you leave me a little room, I'll sit by you.
    GALOMIR. [*Quickly making room.*]
Hey, hey!
    EDRITA. You're surely not afraid of me, are you?
    GALOMIR. Oh, you to blame for all!
    EDRITA.   You say that I'm to blame?!
Whatever has come over you?
    GALOMIR. Your father!
    EDRITA.   Yes, he must be rather angry now;
But when I speak to him, I'll straighten all this out.
    GALOMIR. No, no!
    EDRITA.   Well, after all, we are engaged,
And so you must, you *will*, protect
Me from my father's wrath.
    GALOMIR.   Ha, ha!
    EDRITA. You like that idea, do you?
    GALOMIR. [*Shaking his finger at her.*] You!
    EDRITA.   You don't?
And just because maybe I laughed a bit when you
Went tumbling in the moat? That *was* a fall!
    GALOMIR. [*Rubbing his arm.*]
Ow.
    EDRITA. It still hurts a little?
    GALOMIR. [*Pointing downwards.*] Ouch!
    EDRITA.   Your foot hurts, too.
A husband must get used to lots of things.
Now you've set out and mean to catch them both?
    GALOMIR. [*Grabbing at her.*]
You, you!
    EDRITA. Just me alone? Where did your courage go?
No, no! You have to catch the runaways,
All by yourself. They are not far away!
    GALOMIR. [*Standing up.*]
Oh! Where?
    EDRITA.   Not right in front of you;
And yet not far off. They are two, but you are armed.
Here stands your spear. [*She touches the spear, which falls down;*
    GALOMIR *starts to pick it up.*]

It's all right lying on the ground.
And there is your broad and knightly sword.
  GALOMIR. [*Slapping his sword.*]
Uh-huh!
  EDRITA. I know, your arm is strong. Just recently
You cut a bull's head off with one fell stroke.
The contest was not fair, though. After all,
You had a weapon, he had none.
Next time give up your advantage, and then
Two equals will be in the fight. But even so—
I want now to sit on your other side. [*She does so as he makes
   room for her.*]
Here is your sword, all good and strong. But it's too plain.
What will you give me if I tie a ribbon 'round
Your sword? Perhaps a blue one like the one [*She unties the bow
   around her neck.*]
I wear about my neck. You see? [*She holds it in her hand.*]
  GALOMIR. [*Reaching for her face with his open hand.*]
Ooh!
  EDRITA. You move fast!—I think that it looks very nice.
Pull out your sword and lay it down between
The two of us. They do that at the wedding, too:
A sword lies temporarily
Between the husband and the wife. [GALOMIR *has put the sword
   between them.*]
  EDRITA. [*Winding the ribbon about the hilt of the sword.*]
I'll tie it like this—then like that—and once
Again like this—[*She coughs repeatedly.*]
  GALOMIR.   What?
  EDRITA.   Oh, I must have walked too fast.
Now that looks pretty, don't you think? Oh, yes, how nice! [*She
   claps her hands as if in delight.* LEON *and* ATALUS, *who had
   earlier come into sight, are now close by.*]
  EDRITA. [*Knocking the sword over.*]
Oh dear, it fell.
  GALOMIR. My sword!
  EDRITA.   Well, pick it up.
[*She steps on it with her foot as* GALOMIR *bends down to get it.
   She stands up and speaks to* LEON.]
Come on! His spear is over there: get hold of it. [*Down to
   GALOMIR.*]
Why do you hesitate?
  GALOMIR. [*Still bending down.*] Your foot—

EDRITA. [*Beckoning* ATALUS *to the other side.*]

             You over here.
[*To* GALOMIR.] Oh yes, my foot. It's standing on your sword.
The naughty little foot! [*To* LEON *and* ATALUS.]
       Let's go.
  GALOMIR. [*Raising himself up from the ground.*] Then lift it up.
[*He catches sight of* LEON, *who stands to the left and holds the
  spear up against his chest.*]
Ah! [GALOMIR *sinks down onto the mound. Meanwhile,* ATALUS
  has come from the right and picked up the sword.]
  EDRITA. [*She rises and rushes to* LEON's *side. To* GALOMIR.]
     Don't you move, or else they'll put an end to you.
  ATALUS. Good fortune blows my way, for now I have a sword!
  EDRITA. [*Clapping her hands.*] Oh, this is good; oh, this is good!
              It truly is!
[*To* ATALUS.] Now you: you point that sword at him!
  ATALUS. [*With raised sword.*]   It's done.
  LEON. [*To* GALOMIR.]
I'm sorry that I must direct my words at you
In such a situation. It was not my choice.
It's happened, though, and since it has, I'll use
It to escape. Remain, sir, where you sit;
You're in our power now. [*Taking off his belt.*]
         I'm forced to tie you with
My belt, sir, to the trunk of this big tree.
It will not hold for long against your strength,
But we'll be gone by then and you'll get home all right.
  EDRITA. [*To* LEON.] I'll hold the spear for you, but if he stirs,
It will be back in your two hands at once. [*She points the spear at
  GALOMIR, *but she has the wrong end pointing at him.*]
Just look!—That's wrong! It has to be like this. [*She turns the
  spear around.*]
[*To* ATALUS.] Keep pointing your sword, too! You point that sword
               at him!

While GALOMIR *looks at* ATALUS, *who has come a step closer,* LEON
  quickly slips the belt between GALOMIR's *body and his arms, on
  which* GALOMIR *leans back on the mound for support, and ties
  the arms tightly to the tree.*

GALOMIR. Ah—oh!
  LEON.   No harm will come to you if you submit.
  EDRITA. You tie him tight. He has the strength of many men.

LEON. [*He finishes tying up* GALOMIR.] I think I've tied him well
                                                    enough for now.
Come, Atalus. You're my responsibility. [ATALUS *walks up to him.*]
    EDRITA. I'm not? Then I'll just have to look out for myself.
[*Loudly, but at the same time shaking her head in denial.*]
From here we will go straight into the woods. [GALOMIR *has been
    making violent efforts to free himself.*]
    LEON. He's breaking loose!
    EDRITA. [*To* ATALUS.] You go and see to him! [ATALUS *goes over
to* GALOMIR.]
    EDRITA. [*Softly, to* LEON.] So what if he breaks loose? So what?!
Alone, he won't suffice, since you have weapons now.
And if my father's men come get him in this place,
The low road will be clear; it's shorter, it
Is better, and we'll reach the river bank
Ahead of them. Goodbye, then, Galomir,
And for a long, long time, I hope.
    LEON. And when you reach the father of this girl,
You tell him I did not—
    EDRITA.   You mean that I myself?
That I ran off all by myself? Well, thanks a lot
For your concern with my good name!
Of course I know, though, that you speak the truth.
So let's say nothing: then we'll be most truthful,
And meanwhile we'll make more use of our feet.
Come, Atalus. [*She exits right.*]
    LEON. [*Pulling* ATALUS *after him.*] Yes, come!
    ATALUS. [*Pointing to* GALOMIR.]   He's active still.
I think a little blow to—
    LEON.   What's got into you?
[*He drags him away. Both of them exit right.*]
    GALOMIR. [*Following them with his eyes, then struggling
    furiously against his bonds.*]
Ah—scoundrels—oh—Death! Curses!—Oh, this belt!
[*He tries to reach the knot with his teeth.*]
Can't reach it! Right there is my horn. Blow, blow on it!
[*Bending his head down toward it.*]
Can't reach it, either. [*Struggling.*] Damned scoundrels!
[*He sinks back onto the mound, exhausted. Then suddenly with
    a crafty expression on his face.*]
Aha! [*He has finally succeeded in partly freeing his right arm

from the belt and now struggles to free it completely.]
   Go easy, man! Ah, oh!—
Don't stop!—My arm!—It's free! My arm!
Your arm's free, Galomir! Hey, hey! [*He has succeeded in
 freeing his right arm from its bond and immediately reaches for
 his horn.*]
He blows on it! [*He sounds the horn, then listens.*]
      Hark!—No! [*He frees the other arm and follows
 the trail of the runaways.*]
           There! There!
Into the woods—Oh no, no sword! [*He slaps his hand on the
 empty sheath. He stops at the exit on the right and sounds his
 horn again. An answer comes from far off.*]
Ha, ha! Where men, where?
[*Another answer, closer.*]
         Oh! From there. Come on!
[*Enter one of the men from the castle. It is the* STEWARD; *several
 others follow him on.*]
 STEWARD. It's you?
 GALOMIR.   Yes, yes!
 STEWARD.   You've seen the fugitives?
 GALOMIR. [*Pointing in the direction they took.*]
That way!
 STEWARD. [*Pointing in the other direction.*] Come over here. This
               is the path we take.
 GALOMIR. [*Pointing to the path on the right.*]
There, there!
 STEWARD.   The master ordered us—
 GALOMIR.   No, there!
 STEWARD. If we go your way, they'll escape us, sir.
The other way is faster and
Our paths will cross. We'll catch them then.
 GALOMIR. Saw them myself! Tied up!—The tree. [*Pointing to
 the tree.*]
 STEWARD. They tied you up?
 GALOMIR. [*Indicating the path on the right.*]
        This way. And weapon for me, too.
[*He takes a club from one of the soldiers and brandishes it.*]
Aha!—Let's go!
 STEWARD. All right, if that's what you command.
I tell you, though: I wash my hands
Of this in total innocence. [*They exit right.*]

Scene Change

Open area beside the river, which is visible at the rear of the stage.
On the shore, the FERRYMAN's *cottage. Enter the* FERRYMAN *and*
his HELPER.

FERRYMAN. You say he drove the whole flock off?
HELPER. Yes, Kattwald did. We had them out to pasture.
It's been two days now. As he left,
He grinned and ordered me to say that he
Collects his debts this way as soon as they fall due.
FERRYMAN. Seized my whole flock for such a little debt?
Then I'll do no more work for him from this point on.
These savages! Their insolence is not
To be endured. The Franks pay better and,
Indeed, they are the better people. [*Pointing to a tree from which*
a picture of the crucifixion hangs.]
They gave me as a gift that holy image there,
And if one can predict the crop from just the seed,
Their God's worth more than the Teutonic Wodan.
But first I'll have revenge for this misdeed.
I'll take from Kattwald something he loves most:
His daughter, wife, perhaps the oldest son.
The blood will flow if he won't pay me back
With interest for property
Of mine he had no right to steal.
And now prepare the boat for me. I want
To go across. They say the Franks have once again
Burst forth to try to win the far shore back.
It's always in dispute, now this side, now
The other has the piece of land.
It's only sparsely populated and
Two days are necessary if
You want to travel its perimeter.
Their goal is Metz quite likely, where those devils keep
An inept watch upon the land they claim.
But they won't capture Metz so fast;
Therefore the word is patience still.
Until that time we must suppress our rage.
Except that I won't wait to get back at Kattwald. [*He goes to the*
rear of the stage, where he busies himself at the water's edge.]
EDRITA. [*Entering hastily from the left.*]

We're at the river bank!
[*Calling into the wings.*]
                                        Be sure to hide
Your weapons. In emergency, you can retrieve
Them easily. [*Enter* LEON *and* ATALUS.]
    EDRITA.   Now have I kept my word or not?
[LEON *walks rapidly to the shore of the river; on his return, he*
   catches sight of the tree with the image of the crucifixion and
   kneels down to pray before it.]
How careless to kneel down and pray at such a time!
    ATALUS. He's right to do it; I must do so, too. [*He kneels down.*]
    EDRITA. [*To the* FERRYMAN, *as he comes from the river and*
notices the two men.] Are you the ferryman?
    FERRYMAN.   Indeed I am.
    EDRITA.   But not
The one in serfdom to the Rhenish Count?
    FERRYMAN. The good Count Kattwald, yes.
    EDRITA.   Well, then!
The two men that you see are Kattwald's servants.
They bear a message from his lips to all the land.
So quickly get a boat, a good fast one,
To carry them across and me along with them.
    FERRYMAN. You come from Count Kattwald?
    EDRITA.   We do. I'll give you proof:
[*Lowering her voice.*] The word is "Arbogast."
    FERRYMAN.   Yes, so it is!
Well, that suits me, it truly does. [*Calling to his* HELPER.]
Hey, Notger, come! These worthy people here,
They make this trip for Count Kattwald, the good,
Kind man who guarantees the safety of
Our flocks. Now go prepare the boat.
[*Tipping his cap to* EDRITA.]   Excuse me, please.
I have to give instructions to my man. [*Softly to his* HELPER.]
Start rowing them across, but then delay somehow
Until I can assemble fishermen, some friends—
    LEON. [*Who has risen.*]
Where is the ferryman?
    FERRYMAN.   Right here.
    LEON.   We want to cross.
    FERRYMAN. I know, I know, you're on a special mission for
The count.
    LEON.   What does he say, this man?

EDRITA.   I told
Him what you know yourself: that both
Of you, on orders from Kattwald—
    FERRYMAN. And in this case a humble man like me obeys.
    LEON. If that's the only reason you will do
This deed, and not for pay, not even for
The sake of Him who shines up there, [*Pointing to the image of
    the crucifixion.*]
Then know that we're not in the service of
Count Kattwald, nor moreover are we here
With his consent.
    EDRITA.   Leon!
    LEON.   It's true and I can't help
But say it.
    FERRYMAN. You are not among Count Kattwald's friends,
You say?
    LEON. No, we are not.
    FERRYMAN.   You knelt just now before
The image of the crucifixion in the tree.
Are you perhaps some of those Frankish hostages—?
They asked about one hostage only a short time
Ago.
    LEON. Who asked?
    FERRYMAN.   It's said the inquiry was made
By him who leads the Frankish faithful in Chalons.
    ATALUS. Leon!
    FERRYMAN.   You are awaited over there;
But in between there's hostile ground both far and wide.
    LEON. Well, God will help. Whoever we are, if
You won't take us across the river, we
Will have to try our luck some other place.
    FERRYMAN. Hold on! Do you have money?
    LEON. [*Showing him some coins.*]   Yes, if that will do.
    FERRYMAN. All right, I'll ferry you across myself. And not
Because you're Kattwald's people, no, indeed, because
You're *not*. For if you were, I'd strand you in
The middle of the river. Kattwald is
My enemy; my heart yearns for revenge.
    LEON. [*To* EDRITA.] You see? It isn't wise to be too clever.
    EDRITA. [*Walking away from him and pointing to* ATALUS.]
I'll go with him. What else can I do now?
    FERRYMAN. [*After speaking with his* HELPER, *who leaves again
    at once.*]

Now come, for horsemen roam the area.
If you've escaped, they may well be pursuing you.
Look there!—Be quick!—And give your thanks to Him [*Pointing
   to the image of the crucifixion in the tree.*]
Who guided your feet here and guided what you said
To me as well. [*Exit* LEON, ATALUS, *and* EDRITA.]
   SOLDIER. [*He enters downstage.*] Halt there!
   FERRYMAN.   You halt yourself! I have
A spear and maybe two right in
My boat there. Want to sample them? [*He exits.*]
   SOLDIER. [*Calling back in the direction from which he entered.*]
Hello!
   SECOND SOLDIER. [*He enters at the rear of the stage, left.*]
       Oh, there they are! Look. [*He advances but then retreats,
   shielding his head.*]
                       Blast it! They are armed!
   KATTWALD. [*Entering.*] Where are they! Where now?
   SECOND SOLDIER.   They're already on
The river. See?
   KATTWALD. Go after them.
   SECOND SOLDIER.
Yes, only there's no boat around.
But they must pass close by the sand bar on
The right there; when they do, they'll be within
Our arrows' range.
   KATTWALD.   Then shoot, do shoot! And if you hit
My child, much rather would I have her dead—er, I
Mean, wounded—than have them escape and her with them.
[KATTWALD*'s men have taken up positions along the shore, right.*]
   THIRD SOLDIER. It is no use. They use their strength to fight
The current and they head their boat straight for
The middle of the river.
   KATTWALD. [*Hastening to the edge of the shore.*] I am not to
                          lose
To them! Not them! I have to have revenge! Revenge!
Why, I myself will jump into the river and
If I can't catch them, may I drown!
   THIRD SOLDIER. [*Restraining him.*] Hold on! It may be Galomir
                       will get to them.
The path he took comes out right by a ford,
And then, although they've almost crossed
The river, they will come to harm.

KATTWALD. [*Designating the places on his outstretched arm.*]
I want to bathe my hand, my arm, in blood of theirs.

The curtain falls.

Act 5

*Before the walls of Metz. At the rear of the stage, a large gate, the
    walls on each side of which are partly hidden by trees. At the
    front of the stage, right, a sort of shed with double doors. It is
    before daybreak and still dark.*

LEON. [*He opens the door of the shed and comes out, closing
    the door behind him.*]
The sun delays its rise: it's still dark night.
And dark is my own heart, as dark as all outside. [*Looking back.*]
Like children there they lie asleep,
And like their mother, I keep careful watch.
Were but a share of mother's quiet happiness,
Of joy she gets from work well-done, bestowed on me! [*Coming
    forward.*]
So far, so good. The river's crossed; we're on
That other side that seemed so far away to us,
Though, to be sure, the foe dwells here as well.
Yet something's odd: this district, otherwise
A busy, crowded place, is bleak
And empty; passersby don't stop
To say hello. At least this situation makes
Our going safe; but then again, no one
Is here to point the way for us.
It seems to me this city's name is Metz,
A stronghold where the enemy keeps watch
Upon the land. Once we're beyond this place,
Then we'll be nearing home. I wish that wings
Would speed up our snail's pace, although I dare not wake
The two who sleep; they are exhausted unto death
And pale. Bear up alone, Leon, bear up for all.
And when we finally do stand before
My master!—How his awe-inspiring image
Comes suddenly through night and darkness to
My erring eye! His parting words warned me
Against deceit, and what a mess

We now have made of everything.
A daughter stolen from her father's house.
We stole her! At the least, we let her follow us.
What shall I do before my master's stare?
And what will come of her who followed us,
Who undertook, just like a child,
This venture in all innocence,
Her trust inspired by my truthfulness,
Whose aim was to destroy all trust in me?
I can't believe she loves that other man,
Young Atalus, although, it's true, he's changed:
His nature has improved since we
Departed savage, foreign soil.
At first she seemed to be inclined toward me;
But my rebuffs, my careless, stern admonishments,
Drove her from me to him.—She loves him not,
And yet each word she grants to him runs through
My wretched heart, arousing hate and jealousy.
Just now as we were taking our night's rest,
Her head sank down upon my breast. She slept and as
She drew a deep, deep breath, it sounded like
A sigh. Her head so warm, her breath so sweet, she sent
A cold fear penetrating to my very core:
"Perhaps she thinks of him." Then I got up,
She put her cheek upon a different pillow,
And I went out to talk into the night.
The East grows gray; the day, it seems, awakes.
Perhaps I now can find just where our path left off.
Perhaps in this strange wasteland there will be
A traveler—Hark! Wasn't that somebody's step?
What good is caution, then, where caution but
Reveals an unseen threat? [*Calling softly to the left.*] Is that a
                                              man?
Who walks these parts? It's silent once
Again.—But no. Who goes there? Answer me! [*One of*
KATTWALD's *men appears, walks up behind* LEON, *and seizes
him.*]
SOLDIER. Here is the answer!
LEON.   Treason!
SOLDIER.   You're the traitor, you!
SECOND SOLDIER. [*Entering downstage left.*]
You have him there?
FIRST SOLDIER. [*Struggling with* LEON.] He's getting loose!

SECOND SOLDIER.   I'm coming!
LEON. [*He has broken free.*] Get off of me! Until I've done what I
Set out to do, no one shall capture me. [*He goes to the other side
   of the stage. Enter* KATTWALD'S STEWARD.]
   STEWARD. You've got them?
   FIRST SOLDIER.   There's one.
   STEWARD.   Well, where *he* is, that
Is where the others will be, too. Now come in close.
   GALOMIR. [*He enters.*]
Hah, you! The girl, say where! Oho, my sword! [*He draws his
   sword.*]
STEWARD. Just calm yourself. They cannot get away.
LEON. If you thirst for my blood, well, here I am.
Revenge seeks out the instigator of the crime.
You want the girl, the daughter of your master?
I will request that she go home with you.
And if she goes, that's fine; if not, I'll risk [*Putting his hand on a
   dagger that he carries in his belt.*]
My blood for her the same way I will for
The other one.
   STEWARD.   Where are those two, confess!
No use denying that they're here.
   LEON. I don't deny it and have not done so. Look, here
They are. But keep your distance from the both of them. [*He has
   opened the door of the shed;* ATALUS *and* EDRITA *can be seen
   sleeping on bundles of straw in a half-sitting position.*]
Do you not feel the innocence that hovers right
Above their heads? Their breath is like God's breath,
For, in their sleep, they do abide with him.
Oh sleep, beginning of eternal bliss
That's only interrupted yet again
By dreary waking! When you speak,
Speak softly, gently, lest you wake them up. [*He closes the doors.*]
And one more thing: the first man who comes near
Me, will fall victim to his hasty zeal. [*Putting his hand on his
   dagger again.*]
Though only one will die, the threat
Of death hangs over all of you.
   STEWARD. [*As* GALOMIR *starts to attack* LEON.]
Why do that needlessly? He has a knife;
The other one will help him, too, when he wakes up.
We are, you know, at Metz, strong fortress that belongs
To us. Inside are fetters, dungeons, torture rooms,

And men who'll help us in this hunt,
Which, happily, won't then have any risk.
Someone knock on the gate; we'll stay and guard them here. [*One
     of the men goes up to the gate.*]
　　LEON. Now that they have surrounded me with nets,
There's only One who can give help and Thou art He! [*With arms
     raised toward heaven.*]
'Twas at Thy bidding that I came into this land,
'Twas through my master's mouth that Thou didst speak with me.
From the rich store of his good deeds,
He summoned forth Thy help for me on this, my trip.
Oh, do not take Thy help away before
It's done its good. I know, I seem to ask
For the impossible, but only what
Is not Thy will is called impossible;
Whatever is Thy will is more than possible.
I plead not for myself, no, but for him, for her.
A human life, alas, it isn't much;
A human destiny, however, is a lot.
Protect them from the enemy and from themselves.
The girl, if she goes home to her own kind,
Will grow as wild and wicked as her countrymen.
And Atalus—we both know well, dear Lord, he is
But weak. If he is taken prisoner again,
He will, in his despair, turn from Thy ways. And then
His uncle will, for his part, cross himself and die.
That shall not, must not be—Am I correct or not? [*He falls to his
     knees.*]
　　STEWARD. He is bewildered and addresses clouds and air.
[*Toward the rear.*]
Nobody's come yet?
　　LEON.　　　　　　　Hark! What a familiar sound!
[*From the city can be heard the distant sound of a little bell
     ringing several times.*]
The Christians are the ones who use such pious sounds
To call the faithful in to prayer.
　　STEWARD. You err; there are no Christian folk within.
They worship the Teutonic Wodan there.
They're coming now!
　　LEON.　　　　　　All right, must I then use
My last resort? No longer do I beg
For help, no, I demand Thy help—
I *am* still begging, Lord, I beg!

When I departed from your pious servant,
The lightning flashed inside my heart. It spoke
Of miracles, a miracle that would occur.
And so I want, nay, I demand a miracle!
Keep Thou Thy holy word to me.—Thou shalt not lie! [*He leaps to
his feet. The gate opens; armed* SOLDIERS *come out, among
them a* CAPTAIN *in shining armor.*]
    STEWARD. [*He has started toward the gate and now retreats.*]
Those aren't our men!
    CAPTAIN.   Our enemies, right there!
Go after them!
    STEWARD. [*He keeps on retreating.*] Is this not Metz, strong
                                   fortress that
Belongs to us?
    CAPTAIN.   Two days ago your forces still
Held Metz. A sneak attack by night, and it was ours. [*The sound
of bells is heard again.*]
The pious bells, though set up in all haste,
Resound in clarity with calls to prayer;
They also beckon to the faith all those with love
And hope.
    LEON. [*To* ATALUS *and* EDRITA, *who have come out of the shed.*]
             Did you hear that?
[CHOIR BOYS *come out of the gate.*]
    CAPTAIN.   The holy Bishop, he
Himself, whose diocese needs him back home,
Has come here in the service of the Lord,
To sow the seed of Christian charity.
See, there he is! Surrender both to God and us! [GREGORY *comes
out of the gate.*]
    LEON. [*To* ATALUS.] Your uncle! Run to him!
    ATALUS. [*Running up to* GREGORY.]   Oh, sir! Dear sir!
    GREGORY. My Atalus! My son!—The grace of God—[*They stand
there with their arms about each other.*]
    LEON. [*Taking* EDRITA's *face between his hands.*]
Edrita, look! We are with our own kind at last. [*Letting her go.*]
That may be so, but you're the single stain
    EDRITA. [*Turning away from him.*] I am?
Then I alone can cleanse myself.
    GREGORY. So finally I get to hold you in my arms! [*He raises*
    ATALUS *up as* ATALUS *starts to kneel down before him.*]
I have been very troubled over you, my son,

Not only over how you'd break free from
Your captors, no, but also over you
Yourself, what you will be and do.
A veil has fallen from my eyes: you are
Not as you ought to be. I'd like to see
If wiser care can change that in the time to come.
But tell me, did you get here by yourself?
Was not another youth with you, one whom I sent?

    ATALUS. [*Going up to* LEON.]
Yes, my protector. Here he is, and I
Owe everything to him.

    GREGORY. [*To* LEON.] Hah, you, my madcap lad!
So faithful and so brave! Here is
My hand! To shake, not kiss!—Like this. Well, you
Have told some pretty lies? You've taken lots
Of risks? Deceived the enemy with this and that?
You've played with lies and trickery? Oh yes, I know.

    LEON. It's true that things did not go off as cleanly as
We would have liked. We watched ourselves as much
As we were able to. The only one to be
Completely and at all times true in word and deed
Was God, our helper.

    GREGORY.   In His ways the truth abides. [*To the*
FRANKISH CAPTAIN.]
And therefore in His name I ask that you
Release these men and let them go back home. [*Pointing to*
    GALOMIR *and his men.*]
Unless it is the case that some of them
Feel moved to seek salvation in the bosom of
The Church.—No, they are not so moved.
May God be with you always. Here we practice no
Constraint, for in the end the truth constrains all men.
It has no need for helpers and
Defenders from without. How else,
Then, could it be the truth? Depart in peace.

    GALOMIR. [*Pointing to* EDRITA.] And that one, too!

    STEWARD.   Let's use the freedom they
Have granted us, in all their foolishness,
Lest they decide to take it back. [*He pulls* GALOMIR *along after*
   him. The men follow, escorted by some Frankish SOLDIERS.]

    GREGORY. [*He has taken a few steps toward the city.*]
You still stand there and do not follow me
Inside the city walls?

ATALUS.   There is another one
Who waits upon your word. [EDRITA *steps forward*.]
                              She is the daughter of
My keeper, Count Kattwald.
     GREGORY. [*Sternly*.]   Leon, did you do this?
     LEON. Permit me, master—
     EDRITA.   He will say to you
That he was not the one, and that almost
Against his will I followed after him.
His words are true, too.
     GREGORY. [*To* EDRITA.] What led you to take this step?
     EDRITA. What first moved me to take it, I did not
Know at the time; but now I know.
Yet best that I forget, for now and evermore.
The second reason, nobler, finer than the first,
I knew it then and I will always know.
Just now you offered to my countrymen
Salvation in the Church, but they said no.
Behold one here who wanted it and wants it still.
Receive me in your peaceful company.
     GREGORY. Am I to act without your father's leave?
     EDRITA. If he should come to get her, give him back
The Christian girl, for you would not do that, I trust,
Unless he turned to Christianity himself.
A tiny seed of charity will thus be sown,
From which one day will grow the welfare and
Salvation of my country's folk.
     GREGORY. It is not fitting that I hoard what we all share
So much of; therefore I shall not reject
What you propose.
     ATALUS.   There's one more thing! I wish her well,
Dear sir, and if—
     GREGORY.   Yes, what?
     ATALUS.   If you consent, I want—
     GREGORY. What do I hear? You never were inclined toward that.
     ATALUS. When I lay shackled as a prisoner,
She was the only one who wasn't rough and wild.
Each time she came and went, my spirits were revived.
Then on our journey, she stayed close to me,
She took my arm and also—sir, you see.
     GREGORY. I see that she's a lovely and good-natured girl.
     ATALUS. She is descended from the Rhenish Counts as well.
     GREGORY. And so you think of equally high rank with you?

For any set of ancestors, however old
They are, you don't exchange your first,
The oldest ancestor of all, the One Who lived
Before there even was a sun, Who in
His image made men out of lowly dust.
He also has a coat of arms: man's countenance.
I had, it's true, quite different plans for you,
But if indeed this be God's will— [*To* EDRITA.] And you?

   EDRITA. I mean to live in solitude a while,
But after that I'll do whatever you command.

   GREGORY. Then let the future bring what may; for now,
Hold out your hand to him, your new protector.

   LEON. [*As* ATALUS *puts out his hand and* EDRITA *is in the
process of taking it.*]
Oh, sir!

   GREGORY.   What's this?—Why do you stand so far away?

   LEON. I'll draw near, then, to ask for leave of absence.

   GREGORY. A leave of absence? Why, man?

   LEON.   Traveling becomes
A habit, sir, the moment you have seen the world
A little bit. And then, you know,
I always have been driven by the urge to be
A soldier in the army of the King.

   GREGORY. And that is all?

   LEON.   Yes, that is all.

   GREGORY. There is another reason why you want this leave.

   LEON. In truth, there's not.

   GREGORY.   Thou shalt not lie!

   LEON. You certainly would think a man—

   GREGORY.   Once more:
Woe unto him who lies and on the lies themselves!

   LEON. Well, sir, the girl does mean a lot to me, in fact.
But if she won't have me, let someone else have her.
To look on, though, as she's united with—

   EDRITA. [*Remaining where she is.*]
Leon!

   LEON. Yes, you.

   EDRITA.   Leon and I—

   LEON.   You what?

   EDRITA. I took a liking for you right away, not so?

   LEON. Yet later on there came a bitter change.
You went with Atalus.

   EDRITA.   I had to go with him
When you so cruelly tried to turn me back.

LEON. [*Pointing to* GREGORY.] It was because of him. He would
Not suffer any other action on my part.
Was I supposed to come back home to him
With kidnapped prey, with stolen property?
    EDRITA. You stole my heart, though, and you have it still.
    LEON.   And yet
You want to marry me, a thief?
    EDRITA.   Who, I?
[*Looking trustingly at the* BISHOP *with her hands clasped.*]
                                      Oh, no.
    GREGORY. Who will explain this mixed-up world to me?
They speak the truth, the two of them; they're proud they do.
And she deceives herself and him, while he deceives
Both me and her—and when he lies, it is
Because he's been lied to by other men.
Yet each of them speaks truth: he does, and so does she.
I've noticed that you never can root out bad weeds;
You only pray that wheat grows over them.
[*To* ATALUS.] Things don't look good for us. What do you think, my
                                              son?
    ATALUS. [*After a pause.*]
I think it best to give the girl to him,
The one who rescued me and whom, alas, she loves.
    GREGORY. Quite right, my son, and so that there will be no doubt
About her husband's rank, place, and repute,
Observe that from this day, of nephews I have two!
The King, I'm sure, will grant this favor unto me,
So let Leon now woo this daughter of a count.
Your heart is broken, Atalus?
Lift up your eyes and look at me.
You've been deceived, but in deception's realm, my son!
I know a land where truth completely reigns,
Where lies are seen as one big motley that He named,
When He created man, "ephemerality,"
And that he wrapped around the sinful human race
So that their eyes would not be blinded by
The brilliance of His truth. Now if you want,
Pursue the life that in the past we settled on
For you. You'll find a bliss there that
Deception cannot desecrate, and that
Will keep on growing up until the day you die.
And these two— [*Turning toward them with a gesture of his
    hand.*]
                              May they live in harmony.

As LEON *and* EDRITA *rush into each other's arms
and* GREGORY *starts to leave the stage,
the curtain falls.*

Select Bibliography

Angress, R. K. "*Weh dem, der lügt!*: Grillparzer and the Avoidance of Tragedy." *Modern Language Review* 66, no. 2 (April 1971): 355–64.

Burkhard, Arthur. *Franz Grillparzer in England and America.* Wien: Bergland, 1961.

———. "Grillparzer in English Translation." In *Österreich und die angelsächsische Welt: Kulturbegegnungen und Vergleiche,* edited by Otto Hietsch, 411–17. Wien: Braunmüller, 1960.

Coenen, Frederic E. *Franz Grillparzer's Portraiture of Men.* Chapel Hill: University of North Carolina Studies in the Germanic Languages and Literatures, no. 4, 1951.

Heald, David. "Grillparzer and the Germans." *Oxford German Studies,* 6 (1971–72): 61–73.

Jessen, Myra R. "Conflicting Views in the Evaluation of Grillparzer." *Modern Language Quarterly* 15, no. 1 (March 1954): 67–73.

Jones, Sheila. "*Weh dem, der lügt!* Reconsidered in the Light of Some Basic Character Types in Grillparzer's Work." *New German Studies* 2, no. 3 (Autumn 1974): 171–91. Reprinted in *Essays on Grillparzer,* edited by Bruce Thompson and Mark Ward, 59–79. Hull: German Department at Hull University, 1978.

Kaufmann, F. W. "Grillparzer's Position in Nineteenth-Century Thought." *Modern Language Notes* 53, no. 5 (May 1938): 347–51.

———. "Grillparzer's Relation to Classical Idealism." *Modern Language Notes* 51, no. 6 (June 1936): 359–63.

Krispyn, Egbert. "The Fiasco of *Weh dem, der lügt!*." *German Life and Letters,* n.s. 25, no. 3 (April 1972): 201–9.

Morris, I. V. "Grillparzer's Individuality as a Dramatist." *Modern Language Quarterly* 18, no. 2 (June 1957): 83–99.

Mulholland, Gabrielle. "Some Problems in Translating Grillparzer." *German Life and Letters,* n.s. 19, no. 3 (April 1966): 178–89.

Mullan, W. N. B. *Grillparzer's Aesthetic Theory: A Study with Special Reference to His Conception of the Drama as "Eine Gegenwart."* Stuttgart: Heinz, 1979.

Nolte, Fred Otto. *Grillparzer, Lessing, and Goethe in the Perspective of European Literature.* Lancaster, Pa.: Lancaster Press, 1938.

Papst, E. E. "Franz Grillparzer." In *German Men of Letters: Twelve Literary Essays,* edited by Alex Natan, vol. 1, 101–20. London: Oswald Wolff, 1961.

Politzer, Heinz. "The Once and Future Poet: The Plays of Franz Grillparzer." In *Traditions and Transitions: Studies in Honor of Harold Jantz,* edited by Lieselotte Kurth et al., 210–27. München: Delp'sche Verlagsbuchhandlung, 1972.

Pollak, Gustav. *Franz Grillparzer and the Austrian Drama.* New York: Dodd, Mead, 1907.

Roe, Ian F. "Truth and Humanity in Grillparzer's *Weh dem, der lügt!*." *Forum for Modern Language Studies* 22, no. 4 (October 1986): 289–307.

Skrine, Peter. "Grillparzer and Romantic Verse Drama." In *Grillparzer und die Europäische Tradition,* edited by Robert Pichl et al., 45–55. Wien: Hora-Verlag, 1987.

Stern, J. P. "Grillparzer's Vienna." In *German Studies Presented to Walter H. Bruford,* 176–92. London: George G. Harrap, 1962.

Thompson, Bruce. *Franz Grillparzer.* Boston: Twayne, 1981.

———. "Grillparzer, Revolution, and 1848." In *Essays on Grillparzer,* edited by Bruce Thompson and Mark Ward, 81–91. Hull: German Department at Hull University, 1978.

Ward, M. G. "The Comedy of *Weh dem, der lügt!*." In *Studies in Nineteenth-Century Austrian Literature,* edited by B. O. Murdoch and M. G. Ward, 28–48. Glasgow: Scottish Papers in Germanic Studies, 1983.

Wells, George A. *The Plays of Grillparzer.* London: Pergamon Press, 1969.

Whitaker, Paul K. "The Concept of 'Sammlung' in Grillparzer's Works." *Monatshefte* 41, no. 2 (February 1949): 93–103.

Yates, Douglas. *Franz Grillparzer: A Critical Biography.* Oxford: Basil Blackwell, 1946.

Yates, W. E. *Grillparzer: A Critical Introduction.* Cambridge: Cambridge University Press, 1972.

The Beaver Coat

A Thieves' Comedy in Four Acts

by
GERHART HAUPTMANN

Translated by Bert Cardullo

Translated from the following edition:
Hauptmann, Gerhart. *Der Biberpelz*. In *Sämtliche Werke*, edited by Hans-Egon Hass, vol. 1. Frankfurt am Main: Propyläen Verlag, 1966.

Characters

Von Wehrhahn, Justice of the Peace
Krueger, property owner
Dr. Fleischer
Philipp, his son
Motes
Frau Motes, his wife
Frau Wolff, washerwoman
Julius Wolff, her husband
Leontine ⎱ *their daughters*
Adelheid ⎰
Wulkow, a bargeman
Glasenapp, clerk in von Wehrhahn's court
Mitteldorf, bailiff in von Wehrhahn's court

The action takes place somewhere in the vicinity of Berlin in the late 1880s.

Act 1

A small, narrow, blue-tinted kitchen with a low ceiling. At the left is a window and a crude, wooden door leading outside. In the middle of the rear wall is an empty door frame through which one sees a second room. It contains a high, neatly made bed. Above it hang some cheap photographs in even cheaper frames, prints of oil portraits the size of calling cards, etc. A chair of soft wood stands with its back toward the bed. In the left-hand corner of the kitchen is the stove; above it, on the wall, kitchen utensils hang from a wooden frame. In the right-hand corner are oars and other boating implements; firewood stands in a pile under the window. Scattered about are an old kitchen bench, several stools, etc. It is winter and the moon is shining. On the stove burns a tallow candle in a tin candlestick. LEONTINE WOLFF *sits on a stool next to the stove, asleep, with her head and arms on top of the stove. She is a seventeen-year-old, pretty blond and is wearing the working clothes of a servant girl. She wears a thick woolen shawl over her blue cotton jacket.—For a few seconds there is silence. Then someone is heard trying to unlock the door from the outside, but the key is in the lock on the inside. A knocking on the door follows.*

FRAU WOLFF. [*Still unseen, from outside.*] Adelheid! Adelheid! [*Silence. Then she knocks on the window.*] Open the door, hurry!

LEONTINE. [*Talking in her sleep.*] No, no, I'm not a slave!

FRAU WOLFF. Open up, girl, or I'll come through the window! [*She bangs hard on the window.*]

LEONTINE. [*Waking up.*] Oh, it's you, Mama! I'm coming! [*She unlocks the door.*]

FRAU WOLFF. [*Without putting down the sack she is carrying on her shoulder.*] And what are you doing here?

LEONTINE. [*Sleepily.*] Evening, Mama.

FRAU WOLFF. How did you get in, huh?

LEONTINE. Well, the key was on the top of the goat shed as usual. [*Short pause.*]

FRAU WOLFF. And what do you want here, girl?

LEONTINE. [*With a silly pout.*] Don't you want me home at all no more?

FRAU WOLFF. Do me a favor and don't start fussing, huh? That's just what I need! [*She lets the sack drop from her shoulder.*] Don't you have any idea what time it is? Off with you now and get home to your employer.

LEONTINE. And if I did get back a little late for once—so what!

FRAU WOLFF. Now you just watch yourself, understand? Get going or there's going to be trouble.

LEONTINE. [*Whining and obstinate.*] I ain't going back, Mama!

FRAU WOLFF. [*Surprised.*] You ain't going . . . [*Ironically.*] Well, what do you know about that!

LEONTINE. Well, do I have to be a slave for them people all the time?

FRAU WOLFF. [*Has been busy trying to get a piece of venison out of the sack.*] Oh, so you got to slave for them Kruegers? Why, you poor child!—Don't come to me with fool talk like that, wench! Now get a hold of the bottom of this sack. And don't act so stupid, understand? You won't get away with it around here! I ain't going to learn you to loaf! [*Between both of them, they manage to hang the venison on a doorpost.*] Now I'm telling you for the last time . . .

LEONTINE. I ain't going back to them people. I'd just as soon go drown myself, Mama!

FRAU WOLFF. Well, don't catch cold doing it.

LEONTINE. I'll jump into the river!

FRAU WOLFF. Just make sure you let me know when, and I'll give you a shove so you can't change your mind.

LEONTINE. [*Screams loudly.*] Well, do I have to stand for carrying firewood into the shed at night, two whole loads of it?

FRAU WOLFF. [*Acts astonished.*] No, it ain't possible! They ask you to lug wood in! Such people, I tell you!

LEONTINE. . . . and twenty talers for the whole year? Freeze my hands off for that? And not even enough potatoes and herring to eat?!

FRAU WOLFF. Don't start making speeches now, girl. Here's the key. Go cut yourself some bread. And when you've had enough, on your way you go, understand? The plum jam's on the top shelf.

LEONTINE. [*Takes a large loaf of bread from the drawer and cuts herself a slice.*] Juste, the one who works for the Schulzes, she gets forty talers and . . .

FRAU WOLFF. Don't be in such an awful hurry!—You ain't going to stay with them people forever. They didn't hire you for all eternity.—As far as I'm concerned, you can leave on the first of April. Until then you stay put! Now you got your Christmas money in your pocket, you want to quit, eh? Them's no manners!—And me running into them people all the time. I ain't going to stand for nothing like that!

LEONTINE. You mean because of these rags they put on me?

FRAU WOLFF. And how about the cash you got?

LEONTINE. Oh, sure! Six whole marks!

FRAU WOLFF. Money's money! Never you mind!

LEONTINE. But if I can make more money?

FRAU WOLFF. Hmph, gabbing maybe!

LEONTINE. No, with the sewing machine. I can go to Berlin and sew coats. Emily Stechow's been doing it since New Year's.

FRAU WOLFF. Don't talk to be about that slut! Just let me get my hands on her! I'd show the bitch something! You'd like to be promoted into her class, wouldn't you? Tramping around all night with fellers. Oh, no, girl, just the thought of it! I'd beat you till you'd forget to get up.—There's your father, watch out!

LEONTINE. If Papa beats me, I'll run away. We'll see how well I get along.

FRAU WOLFF. Shut up now! Go and feed the goats. They ain't been milked yet tonight, either. And give the rabbits some hay.

LEONTINE. [*Tries to get out of the house as quickly as possible, but runs into her father at the door and says hastily in passing.*] Evening.

JULIUS WOLFF, *the father, is a ship's carpenter. He is a tall man with slow movements and dull eyes, about forty-three years old.—Without saying a word, he puts the two oars that he has been carrying on his shoulder in the corner and throws down his carpenter's tools.*

FRAU WOLFF. Did you see Barge-Emil? [JULIUS *growls.*] Can't you talk? Yes or no? Is he coming over?

JULIUS. [*Testily.*] Go ahead! Yell a little louder!

FRAU WOLFF. Oh, you're so brave! And you forgot to shut the door.

JULIUS. [*Closes the door.*] What's wrong with Leontine this time?

FRAU WOLFF. Oh, nothing.—What kind of load did Emil have?

JULIUS. Bricks again. What else would he be carrying? Now what's the matter with that girl?

FRAU WOLFF. Half a barge load or a full load?

JULIUS. [*Flying into a rage.*] What in hell's the matter with that wench again, I want to know!

FRAU WOLFF. [*Even louder than* JULIUS.] What Emil's got in his barge is what I want to know! Half a load or a full load?

JULIUS. Aw, go away, a full load.

FRAU WOLFF. Shh, Julius. [*Frightened, she closes the shutters.*]

JULIUS. [*Stares at her, frightened; after a few seconds of silence, in a low voice.*] It's a young forester from Rixdorf.

FRAU WOLFF. Go hide under the bed, Julius! [*After a pause.*] If only you wasn't so terrible dumb. Blowing up like that. You don't understand them things. Just let me worry about the girls. That's not in your jurisfriction. That's in my jurisfriction. If they was boys it'd be different. I wouldn't tell you what to do with them. Everybody's got his own jurisfriction!

JULIUS. Keep her out of my way, then.

FRAU WOLFF. So you want to beat her to a pulp, eh, Julius? Better forget about that! Don't think for a minute I'd let you! I won't let her be beat black and blue. That girl could be our fortune. If you only had some brains for them things!

JULIUS. Then let her look after herself.

FRAU WOLFF. Don't worry about that, Julius. Could be you're going to be surprised. That girl's going to live in a mansion some day, and we'll be happy if she still knows us. What did the doc tell me the other day? "Your daughter's such a beautiful girl," he says, "she could go far on the stage."

JULIUS. Then let her hurry up and get there.

FRAU WOLFF. You got no education, Julius. No, not a trace of it. If it hadn't been for me, what would've become of them girls? I brought them up educated, understand? Education, that's the important thing nowadays. And you don't get it just like that. One thing after another, slowly but surely. Now first, she's got to learn something about housekeeping. Then if she's got a mind to, she can go to Berlin. But she's still much too young for the stage! [*During this speech there has been repeated knocking at the door. Now* ADELHEID's *voice is heard from outside.*]

ADELHEID. Mama! Mama! Open up! [FRAU WOLFF *opens the door for her and* ADELHEID *comes in. She is a tall schoolgirl of fourteen, with a pretty child's face. Her eyes, however, betray early debasement.*] Why didn't you open up, Mama? My hands and feet are frozen stiff.

FRAU WOLFF. Don't start talking a lot of rubbish. Make a fire in the stove so you'll get warm. Where've you been all this time, anyhow?

ADELHEID. Getting Father's boots. You know that.

FRAU WOLFF. And it took you two hours?

ADELHEID. But I didn't leave until seven!

FRAU WOLFF. So you left at seven, did you? It's half past ten now. You didn't know that, eh? You've only been gone three and a half hours, and that ain't much, is it? Now you listen to me, young lady. If you stay out that long once more, and with that lousy cobbler Fielitz at that—you'll see what happens to you!

ADELHEID. Am I supposed to hang around the house all the time?

FRAU WOLFF. Now you just keep still and don't say another word!

ADELHEID. Just because I go over to Fielitz' for a little while . . .

FRAU WOLFF. Are you going to be quiet? And you telling me about Fielitz! He's nothing to be proud of. His trade ain't just mending shoes, you know. When a man's done time twice . . .

ADELHEID. That ain't true . . . That's all a pack of lies. He told me so himself, Mama!

FRAU WOLFF. The whole village knows about it, you silly goose! A regular pimp, that's what he is.

ADELHEID. He even goes to see the Justice of the Peace.

FRAU WOLFF. Sure he does. Because he's a spy. An unformer he is, on top of everything else.

ADELHEID. What's that, an unformer?

JULIUS. [*From the other room, into which he has gone.*] Just one more word! [ADELHEID *turns pale and at once goes quietly to build a fire in the stove.* LEONTINE *enters.*]

FRAU WOLFF. [*Has cut open the venison; she takes out the heart, liver, etc., and hands them to* LEONTINE.] Quick now, wash them off! And don't say a word or there'll be a row. [LEONTINE, *visibly cowed, goes at her task. The girls whisper to each other.*]

FRAU WOLFF. Hey, Julius! What are you doing in there? You've forgotten all about it, eh? And only this morning I told you—about the board that's come loose.

JULIUS. What board?

FRAU WOLFF. You don't remember, huh? That board back on the goat shed. The wind must've torn it loose last night—get going and nail it on, understand?

JULIUS. Aw, that roof'll still be there in the morning.

FRAU WOLFF. Oh no, you don't! None of that! We ain't going to start with that business. [JULIUS *has come back into the kitchen grumbling.*] There, take the hammer! Here's your nails! Now see that you get it done.

JULIUS. You're crazy.

FRAU WOLFF. [*Calling after him.*] If Wulkow comes, how much do you want?

JULIUS. Well, twelve marks at least! [*Exits.*]

FRAU WOLFF. [*Contemptuously.*] Bah, twelve marks! [*Pause.*] Hurry up now so that Papa gets something to eat. [*Short pause.*]

ADELHEID. [*Looking at the venison.*] What is that, Mama?

FRAU WOLFF. A stork! [*Both girls laugh.*]

ADELHEID. A stork? Have they got horns, too? Oh, I know, it's a deer!

FRAU WOLFF. So if you know, why do you go and ask?

LEONTINE. Did Papa shoot it, Mama?

FRAU WOLFF. Now run out and shout it so's the whole town can hear: My father shot a deer!

ADELHEID. You won't catch me doing that. We'd get the cops on us.

LEONTINE. I'm not afraid of Officer Schulz—he tickled me under the chin once.

FRAU WOLFF. Just let him come. We ain't done nothing wrong. If a deer gets shot and it's dying and no one finds it, what happens? The crows eat it. Whether we eat it or the crows do, it's going to get eaten—that much we know. [*Short pause.*] How was that now: firewood you had to carry in?

LEONTINE. Yes, and in this freezing cold! Two cords of wood! And me dog-tired, at half past nine at night.

FRAU WOLFF. So now all that nice wood's lying there in the street?

LEONTINE. Sure, right by the garden gate. That's all I know.

FRAU WOLFF. Now suppose somebody goes—and steals that wood? Then what, tomorrow morning?

LEONTINE. I don't know. I won't be there.

FRAU WOLFF. Are they green logs or dry ones?

LEONTINE. Oh, nice dry logs!—[*Yawns several times.*] Oh, Mama, I'm so worn out. I've just been working my head off today. [*She sits down, obviously exhausted.*]

FRAU WOLFF. [*After a short silence.*] Well, if you want to, stay here tonight. I've changed my mind. And tomorrow morning we'll see.

LEONTINE. I'm just skin and bones, Mama! My clothes hang like a sack on me.

FRAU WOLFF. Hurry up now and get to sleep; up to the bedroom you go, so we don't have no trouble with Papa. He don't understand nothing about things like this.

ADELHEID. Papa always talks so uneducated.

FRAU WOLFF. He just ain't had no education. And it'd be the same with you, too, if I hadn't brought you up educated. [*Holding a pot on the stove, to* LEONTINE.] Come on now, put them in! [LEONTINE *puts the pieces of meat she has washed into the pot.*] There, now go to sleep!

LEONTINE. [*Goes into the back room, but is still visible as she speaks.*] Oh, Mama, that Motes fellow has left Krueger's.

FRAU WOLFF. Didn't want to pay the rent, huh?

LEONTINE. It was like pulling teeth to get it from him every time, Herr Krueger says. So he finally threw him out. He was such a liar and a windbag, and he always acted so high and mighty to Herr Krueger.

FRAU WOLFF. If I had been in Herr Krueger's place, I wouldn't have put up with him this long.

LEONTINE. Just because Herr Krueger used to be a cabinet-maker, Motes always looks down on him so. And Motes has been quarreling with Dr. Fleischer, too.

FRAU WOLFF. Now who'd start a fight with Dr. Fleischer? That I'd like to know! Them people wouldn't hurt a fly.

LEONTINE. The Fleischers won't even let him in the house no more.

FRAU WOLFF. If only you could get in with them people!

LEONTINE. They treat their servants like their own children.

FRAU WOLFF. And his brother in Berlin, he's cashier at a theater.

WULKOW. [*Has knocked at the door several times, and now shouts in a hoarse voice.*] Are you going to let me in?

FRAU WOLFF. Well, sure! Why not? Come on in!

WULKOW. [*Enters; he is a barge captain on the river Spree, is almost sixty years old, and walks with a stoop. He has a yellowish-gray beard that reaches from one ear to the other and under his chin, so that his weatherbeaten face is left showing.*] A pleasant evening, everybody.

FRAU WOLFF. Here he is again, come to cheat the Wolffs a little.

WULKOW. Oh, I wouldn't try that no more.

FRAU WOLFF. Well, that's how it's going to wind up anyhow.

WULKOW. Just the other way 'round, you mean!

FRAU WOLFF. What'll it be next?!—Well, there he stands. Now don't he beat all?

WULKOW. Just tell Julius to watch his step. They're on the look-out for poachers.

FRAU WOLFF. What are you going to pay? That's the main thing. What's the use of all this jabbering?!

WULKOW. I'm telling you. I've just come from Grünau. Heard it there for sure. They shot Fritz Weber; his pants are full of buckshot.

FRAU WOLFF. What are you going to pay, that's what I want to know.

WULKOW. [*Feeling the venison.*] I already got four bucks lying in the boat.

FRAU WOLFF. It won't sink on their account.

WULKOW. It better not! That would be a spectacle. But what if I get stuck with the beasts here, what then? I got to get them into Berlin. It was bad enough working on the river today, and if it keeps on freezing tonight, there'll be no getting away tomorrow. I'll be sitting in the ice with my boat and have them beasts around my neck.

FRAU WOLFF. [*Apparently changing her mind.*] All right, girl, just run down to Schulz, say hello nice to him, and tell him Mother's got something to sell.

WULKOW. Did I say I wasn't going to buy it?

FRAU WOLFF. Don't matter to me who buys it.

WULKOW. But I want to buy it.

FRAU WOLFF. Hey, if you don't like it, you can leave it.

WULKOW. I'm going to buy the meat! How much do you want?

FRAU WOLFF. [*Taking hold of the venison.*] This here piece weighs a good thirty pounds. Oh, at least that, I can tell you. Well, Adelheid! You were here. We could hardly get it hung up on the nail, could we?

ADELHEID. [*Who had not been present.*] I even sprained something lifting it.

WULKOW. Well, thirteen marks ought to pay for it. And I won't even be making ten pfennigs on the deal.

FRAU WOLFF. [*Acts quite astonished; the next moment, she starts doing something else, as if she had forgotten* WULKOW'*s presence. Then, seeming to notice him again, she says.*] Oh yes, I wish you a good trip!

WULKOW. But I just can't give you more than thirteen.

FRAU WOLFF. Let's drop it, all right?

WULKOW. I can't pay no more than that. I'll tell you, I do this only to keep my customers. May God strike me dead, it's as true as I'm standing here. I don't make that much on this whole deal. And if I said fourteen, I'd have to add: that's one mark out of my pocket. But I don't mind, just so you see my good intentions. Fourteen marks it is!

FRAU WOLFF. Forget about it! That's O.K. We can sell that deer— it won't be here tomorrow morning.

WULKOW. Hope nobody sees it hanging there so nice and pretty! Money won't be the issue then.

FRAU WOLFF. That animal was dead when we found it.

WULKOW. Sure, in a trap, I'll bet!

FRAU WOLFF. Nothing of the kind! You'll get nowhere with that talk. You just want people to give you everything for nothing! We slave till we got no breath left. We stand soaking in the snow for hours, not to speak of all the risks we run out there in the pitch dark. That's no fun, I tell you.

WULKOW. I already got them four bucks on my hands, otherwise I'd say fifteen marks quick enough.

FRAU WOLFF. No, Wulkow, we just can't do business today. You can go take a walk now. We worked like dogs to drag it across the lake . . . almost got stuck in the ice. Couldn't go forward or back. We can't give something like that away for nothing.

WULKOW. As if I was going to get rich on the deal! Running a barge is hard work. And pushing stolen goods ain't so great, either. If you get nabbed, I get taken in along with you. Almost forty years I been working. And what've I got to show for it? Rheumatism—that's what! When I get up early in the morning, I whine like a pup. For years I been wanting to buy me a fur coat. All the doctors have told me I should, because I'm suffering so. Never been able to buy one yet, Frau Wolff. Not to this day, sure as I'm standing here!

ADELHEID. [*To her mother.*] Did you hear what Leontine said?

WULKOW. But anyhow, I'll say sixteen. Sixteen marks!

FRAU WOLFF. No, nothing doing! Eighteen! [*To* ADELHEID.] Now what did you say?

ADELHEID. Frau Krueger's bought a fur coat that cost almost five hundred marks. A beaver coat.

WULKOW. A beaver coat?

FRAU WOLFF. Who bought it?

ADELHEID. Why, Frau Krueger, I tell you, as a Christmas present for Herr Krueger.

WULKOW. That girl works for the Kruegers?

ADELHEID. No, not me. My sister does. I'll never work as a servant.

WULKOW. Ah, if only I could have a coat like that. That's the kind of thing I been wanting to get hold of for a long time. I'd even give sixty talers for one. Rather spend the money on a fur coat than on doctor bills and medicine. I'd get some pleasure out of it at least.

FRAU WOLFF. All you have to do is go over to Krueger's, Wulkow. Maybe he'll give it away.

WULKOW. Don't count on it! But like I said, I'm very interested in such a coat.

FRAU WOLFF. Oh, sure. I wouldn't mind having a fur coat myself.

WULKOW. Where do we stand now? Sixteen?

FRAU WOLFF. Nothing doing below eighteen. No less than eighteen, that's what Julius said. I wouldn't dare take sixteen. Once he gets something like that in his head—[JULIUS *comes in.*] Well, didn't you say eighteen, Julius?

JULIUS. What's that I said?

FRAU WOLFF. Must be one of your hard-of-hearing days! You said yourself: nothing under eighteen. You told me not to sell the buck for less.

JULIUS. I said that? . . . Oh sure, that piece of venison. Yes! Right! Hm. And that ain't a bit too much, either.

WULKOW. [*Taking some money out of his pocket and counting it.*] We got to put an end to this. Seventeen marks. Is it a deal?

FRAU WOLFF. You're a real swindler. Just like I said when you came in: he just walks through the door and already he's cheated you.

WULKOW. [*Unfolds a sack that he has kept hidden under his coat.*] Give me a hand now getting that thing in here. [FRAU WOLFF *helps him put the venison into the sack.*] And if by any chance you hear something about—I mean, well—like a fur coat, for instance. I could pay you sixty or seventy talers for it.

FRAU WOLFF. You must be out of your mind! Where am I supposed to get hold of a fur coat?

A MAN'S VOICE. [*Calling from outside.*] Frau Wolff! Frau Wolff! Are you still up?

FRAU WOLFF. [*Is startled, as is everyone else in the room; whispers tensely.*] Quick, put that away! And get into the other room! [*She pushes everybody into the back room and shuts the door.*]

MAN'S VOICE. Frau Wolff! Frau Wolff! Are you already in bed? [FRAU WOLFF *puts out the candle.*] Frau Wolff! Frau Wolff! Are you still up? [*The voice moves off singing.*] The morn glows re-ed, the morn glows re-ed, / Brings the day when I'll be de-ad.

LEONTINE. That's only "Morning Glow," Mama!

FRAU WOLFF. [*Listens for a while, then softly opens the door and listens again. When she is satisfied, she closes the door and relights the candle. Then she lets the others in from the back room.*] It was only Mitteldorf, the bailiff.

WULKOW. What the hell! Fine friends you got!

FRAU WOLFF. You better get going now, Wulkow.

ADELHEID. Mama, Mino's started barking.

FRAU WOLFF. Quick, quick, Wulkow! Get a move on! And out the back way, through the vegetable garden. Julius will open the gate for you. Go on and open it, Julius.

WULKOW. And like I said, if you should run across anything like a beaver coat, why—

FRAU WOLFF. Yes, of course, but hurry!

WULKOW. If the Spree don't freeze up, I'll be getting back from Berlin in three or four days. I'll be down in the same spot again with my boat.

ADELHEID. By the big bridge?

WULKOW. Where I always tie up. Well, Julius, shuffle ahead. [*Both exit.*]

ADELHEID. Mama, Mino's barking again.

FRAU WOLFF. [*At the stove.*] Oh, let him bark. [*A long, drawn-out cry in the distance: "Ferry over!"*]

ADELHEID. Somebody wants to cross the Spree, Mama.

FRAU WOLFF. Well, go on down. Papa's there by the river. [*"Ferry over!" is heard again.*] Bring him the oars. But he better let Wulkow get away first.

[ADELHEID *leaves with the oars. For a while* FRAU WOLFF *is alone, during which time she works energetically. Then* ADELHEID *returns.*]

ADELHEID. Papa had oars down in the boat.

FRAU WOLFF. And who wants to cross this late at night?

ADELHEID. I think it's that stupid Motes.

FRAU WOLFF. What? Who is it, you say?

ADELHEID. It sounded like Motes.

FRAU WOLFF. [*Vehemently.*] Go on down again! Hurry! Tell Papa to come up; that idiot Motes can stay where he is. He don't need to be snooping around my house.

[ADELHEID *goes.* FRAU WOLFF *hides everything that might give away the deer episode. She puts a cover over the pot on the stove.* ADELHEID *comes back.*]

ADELHEID. Too late, Mama. I could hear them talking already.

FRAU WOLFF. Who is it then?

ADELHEID. Like I told you: Motes.

FRAU *and* HERR MOTES *appear, one after the other, in the doorway. Both are of average size. She is an alert young woman of about thirty, modestly but neatly dressed. He has on a green hunting jacket; his face is healthy but indistinctive, and he wears a black patch over his left eye.*

FRAU MOTES. [*Calling into the room.*] My nose is frozen blue, Mother Wolff!

FRAU WOLFF. What do you go traipsing around for in the middle of the night? You got time enough for walks during the day.

MOTES. Nice and warm in here.—Who's got time during the day?

FRAU WOLFF. Why, you!

MOTES. Do you think I have an independent income?

FRAU WOLFF. I'm sure I don't know what you live on.

FRAU MOTES. Oh, don't be so grouchy, Mother Wolff. We just wanted to ask about our bill.

FRAU WOLFF. You asked me more than once about that.

FRAU MOTES. Well, so we're asking yet again. Any harm in that? We have to pay some time.

FRAU WOLFF. [*Surprised.*] You want to pay?

FRAU MOTES. Of course we do. Naturally!

MOTES. Mother Wolff acts quite surprised. You didn't think we'd skip out on you, did you?

FRAU WOLFF. Why, I wouldn't think a thing like that. If you want to, we'll settle right now. The bill comes to eleven marks and thirty pfennigs.

FRAU MOTES. Yes, yes, Mother Wolff, we're coming into some money. People will look at us with envy in their eyes.

MOTES. Smells like roast hare in here, doesn't it?

FRAU WOLFF. Roast cat maybe! That'd be more like it!

MOTES. I'll just take a look-see! [*He is about to lift the cover from the pot.*]

FRAU WOLFF. [*Stopping him.*] No snooping in my pots!

FRAU MOTES. [*Has observed the scene with suspicion.*] Mother Wolff, we've found something.

FRAU WOLFF. I ain't lost nothing.

FRAU MOTES. Here, take a look at these. [*She shows her two wire snares.*]

FRAU WOLFF. [*Without losing her composure.*] Are those what they call snares?

FRAU MOTES. We found them quite near here. Hardly twenty steps from your garden.

FRAU WOLFF. My goodness, the poaching that's going on in these parts!

FRAU MOTES. If you keep a sharp lookout, Mother Wolff, you just might catch the poacher.

FRAU WOLFF. Them things are none of my business!

MOTES. If I ever nab one of those scoundrels, first I'll box his ears and then I'll turn him in. No mercy for such fellows.

FRAU MOTES. Frau Wolff, have you got a few fresh eggs?

FRAU WOLFF. Now? In the middle of winter? They're pretty scarce at the moment.

MOTES. [*To* JULIUS, *who is just coming in.*] Forester Seidel has caught another poacher. He'll be taken to court tomorrow. He's got pluck, that Seidel, that much you've got to give him. If it weren't for my accident, I could be head forester today. Then I'd really let those bastards have it!

FRAU WOLFF. Quite a few have tried that before you and been sorry they did!

MOTES. Yes, but they were afraid, and I'm not! I've already informed on a few of them. [*Fixing a sharp gaze alternately on* FRAU WOLFF *and her husband.*] And I'm just waiting for a few more. They'll walk right smack into my hands one of these days. I hope those snare-setters don't think I don't know who they are. I know them all right!

FRAU MOTES. Have you done any baking, Frau Wolff? We just can't stand bread bought in a bakery.

FRAU WOLFF. I thought you wanted to pay your bill.

FRAU MOTES. I'm telling you, Mother Wolff, Saturday for sure. My husband, you know, has been made editor of the *Journal of Hunting and Forestry.*

FRAU WOLFF. Oh, yes, I know very well what that means.

FRAU MOTES. Yes indeed, Frau Wolff! And we've already moved away from Krueger's.

FRAU WOLFF. You moved because you had to.

FRAU MOTES. We had to? Honey, just listen to that! [*She gives a forced laugh.*] Frau Wolff says we *had* to leave Krueger's!

MOTES. [*Red with anger.*] Some day you'll find out why I moved away from that place. The man's a usurer and a cutthroat.

FRAU WOLFF. I don't know nothing about that. I couldn't say nothing on that subject.

MOTES. I'm just waiting until I get proof. He'd better watch out for me. He and his bosom friend, Dr. Fleischer. Particularly that one! All I'd have to say is one word and they'd put that man behind bars. [*From the beginning of his speech he has been withdrawing to the door, and with his last words he leaves.*]

FRAU WOLFF. The men got to quarreling again?

FRAU MOTES. [*Apparently in confidence.*] My husband is not someone you trifle with. If he gets something into his head, there's no stopping him. And he's on very good terms with the Justice of the Peace, too.—How about the eggs and the bread?

FRAU WOLFF. [*Reluctantly.*] Well, five's all I got left. And a bit of bread. [FRAU MOTES *puts the eggs and half a loaf of bread into her basket.*] Are you satisfied?

FRAU MOTES. Oh, sure. Of course. The eggs are fresh, aren't they?

FRAU WOLFF. As fresh as my hens can lay them.

FRAU MOTES. [*Hurriedly, because she is anxious to catch up with her husband.*] Well, good night then! And next Saturday's money day! [*Exits.*]

FRAU WOLFF. Sure, sure. That'll be fine. [*Closes the door. Under her breath.*] Hurry up and get out of here. Those two, they owe money to everybody. [*Busy with the pot.*] What's it to them what we eat? Let them look into their own affairs. Go to bed now, girl.

ADELHEID. Good night, Mama. [*Kisses her.*]

FRAU WOLFF. Well, ain't you going to kiss Papa good night?

ADELHEID. Good night, Papa. [*Kisses him; he growls.* ADELHEID *leaves.*]

FRAU WOLFF. Always got to tell her to do that. [*Pause.*]

JULIUS. What did you have to give them people all the eggs for?

FRAU WOLFF. Do you want me to make that fellow mad at me? You make him mad at you, Julius, and I'm telling you, he's dangerous. He don't do nothing but spy on people. Come on, sit down and eat! Here's a fork. You just don't understand such things. Better take care of your own business! Leaving them snares right in back of the garden! They was yours, wasn't they?

JULIUS. [*Annoyed.*] Yeah, yeah.

FRAU WOLFF. And that stupid Motes had to find them straight off, too! You ain't going to set no more snares right around the house, you hear? Somebody might get the idea it's us who's setting them.

JULIUS. Aw, stop your jabbering. [*Both eat.*]

FRAU WOLFF. Listen, Julius, there ain't no more wood, neither.

JULIUS. So you want me to go all the way back into the woods, huh?

FRAU WOLFF. Best to get it over with now.

JULIUS. I can't hardly feel my bones no more. I don't care who goes—just leave me alone.

FRAU WOLFF. You men always talk big, but when it comes right down to it, you don't do nothing. I work three times harder than all of you put together. Well, if there's no way you're going tonight, tomorrow you'll just have to go whether you like it or not. How's your climbing irons? Are they sharp?

JULIUS. I lent them to Karl Machnow.

FRAU WOLFF. [*After a pause.*] If only you wasn't such a coward!—Then we'd have us a few cords of wood in a hurry!—And we wouldn't have to work so hard to get them, neither.—We wouldn't even have to walk very far.

JULIUS. Let me eat my food, will you?

FRAU WOLFF. [*Gives him a playful cuff on the head.*] Oh, don't be such a miserable grumbler all the time. Just look, I got something nice for you! [*Gets out a bottle of whiskey and shows it to him.*] See that? I brought it for you. Now you're smiling, all right! [*Pours her husband a glassful.*]

JULIUS. [*Empties the glass; then.*] That sure's . . . in this cold weather, that sure's good!

FRAU WOLFF. Now see, don't I look out for you?

JULIUS. That sure was good. Sure was! [*He pours himself another glass and drinks.*]

FRAU WOLFF. [*After a pause, starts to split wood, eating a few bites in between.*] That Wulkow—he's a real operator. Always acting as if he's bad off.

JULIUS. He should talk, that one—with all the business he does.

FRAU WOLFF. Well, you heard what he said about that beaver coat.

JULIUS. I didn't hear nothing.

FRAU WOLFF. [*Pretending indifference.*] The girl told him about Frau Krueger and how she gave her husband a fur coat as a present.

JULIUS. Well, them people's got the dough.

FRAU WOLFF. That's true. And then Wulkow said—you must have heard him!—if he could get hold of a fur coat like that, he'd pay sixty talers for it.

JULIUS. Let him burn his fingers himself if he wants to.

FRAU WOLFF. [*After a pause, pouring her husband another drink.*] Oh, you might as well have another one.

JULIUS. Pour away . . . pour away—go right ahead. [FRAU WOLFF *gets out a small notebook and leafs through it.*] How much have we saved since July?

FRAU WOLFF. We paid off thirty talers, you know.

JULIUS. And that leaves . . . that leaves . . . how much?

FRAU WOLFF. Still leaves seventy. You don't get very far at this rate. Fifty, sixty talers at one clip—if we could put that much away all at once, we'd soon have this whole place paid for. And then we could borrow a hundred or two and maybe add on a couple of nice rooms. We can't take in no summer boarders the way it is. And summer boarders, that's what brings in the money.

JULIUS. Well, go on . . . What are you—

FRAU WOLFF. [*Resolutely.*] You're just too slow, Julius. Would you've bought the land, huh? Well? And now if we had a mind to sell, we could get at least double what we paid for it. I'm so different from you! If you was only like me . . .

JULIUS. I'm working, but what good does it do?

FRAU WOLFF. With that kind of work you don't get very far.

JULIUS. Well, I can't go stealing! I'd get caught for sure.

FRAU WOLFF. Oh, you're just plain dumb and that's the way you'll always be. Nobody said a thing about stealing. But, nothing ventured, nothing gained. And once you're rich, Julius, and can ride around in your own carriage, nobody's going to ask where your money came from. Of course, if you took it from poor people! But seriously now—if we went over to Krueger's and loaded the two cords of wood on the sleigh and put them in our shed, them people wouldn't be no poorer for it.

JULIUS. Wood? What's this again—about the wood?

FRAU WOLFF. You just don't trouble yourself about nothing. They can work your daughter to death! They wanted her to carry in wood at ten o'clock at night, and that's why she run away. Naturally, you don't care about that. Maybe you'll even give the child a beating and send her back to them people.

JULIUS. Sure!—That's just what I'll do!—What do you think?

FRAU WOLFF. Things like that shouldn't go without being answered. If somebody hits me, I say, hit him back.

JULIUS. Did they go and hit the girl?

FRAU WOLFF. Well, she run away, didn't she? No, no, Julius, there ain't no use trying to do anything with you. Now the wood's just lying out there in the street. And if I was to say: all right, you treat my children bad, I'll take your wood—a fine face you'd make.

JULIUS. I wouldn't do no such thing . . . What do I care about them? I can do more than sit here and eat. And I won't stand for things like that . . . There won't be no more hitting.

FRAU WOLFF. Well, don't just stand there gabbing. Go get the sleigh. Show them people you got some backbone. The whole thing will be over in an hour. Then we can get some sleep. And in the morning you don't need to go into the woods. We'll have more fuel than we can use.

JULIUS. Even if this does get out, I don't give a damn.

FRAU WOLFF. No reason why it should! Just watch you don't wake up the girls.

MITTELDORF. [*From outside.*] Frau Wolff, Frau Wolff, are you still up?

FRAU WOLFF. Sure, Mitteldorf! Come on in! [*She opens the door.*]

MITTELDORF. [*Enters. He wears an overcoat over his shabby uniform. His face has something Mephistophelian about it, and his nose betrays an alcoholic reddening. His demeanor is gentle, almost timid; his speech is slow and dragging and unaccompanied by any change in facial expression.*] Good evening, Frau Wolff.

FRAU WOLFF. Good night, you mean.

MITTELDORF. I was here before, a while ago. First I thought I saw a light, then all of a sudden everything was dark. And nobody answered, neither. But this time I was quite sure I saw a light, and so I thought I'd drop in.

FRAU WOLFF. What did you want, Mitteldorf?

MITTELDORF. [*Has seated himself, thinks a while, and then says.*] That's why I came: I got a message for you from the Justice's wife.

FRAU WOLFF. She wants me to come and do the wash, huh?

MITTELDORF. [*Furrows his brow in deep thought, then says.*] Yes, that's it!

FRAU WOLFF. When does she want me?

MITTELDORF. —Tomorrow.—Tomorrow morning.—

FRAU WOLFF. And you tell me that the night before at twelve o'clock?

MITTELDORF. But tomorrow is laundry day at the Justice's house.

FRAU WOLFF. I got to know that a few days ahead of time, though.

MITTELDORF. Yes, of course. Don't get upset now. I just plumb forgot about it again. I got so many things in my head, it's easy to forget something like that.

FRAU WOLFF. Well, Mitteldorf, I'll manage. We're friends after all. I know you got enough troubles with eleven children at home. You don't need the Justice's wife bawling you out.

MITTELDORF. If you don't come in the morning, Mother Wolff, I'll really get it.

FRAU WOLFF. I'll be there, don't worry. Here, have a drink. You can use one. [*She makes him a hot toddy.*] Just happened to have some hot water on the stove. We still got to go out tonight—over to Treptow for some nice fat geese. We just ain't got the time during the day. That's the way it is with us. Poor people got to slave day and night. Rich ones can spend their time in bed.

MITTELDORF. I got my notice, did you know that? The justice gave me my notice. I ain't keen enough going after people.

FRAU WOLFF. What do they want? Are you supposed to be a bloodhound?

MITTELDORF. I'd just as soon not go home, 'cause when I do, there'll be a fight. She drives me crazy with her bitching.

FRAU WOLFF. Why, just plug your ears!

MITTELDORF. So I go to the tavern once in a while to forget my troubles. That I ain't supposed to do, neither. She won't let me do nothing! I was just sitting there today, and someone treated everybody to a keg—

FRAU WOLFF. But you ain't going to be scared of a woman! If she yells at you, yell at her, and if she hits you, hit her back. Now come over here, you're taller than me. Get them things down for me. And

Julius, you get the sleigh ready. [JULIUS *leaves.*] How many times do I have to tell you? [MITTELDORF *takes ropes and pulley lines down from a high shelf.*] Get the big sleigh ready! Just hand them ropes to me.

JULIUS. [*From outside.*] I can't see a thing.

FRAU WOLFF. What can't you do?

JULIUS. [*Appears in the doorway.*] I can't get that sleigh out all by myself. All kinds of stuff's piled around and on top of it. And without a light I can't do nothing.

FRAU WOLFF. You know, you're really helpless! [*She hastily ties a kerchief around her head and throws a shawl over her shoulders.*] Just wait a minute, and I'll come and help you. Get the lantern there, Mitteldorf! [MITTELDORF *takes down a lantern with difficulty and gives it to* FRAU WOLFF.] That's it, thanks. [*She puts the burning candle in the lantern.*] That goes in here, and now we're ready to go. I'm coming—I'll help you pull the sleigh out. [*She goes ahead carrying the lantern.* MITTELDORF *follows. When she reaches the door she turns around and hands the lantern to* MITTELDORF.] You can hold the light for us a bit!

MITTELDORF. [*Holding the lantern and singing to himself, exits.*] The morn glows re-ed, the morn glows re-ed . . .

Curtain

Act 2

The courtroom of Justice of the Peace VON WEHRHAHN: *a large, bare, whitewashed room with three windows in the rear wall. The entrance is in the left wall. At the wall to the right stands a long table covered with books, legal documents, etc.; behind it is the Justice's bench. Near the center window are a table and chair for the clerk. On the right and toward the front is a wooden book-case, so positioned that it is within reach of the Justice when he sits in his chair. Shelves full of documents cover the left wall. Down front, beginning at the wall to the left, six chairs stand in a row, their backs to the audience.—It is a clear winter morning. The clerk,* GLASENAPP, *sits scribbling at his desk. He is a sorry-looking, bespectacled figure. Justice of the Peace* VON WEHRHAHN *enters briskly, carrying a file of documents under his arm.* WEHRHAHN *is about forty years old and wears a monocle. He gives the impression of belonging to the landed gentry. His official garb consists of a black frock coat, buttoned all the way up, and high boots that are pulled over his trousers. He speaks in what is almost a falsetto voice and carefully cultivates a military succinctness of expression.*

WEHRHAHN. [*Offhand, as if he were terribly busy.*] Morning!

GLASENAPP. [*Getting up.*] Your servant, Herr Justice!

WEHRHAHN. Anything happened, Glasenapp?

GLASENAPP. [*Standing, leafing through some papers.*] I wish to report, Herr Justice—first, there was . . . yes! The innkeeper Fiebig. He asks for permission, Herr Justice, to have music and dancing at his inn next Sunday.

WEHRHAHN. Fiebig? Isn't that . . . perhaps you can tell me. Didn't he recently rent his hall . . . ?

GLASENAPP. To the Liberals. Quite right, Herr Baron!

WEHRHAHN. The same Fiebig?

GLASENAPP. Yes, indeed, Herr Baron!

WEHRHAHN. We'll just have to curb him a bit. [BAILIFF MITTELDORF *enters.*]

MITTELDORF. Your servant, Herr Baron!

WEHRHAHN. Look here: once and for all—when I'm on duty I'm the Justice of the Peace.

MITTELDORF. Yes sir. As you wish, Herr Bar—Herr Justice, I meant to say.

WEHRHAHN. Try to remember that now: the fact that I'm a baron is beside the point. It doesn't matter at all here. [*To* GLASENAPP.] Now please, I'd like to hear what else you have to report. Has Motes, the writer, been in?

GLASENAPP. Yes, Herr Justice.

WEHRHAHN. So he was here? I confess that he has strongly aroused my curiosity. I trust he intends to come back?

GLASENAPP. He'll be here again around half-past eleven.

WEHRHAHN. Did Motes by chance say anything to you, Glasenapp?

GLASENAPP. He came in the matter of Dr. Fleischer.

WEHRHAHN. Now I want you to tell me, Glasenapp, do you know this Dr. Fleischer?

GLASENAPP. All I know is he lives in Krueger's house.

WEHRHAHN. How long has the man been in this district?

GLASENAPP. I've only been here since September.

WEHRHAHN. Oh, that's right. You came at the same time I did, about four months ago.

GLASENAPP. [*Glancing at* MITTELDORF.] From what I gather, though, Dr. Fleischer has been living here two years.

WEHRHAHN. [*To* MITTELDORF.] I don't suppose you would know anything about that?

MITTELDORF. At your service, sir—he came here a year ago this past September.

WEHRHAHN. Is that so? The man moved here then?

MITTELDORF. At your service, sir—from Berlin, Herr . . . Herr Justice.

WEHRHAHN. Do you have any more information about this individual?

MITTELDORF. I just know a brother of his is the cashier at a theater.

WEHRHAHN. I didn't ask about his brother. What does the man do?—What's his occupation? Who is he?

MITTELDORF. Well, I can't tell you for sure. People do say that he's sick, though. Seems he's got diabetes.

WEHRHAHN. I don't care what he's got. As far as I'm concerned, he can spit molasses if he feels like it.—What does he do?

GLASENAPP. [*Shrugs his shoulders.*] He calls himself a privy tutor.

WEHRHAHN. Private, private! Not privy! Private tutor.

GLASENAPP. Hugk, the bookbinder, has books of his. He gets some bound every week.

WEHRHAHN. I'd like to see some time what the man reads.

GLASENAPP. The postman says he subscribes to twenty newspapers. Some democratic ones, too.

WEHRHAHN. Tell Hugk to come and see me.

GLASENAPP. Right away?

WEHRHAHN. When it's convenient. Tomorrow or the next day. He might bring a few of those books along with him. [*To* MITTELDORF.] You seem to be sleeping when you should be awake—or perhaps this Fleischer has good cigars and gives them to the right people.

MITTELDORF. Herr Justice!

WEHRHAHN. All right, never mind. I'll look into these people myself. My predecessor here just let things get out of control. Well, that'll all be changed in due time. It is disgraceful for a police official to allow himself to accept favors from anyone. You wouldn't understand that, of course. [*To* GLASENAPP.] Motes didn't say anything specific, did he?

GLASENAPP. He didn't tell me anything specific. He said that the Herr Justice would know . . .

WEHRHAHN. I just know in a very general way. I've had my eye on that man for some time. Dr. Fleischer, I mean. Herr Motes simply confirmed for me that my judgment of the fellow was quite correct.—What kind of a reputation does this Motes have? [GLASENAPP *and* MITTELDORF *look at each other.* GLASENAPP *shrugs his shoulders.*] Borrows all over the place, does he?

GLASENAPP. He says he has a pension.

WEHRHAHN. A pension?

GLASENAPP. He got shot in the eye, you know.

WEHRHAHN. Then it would be some kind of compensation for damages.

GLASENAPP. Begging your pardon, Herr Justice. I think the man has mostly the damages. No one's ever seen him with any money.

WEHRHAHN. [*Amused.*] Is there anything else of importance?

GLASENAPP. Only minor matters, Herr Justice. Somebody's given notice—

WEHRHAHN. Very well, very well. Have you ever heard that Fleischer talks too much?

GLASENAPP. No, I don't believe I have.

WEHRHAHN. Because that's what I've been told. That he makes illegal speeches about all sorts of people in high places. Well, we'll see about that. Right now, we've got to get down to work. Mitteldorf, do you have anything?

MITTELDORF. Seems a theft was committed last night.

WEHRHAHN. A theft? Where?

MITTELDORF. At Krueger's.

WEHRHAHN. What was stolen?

MITTELDORF. Firewood.

WEHRHAHN. When? Last night?

MITTELDORF. Last night.

WEHRHAHN. Who told you this?

MITTELDORF. I heard it from . . . from . . .

WEHRHAHN. Come on now, who told you?

MITTELDORF. I heard it . . . I heard it from Herr Fleischer.

WEHRHAHN. So, you're on speaking terms with him?

MITTELDORF. Herr Krueger himself told me, too.

WEHRHAHN. That man is a chronic complainer. Every week he writes me at least three letters. Either somebody has cheated him, or smashed his fence, or moved the boundary marker on his property. It's one annoyance after another.

MOTES. [*Enters; he laughs almost continuously in a nervous way as he talks.*] Your servant, Herr Justice.

WEHRHAHN. Ah, there you are. Glad that you could come. Perhaps you can tell me right away: has something been stolen from Krueger's?

MOTES. I don't live there anymore.

WEHRHAHN. And you haven't otherwise heard anything, Herr Motes?

MOTES. Oh, I've heard something about it, but nothing very definite. When I passed by his house just now, they were both looking for tracks in the snow.

WEHRHAHN. Is that right? Dr. Fleischer is helping him—then I suppose those two are pretty good friends, eh?

MOTES. As close as you can get, Herr Justice.

WEHRHAHN. Yes. Now, as for this man Fleischer—he interests me most of all. Please sit down.—I can tell you, I lay awake half the night. Couldn't sleep because of this business. You wrote me a letter that's got me all worked up.—That's a matter of temperament, to be sure. My predecessor in this position, it wouldn't have bothered him one bit.—For my part, I've made a firm resolution to see this matter through. My mission here is to investigate and clean house. What rubbish hasn't accumulated under the protection of my honorable predecessor?! Dubious characters, political outcasts, enemies of King and country. I'll make those people squirm!—Now then, Herr Motes, you're a writer?

MOTES. Yes, sir, on matters dealing with forestry and hunting.

WEHRHAHN. Then you write for the appropriate professional journals, I take it. And are you able to earn a living at it?

MOTES. If one is established as I am, Herr Baron, it can be done. I make a nice living, I'm happy to say.

WEHRHAHN. You're a trained forester, are you?

MOTES. I attended the Forestry Academy, Herr Justice. I studied in Eberswalde. Then shortly before the final examination, I met with misfortune . . .

WEHRHAHN. Yes, of course, you're wearing an eye patch.

MOTES. I lost my eye hunting, Herr Baron. Buckshot hit me in the right eye; unfortunately, I never found out who did it. And so I had to give up my career.

WEHRHAHN. You don't get a pension, then?

MOTES. No. But I've managed to get along pretty well. My name is already fairly well known.

WEHRHAHN. Hm.—Do you know my brother-in-law by any chance?

MOTES. Chief Forester von Wachsmann? Yes, indeed. I correspond with him quite a bit, and, in addition, we're members of the same club: The Society for the Breeding of Pointers.

WEHRHAHN. [*Fairly sighing with relief.*] Ah, so you really do know him?! I'm delighted to hear that. That makes things much easier, since it gives us a basis for mutual trust. There's no longer anything to stand in our way, Herr Motes.—You wrote me in your letter that you have had the opportunity to observe this Dr. Fleischer. Tell me now what you know about him.

MOTES. [*Clearing his throat.*] When I . . . when I went to live in Krueger's house about a year ago, Herr Baron, I didn't have any idea of the kind of people I'd come into contact with.

WEHRHAHN. You didn't know either Krueger or Fleischer?

MOTES. No, but you know how it is when everybody's living in one house. I couldn't keep to myself entirely.

WEHRHAHN. What sort of person used to show up there?

MOTES. [*With a significant gesture.*] Oh, *that* sort!

WEHRHAHN. I understand.

MOTES. Every Tom, Dick, and Harry. Democrats, of course.

WEHRHAHN. Were there regular meetings?

MOTES. Every Thursday, as far as I know.

WEHRHAHN. We will certainly want to keep an eye on that place.—And now you no longer associate with these people?

MOTES. Finally I just couldn't stand it anymore, Herr Justice.

WEHRHAHN. It was pretty disagreeable, eh?

MOTES. The whole business had become utterly repulsive to me.

WEHRHAHN. All these subversive goings-on, the impudent mocking of people in high places—in the end you just couldn't put up with all that for another moment?

MOTES. I stayed because I thought, who knows, I might be able to do some good.

WEHRHAHN. Finally, though, you did give notice?

MOTES. Yes, Herr Baron, and I moved out.

WEHRHAHN. And now you've decided . . .

MOTES. I considered it my duty.

WEHRHAHN. . . . to inform the authorities.—I think that's very commendable.—So Dr. Fleischer used a certain kind of expression—we'll make a record of all this later, of course—a certain kind of expression in reference to an individual who stands in high esteem with all of us.

MOTES. He certainly did do that, Herr Baron.

WEHRHAHN. You would be prepared, if necessary, to state that under oath?

MOTES. I would.

WEHRHAHN. You may have to, you know.

MOTES. Yes sir, Herr Baron.

WEHRHAHN. It would be best, naturally, if we could get an additional witness.

MOTES. I could look around, Herr Baron. Only the man throws his money around so, that it's . . .

WEHRHAHN. Oh, wait a minute, here comes Krueger. I'd rather get him out of the way first. In any event, I'm most grateful for your energetic assistance. One really has to rely on the help of people like you if one is to accomplish anything these days.

KRUEGER. [*Enters hastily and in a state of excitement.*] Dear God! Dear God! Good day, Herr Justice.

WEHRHAHN. [*To* MOTES.] If you will excuse me a moment! [*Arrogantly inquiring of* KRUEGER.] And what do you want?

KRUEGER *is a small man, somewhat hard of hearing and almost seventy years old. He walks with a slight stoop, the left shoulder a little lower than the right. But he is otherwise still quite active and punctuates his remarks with vigorous gestures. He wears a fur cap, which he has removed in the courtroom, a brown winter overcoat, and a thick wool scarf around his neck.*

KRUEGER. [*Bursting with anger, shouts.*] I've been robbed, Herr Justice! [*Catching his breath, he wipes the perspiration from his forehead with a handkerchief and stares straight at the Justice's mouth, as people who are hard of hearing are wont to do.*]

WEHRHAHN. Robbed? Is that so!

KRUEGER. [*Already irritated.*] That's right, robbed! I've been robbed! Two cords of wood have been stolen from me.

WEHRHAHN. [*Looking around at those present with a half-smile on his face, he makes light of the situation.*] Nothing like that has happened around here of late.

KRUEGER. [*His hand at his ear.*] What? Nothing's happened?! Good God! Do you think I came here just for the fun of it?

WEHRHAHN. You don't have to get insulting. What's your name, by the way?

KRUEGER. [*Taken aback.*] What's my name?

WEHRHAHN. Yes, your name.

KRUEGER. You still don't know my name? I think we've already had the pleasure of meeting.

WEHRHAHN. Sorry. I just can't remember. It wouldn't make a bit of difference in this case, anyway.

KRUEGER. [*Resigning himself.*] My name is Krueger.

WEHRHAHN. A property owner, by any chance?

KRUEGER. [*Vehemently, ironically, and hastily.*] Indeed! Property owner and homeowner, too.

WEHRHAHN. Do you have any identification?

KRUEGER. I-Identification? My name is Krueger. There's no need to make a big issue of it. I've been living here for thirty years. Why, any child on the street can tell you who I am.

WEHRHAHN. I don't care how long you've been living here. All I want is some proof of your identity. Are you acquainted with this—gentleman, Herr Motes? [MOTES *half rises with an angry expression on his face.*] Ah, I understand. Please be seated. What do you say, Glasenapp?

GLASENAPP. Yes, sir. At your service. He's Herr Krueger all right, a property owner in this district.—

WEHRHAHN. Very well.—Now you say some wood has been stolen from you?

KRUEGER. Yes. Wood. Two cords of pine logs.

WEHRHAHN. Did you have the wood stored in your shed?

KRUEGER. [*Becoming vehement again.*] That's something else again! That's the substance of another complaint I have to make.

WEHRHAHN. [*Directs a quick and ironical laugh toward the others, then casually remarks.*] Another one already?

KRUEGER. What did you say?

WEHRHAHN. Nothing. Go ahead with your statement, if you please. So the wood wasn't in the shed?

KRUEGER. The wood was in the garden. In front of the garden, that is.

WEHRHAHN. In other words, it was on the street?

KRUEGER. It was on my property, outside the garden fence.

WEHRHAHN. So that anybody could get to it with no trouble?

KRUEGER. And that is precisely the fault of the servant girl. She was supposed to put the wood in the shed last night.

WEHRHAHN. And she forgot all about it?

KRUEGER. She refused to do it. And when I insisted, she ended up running away. I'll bring suit against her parents for this. I demand full damages.

WEHRHAHN. You may do as you please, but it probably won't get you very far. Now is there anyone you suspect of the theft?

KRUEGER. No. They're all a bunch of thieves around here.

WEHRHAHN. Please, try not to generalize. You really have to give me a lead of some kind.

KRUEGER. I'm not going to accuse someone just like that.

WEHRHAHN. Besides yourself, who lives at your house?

KRUEGER. Dr. Fleischer.

WEHRHAHN. [*Pretending that he is trying to recall something.*] Dr. Fleischer? Dr. Fleischer? Isn't that the man—? who . . .

KRUEGER. . . . is very learned. He is a very learned man, indeed.

WEHRHAHN. And the two of you are intimate friends?

KRUEGER. It's my business who my intimate friends are. That's got nothing to do with what we're talking about, it seems to me.

WEHRHAHN. How am I going to find out anything if you keep on like this? You have to give me a clue at least.

KRUEGER. I have to? Good God! I have to? Two cords of wood have been stolen from me. All I do is come to report the theft and—

WEHRHAHN. But you must have some idea of who did it. *Somebody* must have stolen the wood.

KRUEGER. Wha—? Yes—I didn't do it! That much we know for sure.

WEHRHAHN. But my dear man . . .

KRUEGER. Wha—? Krueger's the name.

WEHRHAHN. [*Giving in, apparently bored.*] Ah—well, Glasenapp, file a report on this incident.—Now what's this about the servant girl, Herr Krueger? The girl ran away?

KRUEGER. Yes, that's exactly what she did—right back to her parents.

WEHRHAHN. Do her parents live in this place?

KRUEGER. I'm not concerned with her face.

WEHRHAHN. I asked if the girl's parents lived here.

GLASENAPP. She's the daughter of Frau Wolff, the washerwoman.

WEHRHAHN. The Frau Wolff who's doing our laundry today, Glasenapp?

GLASENAPP. The same, Herr Justice.

WEHRHAHN. [*Shaking his head.*] Very strange indeed!—She's a hard-working, honest person. [*To* KRUEGER.] Is that right? Frau Wolff's daughter?

KRUEGER. I'm telling you: she's the daughter of Frau Wolff, the washerwoman.

WEHRHAHN. And did the girl come back?

KRUEGER. She hasn't come back yet.

WEHRHAHN. Then let's just call in Frau Wolff herself. Hey, Mitteldorf! You're not too tired, are you? Well, walk across the yard and tell Frau Wolff to come here right away. Please sit down, Herr Krueger.

KRUEGER. [*Sitting down, sighs.*] Lord, what a life!

WEHRHAHN. [*In an undertone to* MOTES *and* GLASENAPP.] I'm really curious to see what comes out of this. Something's not quite right here. I think very highly of Frau Wolff. That woman works like four men. My wife says that if she can't get Frau Wolff to do the washing, she has to hire two women in her place.—The opinions she expresses aren't half bad, either.

MOTES. But she wants to see her daughters on the stage . . .

WEHRHAHN. Oh, well, she may have a screw loose on that point. But her basic character is sound. What have you got there, Herr Motes?

MOTES. Wire snares. I'm taking them to Forester Seidel.

WEHRHAHN. Let me see one of those things. [*He holds one up and examines it closely.*] That would slowly choke an animal to death all right. [FRAU WOLFF *enters,* MITTELDORF *behind her. She is drying her hands, which are still wet from doing the wash.*]

FRAU WOLFF. [*Freely and cheerfully, with a quick glance at the snares.*] Here I am. What's up? What do you want me for?

WEHRHAHN. Frau Wolff, do you know this gentleman?

FRAU WOLFF. Well, which one? [*Pointing her finger at* KRUEGER.] Him there? That's Herr Krueger. I should know him, I think. Good morning, Herr Krueger.

WEHRHAHN. Your daughter works at Herr Krueger's house?

FRAU WOLFF. Who? My daughter? Sure! Leontine. [*To* KRUEGER.] I should say did work—she ran away from you, after all.

KRUEGER. [*Furiously.*] She certainly did!

WEHRHAHN. [*Interrupting.*] Now wait a minute.

FRAU WOLFF. What's been going on between you two?

WEHRHAHN. Frau Wolff, now listen to me. Your daughter must go back to the Kruegers at once.

FRAU WOLFF. Oh, no, we're going to keep her home now.

WEHRHAHN. That won't be as easy as you think. Herr Krueger has the right, if necessary, to ask the police for assistance. And if it came to that, we'd have to bring your daughter back by force.

FRAU WOLFF. It's just that my husband got this idea into his head that he won't let the girl leave no more. And once my husband gets something into his head . . . God, you men get so awful furious sometimes!

WEHRHAHN. Well, let that go for the time being, Frau Wolff. How long has your daughter been at home?

FRAU WOLFF. Since last night.

WEHRHAHN. Fine. Since last night. Seems she was supposed to carry firewood into the shed and refused to do it.

FRAU WOLFF. What? Refused! That girl don't refuse no work. I wouldn't let her get away with that!

WEHRHAHN. You heard what Frau Wolff said.

FRAU WOLFF. That girl's always been willing. If she ever refused to give me a hand just once, I'd . . .

KRUEGER. She refused to carry in the wood.

FRAU WOLFF. Why, sure, dragging in wood at half-past ten at night! Anybody that'd make a mere child do that—

WEHRHAHN. The important thing, Frau Wolff, is that the wood remained outside, and it was stolen last night. Now will—

KRUEGER. [*Can no longer contain himself.*] You are going to replace that wood, Frau Wolff!

WEHRHAHN. We'll decide on that, if you'll just wait.

KRUEGER. You are going to replace every last penny of it!

FRAU WOLFF. Is that so? You sure got a new way of doing things! Did I steal your blasted wood?

WEHRHAHN. Let the man calm down first, Frau Wolff.

FRAU WOLFF. Hey, if Herr Krueger starts with stuff like that, paying for wood and such things, he'll get nowhere with me. I'm always kind enough to folks. Nobody can complain about me. But if I got to—why not?—I'm going to speak my piece and no bones about it. I do my duty and that's all. There ain't a person in town that can say a word against me. But I ain't going to let nobody walk all over me!

WEHRHAHN. Please don't get all worked up, Frau Wolff. There's really no cause for it. Just keep calm, quite calm. After all, it isn't as if we don't know you. No one is going to deny that you are a decent, hard-working woman. Now let me hear what you have to say in answer to the plaintiff.

KRUEGER. She can't possibly have anything to say!

FRAU WOLFF. That's the limit, I tell you! Ain't the girl my daughter? And I got nothing to say in response? If it's a fool you take me for, you don't know Mother Wolff. I'm not going to keep quiet for nobody, not even for the Justice, much less for you, believe me!

WEHRHAHN. I can well understand that you're upset, Frau Wolff, but if you want to help matters, I'd advise you to remain calm.

FRAU WOLFF. Here I've been working for them people, doing their laundry for ten years. Always got along just fine with each other. And now all of a sudden it comes to this. I ain't going to work for you no more, and that's a fact!

KRUEGER. We don't need you. There are other women who can do the wash.

FRAU WOLFF. And you can get somebody else to sell the fruit and vegetables from your garden.

KRUEGER. Don't you worry, I can get rid of them.—Why didn't you just wave a stick at that girl of yours and chase her back to me?

FRAU WOLFF. I won't permit my daughter to be abused.

KRUEGER. And just who's been abusing your daughter, I'd like to know?

FRAU WOLFF. [*To* WEHRHAHN.] The girl's nothing but skin and bones.

KRUEGER. Then she shouldn't stay out dancing all night long.

FRAU WOLFF. She's so exhausted, she's been sleeping like a log all day.

WEHRHAHN. [*Past* FRAU WOLFF *to* KRUEGER.] Where did you buy that firewood, by the way?

FRAU WOLFF. Is this thing going to drag on much longer?

WEHRHAHN. Why do you ask, Frau Wolff?

FRAU WOLFF. On account of the laundry. Can't get that done if I'm standing around here all day.

WEHRHAHN. I can't worry about that, Frau Wolff.

FRAU WOLFF. Oh? And your wife? What'll she say? You better go talk to her about it, Herr Justice.

WEHRHAHN. We'll be finished in another minute, anyway.—Tell us now, Frau Wolff, since you know everyone in town, who do you think might have done it? Who possibly could have stolen that wood?

FRAU WOLFF. I really couldn't say, Herr Justice.

WEHRHAHN. And you didn't notice anything suspicious last night?

FRAU WOLFF. I wasn't even home last night. I had to go over to Treptow to buy geese.

WEHRHAHN. About what time was that?

FRAU WOLFF. A little after ten. Mitteldorf, he was there when we left.

WEHRHAHN. And you didn't run into a sleigh carrying wood?

FRAU WOLFF. No, not that I know of.

WEHRHAHN. What about you, Mitteldorf, did you notice anything?

MITTELDORF. [*After some thought.*] No, I didn't observe nothing suspicious.

WEHRHAHN. Of course not. I might have known. [*To* KRUEGER.] So where did you buy the wood?

KRUEGER. Why do you have to know that, I'd like to ask?

WEHRHAHN. I think you'd better leave that to me.

KRUEGER. From the Forestry Administration, naturally.

WEHRHAHN. That isn't so natural at all. There are private wood dealers, you know. I for one buy my wood at Sandberg's. Why shouldn't you buy yours from a dealer? More often than not, it's cheaper.

KRUEGER. [*Impatiently.*] I don't have any more time, Herr Justice.

WEHRHAHN. What's that about time? You haven't got time? Did you come to see me or the other way around? Am I taking up your time, or are you taking up mine?

KRUEGER. That's your job. That's what you're here for.

WEHRHAHN. Maybe I should shine your shoes while I'm at it.

KRUEGER. And maybe I'm the one who's the thief here. I won't stand for that tone of voice from you!

WEHRHAHN. Now look here . . . Don't you shout at me!

KRUEGER. You're the one who's shouting, sir!

WEHRHAHN. You're half deaf, I have to shout.

KRUEGER. You shout all the time. You shout at everyone who comes in here.

WEHRHAHN. I don't shout at anybody! Be quiet!

KRUEGER. You carry on around here as if you were God–knows–who. Pestering everybody in town.

WEHRHAHN. You haven't seen anything yet, just wait. I'll make you a good deal more uncomfortable before I'm through.

KRUEGER. That doesn't impress me one bit. You'd like to think you're important. Putting on airs all the time. Acting as if you were the king himself . . .

WEHRHAHN. I *am* king around here!

KRUEGER. [*Roaring with laughter.*] Ha, ha, ha, ha! Forget about that. As far as I'm concerned, you're nobody at all. You're just a plain old justice of the peace. And you still have to learn how to become that.

WEHRHAHN. Mister, if you don't be quiet at once . . .

KRUEGER. Then you'll have me arrested, is that it? I wouldn't advise you to do that. You might put yourself in a dangerous position.

WEHRHAHN. Dangerous position? [*To* MOTES.] Did you hear that? [*To* KRUEGER.] You can scheme and agitate all you want, you and your charming friends, but you won't get me to budge an inch.

KRUEGER. Good God! Scheme against you? I? You're much too unimportant for that. If you don't change your tactics, though, believe me, you'll cause so much trouble that you'll make things quite impossible for yourself.

WEHRHAHN. [*To* MOTES.] One must make allowances for his age, Herr Motes.

KRUEGER. I request that you take my deposition.

WEHRHAHN. [*Digging among his papers.*] Please be good enough to put it in writing yourself and send it in. I don't have the time just now. [*Dumbfounded,* KRUEGER *looks at* WEHRHAHN, *then turns violently and leaves the room without saying a word.*]

WEHRHAHN. [*After a moment of embarrassed silence.*] People come in here with such trifles!—Bah! [*To* FRAU WOLFF.] You can get back to your washing now. I tell you, my dear Motes, they really make it hard to do this job. If one weren't dedicated to one's work, one would be sorely tempted sometimes just to throw in the towel. So the watchword has to be: courage! Stay at your post! After all, what is it we're fighting for? The supreme welfare of the nation!—

Curtain

Act 3

FRAU WOLFF's *house, about eight o'clock in the morning. Water for coffee is boiling on the stove.* FRAU WOLFF *is sitting on a footstool and counting out money on the seat of a chair.* JULIUS *comes in carrying a dead rabbit.*

JULIUS. For God's sake, put that money away!

FRAU WOLFF. [*Absorbed in her calculations, gruffly.*] Oh, don't bother me! [*Silence.* JULIUS *throws the rabbit onto a stool; then, unable to make up his mind what to do next, he picks up one thing after another. Finally he starts polishing his boots. A hunting horn is heard in the distance.*]

JULIUS. [*Listens, then anxiously and excitedly.*] I told you to put that money away!

FRAU WOLFF. Leave me alone, Julius. Just let that stupid Motes blow his fool horn. He's out in the woods and ain't thinking about nothing.

JULIUS. You'll land us all in the slammer yet!

FRAU WOLFF. Stop talking nonsense. The girl's coming!

ADELHEID. [*Enters, just having awakened.*] Good morning, Mama!

FRAU WOLFF. Did you sleep well?

ADELHEID. You were out last night, weren't you?

FRAU WOLFF. You must have been dreaming.—Now get a move on and bring some wood in! Hurry up! [ADELHEID, *playing ball with an orange, goes toward the door.*]

FRAU WOLFF. Where did you get that orange?

ADELHEID. From Schoebel, the grocer. [*Exits.*]

FRAU WOLFF. You shouldn't take no presents from that fellow!— Come over here, Julius, and listen to me! There's fifty-nine talers. It's always the same with that Wulkow. He always has to cheat you out of one at least, 'cause he said he was going to give us sixty.—I'm putting the money in this bag, understand? Now go and get a shovel and dig a hole at the back of the goat shed. But make sure it's under the feed box where it's nice and dry. Then put the bag in the hole, you hear? And lay a flat stone over it. Don't be so long about it, neither.

JULIUS. I thought you were going to make a payment to Fischer.

FRAU WOLFF. Just go and do as I tell you. And don't take forever, you understand?

JULIUS. Don't make me mad, or you'll be sorry you did. I don't like the idea of that money staying around the house.

FRAU WOLFF. So what would you do with it?

JULIUS. Take it and give it to Fischer. You said we were going to pay him something with it.

FRAU WOLFF. You're the biggest fool I ever laid eyes on! If you didn't have me, you'd be lost.

JULIUS. Keep on yelling at me! That's right.

FRAU WOLFF. A person's got to yell at you, you're so dumb. If you didn't talk so stupid, I wouldn't have to yell at you. If we take that money to Fischer now, you just watch what happens to us.

JULIUS. That's what I've been saying all along! To hell with this whole business! What's the good if I've got to go to jail?

FRAU WOLFF. Now it's about time you shut up!

JULIUS. Could you scream a little louder?

FRAU WOLFF. I'd need another mouth for that. And you're already carrying on enough for the both of us . . . I don't for the life of me know why, about a little thing like this. Just look after yourself and don't worry about me. Did you throw the key in the river yet?

JULIUS. Have I been down to the river yet today?

FRAU WOLFF. Then it's about time you got going. Do you want them to find the key on you? [JULIUS *is about to go.*] No, wait a minute, Julius! Give me that key!

JULIUS. What are you going to do with it?

FRAU WOLFF. [*Taking the key.*] That's my business, not yours. [*She hides the key on her person, puts coffee into the grinder, and starts to grind.*] Go do what you have to in the shed now. Then you can come and have coffee.

JULIUS. [*Savoring the coffee.*] If only I'd known that before! [JULIUS *leaves.* ADELHEID *enters, carrying a large apronful of firewood.*]

FRAU WOLFF. Where did you get that wood?

ADELHEID. From that new pile of logs, where else?

FRAU WOLFF. You ain't supposed to touch that new wood.

ADELHEID. [*Drops the wood to the floor in front of the stove.*] It won't do no harm, Mama, if some of it gets used.

FRAU WOLFF. What do you know about it? What's the big idea? You who ain't even dry behind the ears yet!

ADELHEID. I know where it's from!

FRAU WOLFF. What do you mean, girl?

ADELHEID. I mean the wood.

FRAU WOLFF. Don't talk rubbish. We bought that wood at an auction.

ADELHEID. [*Playing ball with her orange.*] Oh, sure. If only that was true! You stole it.

FRAU WOLFF. What did you say?

ADELHEID. You stole it. That's the wood from Krueger's, Mama. Leontine told me so.

FRAU WOLFF. [*Boxes her ears.*] That's what I got to say to that! We ain't no thieves. Now go and do your homework. And do it right, I tell you. I'll come in later to look at it.

ADELHEID. [*Goes into the other room.*] I thought I could go skating.

FRAU WOLFF. And your confirmation class, have you forgotten all about that?

ADELHEID. That's not till Tuesday.

FRAU WOLFF. It's tomorrow, thank you. You go and study your Bible verses. I'll come in later and hear you say them.

ADELHEID. [*Can be heard yawning loudly in the other room; then she says.*] Jesus said to his disciples, whoever has no spoon shall eat with his fingers. [JULIUS *enters.*]

FRAU WOLFF. Well, did you do the job proper, Julius?

JULIUS. If you don't like the way I did it, do it yourself.

FRAU WOLFF. God knows, that would be the best way of doing things. [*She pours coffee both for* JULIUS *and herself and puts the cups, along with bread and butter, on a wooden chair.*] Here, drink your coffee.

JULIUS. [*Sitting down and cutting himself some bread.*] I sure hope Wulkow got away all right.

FRAU WOLFF. Why wouldn't he, with the thaw we're having?

JULIUS. You call this a thaw?

FRAU WOLFF. Even if it is freezing a bit, he ain't going to get stuck. I'll bet he's quite a ways up the canal by now.

JULIUS. I only hope he ain't still down by the bridge.

FRAU WOLFF. I don't really care where he is.

JULIUS. That Wulkow, one of these days he's going to get himself into a hell of a mess, you can take it from me.

FRAU WOLFF. That's his business, not ours!

JULIUS. Trouble is, we're all in this together. Just let them find that fur coat on his boat.

FRAU WOLFF. Fur coat? What are you talking about?

JULIUS. Krueger's fur coat, what do you think?

FRAU WOLFF. Stop talking such trash, you understand? You'll put your foot in your mouth yet, gabbing about everybody else's business!

JULIUS. But this concerns me, too.

FRAU WOLFF. The hell it does! It's none of your business. It's my affair, not yours. You ain't even a man; an old woman, that's what you are.—Here's some money for you, now get out of my way. Go on over to Fiebig's and drink some whiskey. Have a fine time of it the whole day, for all I care. [*Knocking at the door.*] Come in! Come in, whoever it is.

DR. FLEISCHER *enters with his five-year-old son. Fleischer is twenty-seven years old, has coal-black hair, a beard and mustache that are just as black, deep-set eyes, and a voice that is soft as a rule. He wears a suit cut in the style of the "reform clothing" advocated by Jäger. He displays at every moment a touching concern for his child.*

FRAU WOLFF. [*Jubilantly.*] Oh, my, Philipp's come to visit us! That's real nice. That means a lot to me, I can tell you. [*She takes the child and removes his overcoat.*] Come on now, take off your coat. It's warm in here—you won't freeze.

FLEISCHER. [*Anxiously.*] Frau Wolff, I think there's a draft. I'm positive there's one.

FRAU WOLFF. Oh, he ain't so frail as all that. A little draft won't hurt the boy.

FLEISCHER. But it will, I assure you. You have no idea. That boy'll catch cold in a second. Keep moving, Philipp. Keep moving around. [PHILIPP *shrugs his shoulders in defiance and screams.*]

FLEISCHER. Yes, Philipp, you see, otherwise you'll get sick. You just need to walk up and down slowly.

PHILIPP. [*Stubbornly.*] But I don't want to!

FRAU WOLFF. Oh, let him be.

FLEISCHER. Well, all right. Good morning, Frau Wolff.

FRAU WOLFF. Good morning, Dr. Fleischer. I'm glad to see you here again.

FLEISCHER. Good morning, Herr Wolff.

JULIUS. And a very good morning to you, Herr Fleischer.

FRAU WOLFF. Well, make yourself at home. Have a seat.

FLEISCHER. We really can't stay long.

FRAU WOLFF. Having such nice visitors first thing in the morning, I know we're going to have a good day today. [*Kneeling in front of the boy.*] Ain't that so, little fellow? You're going to bring us luck, right?

PHILIPP. [*Excitedly.*] I've been to the zoo, and I saw storks, and they bit each other with their golden bills.

FRAU WOLFF. No, not really! You're telling me stories. [*Hugging and kissing the boy.*] Boy, oh boy, I could just eat you. Herr Fleischer, I'm keeping this boy. He's my boy. You're my boy, ain't you? How's your mommy, huh?

PHILIPP. She's fine, and she says hello, and she wants to know will you come and do the laundry tomorrow morning.

FRAU WOLFF. Well, just listen to that. What a boy. He can already deliver messages. [*To* FLEISCHER.] Won't you sit down a bit?

FLEISCHER. The boy's been nagging me to take him boating. Do you think it will be all right?

FRAU WOLFF. Why, sure. There's no ice on the Spree. The girl can row you two around a little.

FLEISCHER. He won't give me a moment's peace about it. He just got it into his head that he has to ride in a boat.

ADELHEID. [*Appearing in the door of the other room, beckons to* PHILIPP.] Come, Philipp, I'll show you something nice. [PHILIPP *lets out a scream in defiance.*]

FLEISCHER. Now, Philipp, don't be naughty!

ADELHEID. There, look at the pretty orange! [*Beaming,* PHILIPP *takes a few steps toward* ADELHEID.]

FLEISCHER. Run along then, but no begging!

ADELHEID. Come on, we'll eat it together. [*She takes a few steps toward the child, grabs him by the hand, holds the orange in front of him with the other hand, and both go, united, into the other room.*]

FRAU WOLFF. [*Following the boy with her eyes.*] Ah, that boy, I could just sit and look at him all day long. I don't know, when I see a boy like that . . .—[*She wipes her eyes with a corner of her apron.*]—I just feel like crying.

FLEISCHER. Didn't you ever have a son?

FRAU WOLFF. Yes, I did. But what good does it do me now? I can't bring him back to life.—You see—things like that—that's life. [*A pause.*]

FLEISCHER. One can't be careful enough with children.

FRAU WOLFF. You can be as careful as you like—what's going to happen is going to happen. [*Shaking her head. Pause.*] What trouble did you have with Herr Motes?

FLEISCHER. I? None at all. What trouble am I supposed to have had with him?

FRAU WOLFF. Oh, nothing special.—

FLEISCHER. How old is your daughter now?

FRAU WOLFF. She'll be finishing school come Easter. Why? Would you like her to go to work for you, Herr Fleischer? I wouldn't mind one bit letting you have her.

FLEISCHER. Why not? That wouldn't be a bad idea at all.

FRAU WOLFF. She's grown to be a strong girl. Even if she is still young, I tell you, she can work as hard as anybody. And mind you: sometimes she's a little bitch, sometimes she just don't know what's good for her. But dumb she ain't. I think she's even got genius in her.

FLEISCHER. Hm, that may well be.

FRAU WOLFF. Just let her recite something for you once—a poem or what not. I can tell you, Doctor, it'll give you goose bumps. You call her over some time when you got company from Berlin. I know you always got all kinds of writers coming to see you. She ain't bashful, either; she'll start right in. She recites so beautiful!—[*Her tone changes.*] Now I'd like to give you some good advice. You won't take offense, though, will you?

FLEISCHER. I never take offense at good advice.

FRAU WOLFF. First thing, then: don't keep giving away so much stuff! Nobody thanks you for it. Ingratitude's all you get.

FLEISCHER. But I don't give very much away, Frau Wolff.

FRAU WOLFF. Never mind, I know. And don't talk so much—it just makes people suspicious. Right away they say: he's a democrat. Always be real careful about what you say.

FLEISCHER. How am I to take that, Frau Wolff?

FRAU WOLFF. You can take it any way you want to. But you got to be very careful when it comes to talking, or you'll be sitting in the clink before you know it.

FLEISCHER. [*Turns pale.*] Now don't talk nonsense, Frau Wolff.

FRAU WOLFF. No, no, I say this in all seriousness.—And be careful around that man, whatever you do.

FLEISCHER. Around what man?

FRAU WOLFF. The same one we were talking about a little while ago.

FLEISCHER. Motes, you mean?

FRAU WOLFF. I ain't mentioning no names. You had some trouble with him, didn't you?

FLEISCHER. I have nothing to do with him anymore.

FRAU WOLFF. You see? Just what I thought!

FLEISCHER. But nobody can blame me for that, Frau Wolff!

FRAU WOLFF. That's not what I'm blaming you for.

FLEISCHER. It would be a fine thing, wouldn't it, to associate with a swindler, a notorious swindler!

FRAU WOLFF. The man is a swindler. You're right there.

FLEISCHER. Now he's moved to Frau Dreier's—Cake-Dreier, they call her. That poor woman had better watch out. Whatever she has, she'll lose it for sure. With a fellow like that . . . real jailbird material . . .

FRAU WOLFF. Sometimes, you know, he says things . . .

FLEISCHER. Is that right?! About me? I'm curious.

FRAU WOLFF. It seems you said something bad about some high-up person or other.

FLEISCHER. Hm. You don't have anything more specific than that, do you?

FRAU WOLFF. Him and Wehrhahn, they put their heads together an awful lot—that's for sure. But I tell you what. Why don't you go and see Mother Dreier? The old hag already smells a rat. First they talk to you so nice and sweet, then they want you to do anything they say.

FLEISCHER. Oh, for heaven's sake! This is all a bunch of foolishness.

FRAU WOLFF. You just get yourself over to the Dreier woman. It can't do no harm. She told me some story . . . Seems Motes tried to get her to perjure herself. If that's true, you'd have that fellow right where you wanted him, wouldn't you?

FLEISCHER. I could go over there, I suppose. But then, I don't really care. What's the world coming to if a fellow like that . . . just let him try!—Philipp, Philipp! Where are you? We have to go.

ADELHEID'S VOICE. Oh, but we were looking at such pretty pictures.

FLEISCHER. By the way, what do you think of that other business?

FRAU WOLFF. What other business?

FLEISCHER. You mean you haven't heard yet?

FRAU WOLFF. [Uneasily.] No, like I told you.—[Impatiently.] Hurry and go, Julius, so you'll be back in time for lunch. [To FLEISCHER.] We killed a rabbit this morning. Ain't you ready yet, Julius?

JULIUS. Just let me find my cap, will you?

FRAU WOLFF. I can't stand it when people take so long to do something. Always figuring they can put off till tomorrow what they don't do today. With me, things got to move!

FLEISCHER. Last night at Krueger's there was . . .

FRAU WOLFF. That's enough! Don't mention that man's name to

me! I'm so damn mad at him. He hurt my feelings something awful. The way the both of us used to get along, and then he up and says such bad things about me in front of all them people. [*To* JULIUS.] Well, are you going or not?

JULIUS. I'm going already; just keep your shirt on. I bid you good morning, Herr Fleischer.

FLEISCHER. Good-bye, Herr Wolff. [JULIUS *leaves.*]

FRAU WOLFF. Now, as I was saying—

FLEISCHER. Yes, you two had quite a fight about the firewood that was stolen from him, didn't you? He's been sorry about it ever since.

FRAU WOLFF. Him sorry!

FLEISCHER. No, it's true, Mother Wolff. And after this new business, he's even more sorry. He really thinks very highly of you. It would be best if the two of you made up.

FRAU WOLFF. He could have come to me first and talked reasonable, but no, he has to run to the police right away!

FLEISCHER. That poor old couple has been getting the worst of it lately. First the wood a week ago, and now the fur coat . . .

FRAU WOLFF. What? O.K., out with the big news.

FLEISCHER. There's been another robbery at Krueger's.

FRAU WOLFF. Robbery? No fooling!

FLEISCHER. Yes, and a brand-new fur coat this time.

FRAU WOLFF. You want to know something? I'm not going to stay in this place much longer. There must be a gang of thieves around here! Why, it just ain't safe no more! Tch, tch. Some people! It's hard to believe.

FLEISCHER. You can imagine the fuss that this has created.

FRAU WOLFF. You can't blame folks, can you?

FLEISCHER. And pretty expensive that coat was, too—mink, I believe.

FRAU WOLFF. Is that anything like beaver, Herr Fleischer?

FLEISCHER. It may well have been beaver, for all I know. They were quite proud of it.—And still, I couldn't help laughing to myself. When something like that happens, it's always just a bit comical.

FRAU WOLFF. You're being really cruel, Herr Fleischer. Such a thing is nothing to laugh about.

FLEISCHER. You mustn't think I don't feel sorry for the Kruegers.

FRAU WOLFF. What kind of person could do a thing like that? I just can't get it through my head . . . how someone goes and takes things that belong to other people!—No, I'd rather work till I drop.

FLEISCHER. Do you think you might sort of keep your ears open a little? I believe the fur coat is still in this area.

FRAU WOLFF. You suspect anybody?

FLEISCHER. There's a woman . . . she did the cleaning at Krueger's.

FRAU WOLFF. Frau Mueller?

FLEISCHER. Is that the one with the big family?

FRAU WOLFF. She has a big family, all right, but steal . . . no. Pilfer a little, yes!

FLEISCHER. Krueger's fired her, of course.

FRAU WOLFF. But it's got to come out who the real thief is, for goodness' sake. Otherwise the devil himself has a hand in the whole thing. Oh, if only I was Justice of the Peace! That man is really dumb—the dumbest! I can see more with my eyes closed than he can with both eyes wide open and that monocle over one of them to boot.

FLEISCHER. I almost believe you could.

FRAU WOLFF. I can tell you that, if I had to, I could steal the chair out from under his behind.

FLEISCHER. [*Laughs, gets up, and calls into the other room.*] Come on, Philipp. Come, we have to go now. Good-bye, Mother Wolff.

FRAU WOLFF. Put something on, Adelheid, and go take them for a little boat ride.

ADELHEID. [*Enters, buttoning the last buttons on her coat; she leads* PHILIPP *by the hand.*] I'm all ready. [*To* PHILIPP.] Come now and I'll carry you in my arms.

FLEISCHER. [*Worried, helping the boy on with his coat.*] Let's bundle him up well. He catches cold so easily. And it's going to be windy out on the river.

ADELHEID. I'll go ahead and get the boat ready.

FRAU WOLFF. How's your health these days?

FLEISCHER. Much better since I've been living out here.

ADELHEID. [*Calling from the door.*] Mama, Herr Krueger's coming.

FRAU WOLFF. Who?

ADELHEID. Herr Krueger.

FRAU WOLFF. It ain't possible!

FLEISCHER. Oh, that's right, he said he was going to drop by to see you this morning. [*Exits.*]

FRAU WOLFF. [*Glancing quickly at the pile of wood, starts energetically clearing it away.*] Come on, girl, help me get this wood out of sight.

ADELHEID. But why, Mama? Oh. On account of Herr Krueger.

FRAU WOLFF. Why else, you silly goose! Is this the way a proper house should look? And especially on a Sunday morning? What will Herr Krueger think of us? [KRUEGER *appears, sweating and puffing.* FRAU WOLFF *calls out to him.*] Don't look around, Herr Krueger. The house is a terrible mess.

KRUEGER. [*Blurts out.*] Good morning! Good morning! Don't worry about that. You go out to work all week long, so your house can't very well be spic and span on Sunday. You're a good woman, Frau Wolff. An honest woman. I say let's just forget about what happened between us.

FRAU WOLFF. [*So touched that at times she has to wipe her eyes with the corner of her apron.*] I never had nothing against you. I always liked working for you. But then you got so mad, I couldn't help getting mad right back. I sure am sorry about it, though.

KRUEGER. Come on back then and wash for us. Where's your daughter Leontine?

FRAU WOLFF. She went to take some cabbage over to the postmaster.

KRUEGER. Send the girl back to us. We'll give her thirty talers instead of the twenty she's been getting. We've always been satisfied with her. Let's forgive and forget everything. [*He extends his hand and* FRAU WOLFF *shakes it.*]

FRAU WOLFF. We could have done without this whole affair. The girl is still a foolish child, I'm afraid. Us old folks, we've always gotten along just fine.

KRUEGER. Then the matter is settled! [*Catching his breath.*] Well, my mind's at rest about that, anyhow. Now—tell me something. You know what's happened to me this time. What do you think about it?

FRAU WOLFF. Oh, well, you know . . . what is there to say about such a thing?

KRUEGER. And here we have this Herr von Wehrhahn—harassing honest citizens, playing dirty tricks, making a general nuisance of himself. What that man doesn't stick his nose into!

FRAU WOLFF. He sticks it everywhere but where it belongs.

KRUEGER. I'm on my way to his court right now to make a report, and I'm not going to quit until this thing is cleared up.

FRAU WOLFF. Don't you let the matter rest, Herr Krueger.

KRUEGER. Frau Wolff, if I have to turn this town upside down, I'm going to get my fur coat back!

FRAU WOLFF. What this place needs is a good cleaning out. We won't get no peace here until then. They're liable to steal the roof from over your head if you're not careful!

KRUEGER. For heaven's sake, just think! Two thefts in two weeks!

Two cords of wood, just like the stuff you got there. [*He picks up a piece of wood.*] Good, expensive wood, Frau Wolff.

FRAU WOLFF. Oh, I get so mad I could scream. We got some kind of gang among us, and it's a damn shame, that's what it is! What next!

KRUEGER. [*Furiously waving the piece of wood in the air.*] And if I have to spend a thousand talers to do it, I'll find those thieves! They'll all wind up in jail!

FRAU WOLFF. What a relief that would be. Honest to God!

Curtain

Act 4

The courtroom of the Justice of the Peace. GLASENAPP *sits at his desk.* FRAU WOLFF *and* ADELHEID *are waiting for the* JUSTICE. ADELHEID *holds in her lap a small package wrapped in linen.*

FRAU WOLFF. He's taking his time again today.

GLASENAPP. [*Writing.*] Patience! Patience!

FRAU WOLFF. Well, if he's going to be so late again, then he won't have no time for us today, neither.

GLASENAPP. Good God! You and your trifles! There are a lot more important things we have to do.

FRAU WOLFF. Humph, fine things they are, too, I bet.

GLASENAPP. That's no way to talk! It won't get you anywhere here!

FRAU WOLFF. Go ahead and put on a few more airs. The girl was sent here by Krueger.

GLASENAPP. That fur coat business again, I suppose?

FRAU WOLFF. That's right. What of it?

GLASENAPP. The old geezer's really got himself something to talk about this time. Now he can stir things up to his heart's content, the bowlegged nuisance.

FRAU WOLFF. Nuisance yourself! Better see that you find out something about this business!

MITTELDORF. [*Appears in the door.*] He wants you to come right over, Glasenapp. Wants to ask you something, the Justice does.

GLASENAPP. One interruption after another. [*Throws down his pen and goes out.*]

FRAU WOLFF. Good morning, Mitteldorf.

MITTELDORF. Good morning!

FRAU WOLFF. What's keeping the Justice so long?

MITTELDORF. He's writing enough to fill up a book, Mother Wolff. Important stuff, too, I can tell you. [*Confidentially.*] You know, something's in the air.—What, I don't know yet. But there's something, that's for sure . . . Just pay attention and you'll find out. There's going to be some commotion, and when it starts, Mother Wolff, look out. No, like I said, I don't know nothing about it. It's all new to me. Everything's new. And I can never figure out new developments. But something's got to give. It can't go on like this. The whole place has got to be cleaned up. I'm just not in the know anymore. The Justice we used to have, the one who died—why, he was a bum compared with this one. Oh, I could tell you some stories, but I ain't got no time. The baron's waiting for me. [*He starts to leave but, on reaching the door, he turns and says.*] There's going to be some commotion, Mother Wolff, you can take my word for it! [*Exits.*]

FRAU WOLFF. Well, if he ain't gone nuts. [*Pause.*]

ADELHEID. What am I supposed to say? I forgot.

FRAU WOLFF. What did you say to Herr Krueger?

ADELHEID. Why, that I found this here package.

FRAU WOLFF. Right. You don't need to say more than that, neither. Be firm and speak up. You sure know how to wag your tongue pretty good most of the time.

WULKOW. [*Enters.*] Good morning, everybody!

FRAU WOLFF. [*Stares at* WULKOW; *she is speechless for a moment, then.*] I can't believe it! Wulkow, are you out of your mind? What do you think you're doing here?

WULKOW. Er, my wife just had a baby . . .

FRAU WOLFF. What did she have?

WULKOW. A little girl. So I had to come here and get her registered.

FRAU WOLFF. And I thought you'd be way up the canal by now.

WULKOW. I wouldn't mind one bit if I was, Frau Wolff! If I had my way, that's exactly where I'd be. I got away quick enough. But when I come to the locks, there was no getting any further on account of the ice. I waited and waited for the Spree to open up. Two days and two nights I laid there till finally this thing with my wife started. Then there was nothing I could do but turn back.

FRAU WOLFF. So you got your boat down by the bridge again?

WULKOW. Like always. Where else would I put it?

FRAU WOLFF. Well, stay away from me then.

WULKOW. I only hope nobody suspects nothing yet.

FRAU WOLFF. [*To* ADELHEID.] Go get ten pfennigs' worth of thread at the store.

ADELHEID. I'll get it on the way home.

FRAU WOLFF. You'll get it now, and don't talk back!

ADELHEID. I ain't a baby no more, you know. [*Exits.*]

FRAU WOLFF. So you were laid up at the locks, huh?

WULKOW. For two whole days, like I told you.

FRAU WOLFF. [*Suddenly.*] Why didn't you get a picture frame put around it, smart guy? Wearing that fur coat in broad daylight!

WULKOW. Me? Wearing the coat?

FRAU WOLFF. Yes, you were wearing it, and in broad daylight, too. For the whole place to see what a nice new fur coat you got.

WULKOW. That was way out where the canal runs through the middle of the fields.

FRAU WOLFF. It was at the locks—a quarter of an hour from our house! My girl saw you there. She was out rowing Dr. Fleischer around, and he got suspicious right away.

WULKOW. I don't know nothing about that. It's no concern of mine. [*Someone is heard approaching.*]

FRAU WOLFF. Sh! Be careful now, Wulkow.

GLASENAPP. [*Enters hurriedly, somewhat in the manner of the* JUSTICE; *in an arrogant tone, he asks* WULKOW.] And what do you want?

WEHRHAHN. [*Still outside.*] What is it, girl? You've come to see me? All right, go on in. [WEHRHAHN *lets* ADELHEID *enter ahead of him and then follows.*] I don't have much time today, though. Ah, yes, you're Frau Wolff's little girl, aren't you? Well, sit down then. What do you have there?

ADELHEID. I got this package . . .

WEHRHAHN. Wait just a moment . . . [*To* WULKOW.] And what do you want?

WULKOW. I'd like to report a birth.

WEHRHAHN. Something for the public registry. Get the books, Glasenapp. But first I want to attend to this other matter. [*To* FRAU WOLFF.] What's your daughter's problem? Did Krueger slap her again?

FRAU WOLFF. No, he ain't gone that far.

WEHRHAHN. What's the trouble, then?

FRAU WOLFF. It's about this here package . . .

WEHRHAHN. [*To* GLASENAPP.] Hasn't Motes come yet?

GLASENAPP. No, not yet.

WEHRHAHN. I can't understand that! Well now, girl, what is it?

GLASENAPP. It's about the stolen fur coat, Herr Justice.

WEHRHAHN. Oh, yes. I can't possibly attend to that today. No one can do everything at once! [*To* FRAU WOLFF.] She can tell me about it tomorrow.

FRAU WOLFF. She's already tried to talk to you twice.

WEHRHAHN. Then she can try for a third time in the morning.

FRAU WOLFF. But Herr Krueger won't let her have no peace no more.

WEHRHAHN. What does Krueger have to do with this?

FRAU WOLFF. The girl went to him with the package.

WEHRHAHN. What kind of wrapping is that, anyway? Let me see the thing.

FRAU WOLFF. It's connected in some way with that fur coat business. I mean, that's what Herr Krueger thinks.

WEHRHAHN. Well, what's inside it?

FRAU WOLFF. A green vest of Herr Krueger's.

WEHRHAHN. And you found this?

ADELHEID. Yes, I found it, Herr Justice!

WEHRHAHN. Where did you find it?

ADELHEID. It was when I was walking to the train station with Mama. I was just walking along, and there . . .

WEHRHAHN. That'll do for now. [To FRAU WOLFF.] Leave the package here for the time being, and we'll get back to it tomorrow.

FRAU WOLFF. Oh, that's fine with me, but . . .

WEHRHAHN. It's not fine with somebody else?

FRAU WOLFF. It's just that Herr Krueger is so anxious about this.

WEHRHAHN. Herr Krueger, Herr Krueger!—I don't care one bit what he thinks. That man is getting to be a real pest. You simply can't hurry matters like this. Hasn't he put up a reward, and haven't we put an official notice about it in the paper?

GLASENAPP. The way he figures, we're still not doing enough.

WEHRHAHN. What does that mean: not doing enough? We took down the facts of the case. He suspected his cleaning woman, and we searched her house. What more does he want? The man should just hold his tongue. Now, as I said, I'll have time for you tomorrow.

FRAU WOLFF. It's all the same to us. We'll be back.

WEHRHAHN. Very well then, tomorrow morning.

FRAU WOLFF. Good-bye.

ADELHEID. [Curtsies.] Good-bye. [FRAU WOLFF and ADELHEID leave.]

WEHRHAHN. [Leafing through his files, to GLASENAPP.] I'm really curious to see what will come of this. Herr Motes now says he can produce a witness. He claims that Frau Dreier, the old cake lady, was present once when Fleischer made one of his disrespectful remarks. Tell me, how old is this Dreier woman?

GLASENAPP. Somewhere around seventy, Herr Justice.

WEHRHAHN. A bit touched in the head, you think?

GLASENAPP. Well, that depends on how you look at it. I think she's still got her wits about her.

WEHRHAHN. I can't tell you, Glasenapp, what great satisfaction it would give me to really clamp down hard on this bunch. Just so they get an idea of the kind of man they're dealing with. Who wasn't present at the Kaiser's birthday celebration? Fleischer, of course. That man is capable of absolutely anything, I don't care how innocent the expression on his face. We know them, these wolves in sheep's clothing. They wouldn't hurt a fly, but if they feel they have to, those bastards will blow up entire cities. They're going to find the going a little rough around here, though!

MOTES. [*Enters.*] Your servant!

WEHRHAHN. Well, how do things stand?

MOTES. Frau Dreier will be here about eleven o'clock.

WEHRHAHN. This affair will create quite a stir; people are going to make a good deal of noise. They'll say, "Wehrhahn sticks his nose everywhere." Well, thank God, I'm ready for them. After all, I'm not here to have a good time. And my superiors didn't put me in this position for their private amusement. These people think that a Justice of the Peace is nothing more than a glorified jailer. In that case they can let somebody else try to do my job. But the gentlemen who appointed me know very well what my qualifications are. They also know how seriously I take my work; I look upon this office as a sacred calling. [*Pause.*] The report for the state's attorney is ready. If I send it off by noon today, a warrant for Fleischer's arrest will be here the day after tomorrow.

MOTES. They'll really come down on me now.

WEHRHAHN. You know, my uncle is a chamberlain. I'll speak to him about you. Confound it all! Here comes Fleischer! What does he want? Did he smell a rat by any chance? [*There is knocking at the door.* WEHRHAHN *shouts.*] Come in!

FLEISCHER. [*Enters, pale and excited.*] Good morning! [*He receives no answer.*] I would like to make a report in connection with the recent theft.

WEHRHAHN. [*With his most penetrating official stare.*] You are Dr. Joseph Fleischer?

FLEISCHER. That's right. My name is Joseph Fleischer.

WEHRHAHN. And you want to make a report?

FLEISCHER. Yes, with your permission. I have observed something that may help you to track down the fur coat thief.

WEHRHAHN. [*Drums on the table with his fingers and looks around at the others with an expression of mock surprise, causing them to smile; indifferently.*] Now then, what have you observed that's so terribly important?

FLEISCHER. Of course, if you have decided beforehand not to place any value on my information, I should prefer . . .

WEHRHAHN. [*Quickly, arrogantly.*] What would you prefer?

FLEISCHER. I should prefer to remain silent.

WEHRHAHN. [*Turns silently, as if he did not understand, to* MOTES; *then, changing his tone, he says offhandedly.*] My time is somewhat in demand. I'll have to ask you to be brief.

FLEISCHER. My time is also taken up. Nevertheless I considered it my duty . . .

WEHRHAHN. [*Interrupting him.*] You considered it your duty. Very good. Now just tell me what you know.

FLEISCHER. [*Controlling himself.*] Yesterday I went boating. I got the boat from Frau Wolff. Her daughter sat up front and did the rowing.

WEHRHAHN. Is that really essential to this case?

FLEISCHER. It certainly is—in my opinion.

WEHRHAHN. [*Impatiently drumming with his fingers.*] All right, all right! Let's get on with it.

FLEISCHER. We rode into the vicinity of the locks. A river barge was laid up there. The ice was pretty thick at that point, so the barge probably got stuck.

WEHRHAHN. Hm, is that so! Well, that is of little interest to us. What's the point of this story?

FLEISCHER. [*Restraining himself with great effort.*] I must confess that this method . . . Here I am coming to you of my own free will, to volunteer my services to the authorities . . .

GLASENAPP. [*Impertinently.*] The Justice doesn't have the time. As few words as possible, please. Make it short and sweet.

WEHRHAHN. [*Vehemently.*] Get to the point! The point! What is it you want?

FLEISCHER. [*Controlling himself.*] I am eager to see this matter cleared up. And in the interest of old Herr Krueger, I shall . . .

WEHRHAHN. [*Yawning, uninterested.*] The sun's blinding me. Pull down the shades.

FLEISCHER. There was an old bargeman on that boat—probably the owner.

WEHRHAHN. [*Yawning, as before.*] Yes, most likely.

FLEISCHER. This man sat on deck wearing a fur coat, which from a distance looked like beaver.

WEHRHAHN. [*As before.*] Maybe it was marten.

FLEISCHER. We came as close to him as we could go so that I'd be able to get a good look. He was a sorry-looking, dirty fellow, and that fur coat just didn't look as if it had been made for him. It was brand-new, too . . .

WEHRHAHN. [*Appears to come to his senses.*] I'm listening, I'm listening.—Well? And then? What else?

FLEISCHER. What else? That's all.

WEHRHAHN. [*Thoroughly alert by now.*] I thought you wanted to report something. You said it was very important.

FLEISCHER. I have told you what I came to tell you.

WEHRHAHN. You have told us a story about a bargeman who was wearing a fur coat. Now it so happens that bargemen sometimes wear such coats. That's no great revelation.

FLEISCHER. You may think what you wish about it. Under the circumstances, I have no more to say. [*Exits.*]

WEHRHAHN. Have you ever seen anything like it? On top of everything, the man is hopelessly stupid. A bargeman is wearing a fur coat. So what? Has this guy suddenly gone crazy? I own a beaver coat myself. Surely that doesn't make me a thief by any stretch of the imagination.—[*To* MITTELDORF, *who is standing at the door.*] Confound it! What is it now? Isn't there going to be a moment's peace today? Don't let anyone else in! Herr Motes, I wonder if you would be good enough to go over to my private residence. We'll be able to talk there without being disturbed.— Here comes Krueger for the umpteenth time. He's got ants in his pants, that man. If he continues to bother me, I'll throw the old fool out on his ear one of these days! [KRUEGER *appears in the doorway, accompanied by* FLEISCHER *and* FRAU WOLFF.]

MITTELDORF. [*To* KRUEGER.] You can't see the Justice now, Herr Krueger.

KRUEGER. Oh no? Can't see him, indeed! Never mind such talk. [*To the others.*] In we go. Follow me. I'll find out about this. [*All three enter,* KRUEGER *leading the way.*]

WEHRHAHN. A little more quiet, please! Can't you see that I'm busy?

KRUEGER. Go right ahead. We can wait. And when you get through you'll be busy with us.

WEHRHAHN. [*To* MOTES.] Please, then, wait at my private residence. And if you should run into Frau Dreier, tell her I'd prefer to question her there, too. You can see for yourself—it's impossible to get anything done here.

KRUEGER. [*Pointing to* FLEISCHER.] This gentleman also has information from Frau Dreier. And he can even present it in written form.

MOTES. Your servant, sir. I had best take my leave. [*Exits.*]

KRUEGER. It's a good thing he took his leave.

WEHRHAHN. You will kindly keep your observations to yourself.

KRUEGER. I'll say even more: that man is a swindler!

WEHRHAHN. [*Pretends not to have heard the remark; to* WULKOW.] Now then, what is it? I'll take care of you first. Oh, yes. The books, Glasenapp!—No, wait a minute. I want to get rid of him first. [*To* KRUEGER.] I'll attend to your business first.

KRUEGER. Yes, I would most urgently ask you to do so.

WEHRHAHN. Let's drop the "most urgently," if you don't mind. Now what do you request?

KRUEGER. Request, nothing! I don't want to request a thing. I'm here to demand what I consider my right.

WEHRHAHN. And what right would that be?

KRUEGER. My proper right, Herr Justice. The right that I have as the victim of a theft to obtain the assistance of the authorities in recovering my stolen property.

WEHRHAHN. Have you been refused such assistance?

KRUEGER. Oh, no, not at all. You would never do that, of course. But I notice that nothing has happened yet! No progress has been made in the case.

WEHRHAHN. Do you think that crimes are solved just like that?

KRUEGER. No, I don't think anything of the kind, Herr Justice. I probably wouldn't have come here if I did. But I have definite evidence that you're not doing anything about my case.

WEHRHAHN. I think I would be amply justified in cutting you short right now. It really goes beyond the extent of my duties to listen to any more of this sort of thing. For the time being, however, you may continue.

KRUEGER. You can't cut me short, anyway. As a Prussian citizen I have certain rights. And even if you cut me short here, there are other places where I could speak out. I repeat: you're not doing a thing about my case.

WEHRHAHN. [*Seemingly perturbed.*] All right, go ahead and prove it.

KRUEGER. [*Pointing to* FRAU WOLFF *and her daughter.*] This woman here came to see you because her daughter had found something. Although she is a poor woman and has to work, Herr Justice, she managed to take the trouble. You sent her away once before, and today she came again, and . . .

FRAU WOLFF. But he didn't have no time, the Justice.

WEHRHAHN. Go on, please!

KRUEGER. I certainly will. I'm not through by a long shot. What

294   *THE BEAVER COAT*

did you tell this woman? You simply told her you didn't have time for the case at present. You didn't even question her daughter! So you don't know the slightest thing about the matter; you know nothing at all about the entire incident.

WEHRHAHN. I must ask you to control yourself a little.

KRUEGER. I am under control—very much so. In fact, too much so, Herr Justice. I'm far too controlled a man for my own good. Otherwise I'd react quite differently to something like this. What kind of an investigation is this? This gentleman here, Herr Fleischer, comes to you to report something that he has observed. He saw a bargeman wearing a beaver coat, and . . .

WEHRHAHN. [*Holding up his hand.*] Wait a minute! [*To* WULKOW.] You're a bargeman, aren't you?

WULKOW. Yes sir, I've been out on the river for thirty years.

WEHRHAHN. Are you nervous? You've really got a twitch there.

WULKOW. I've had a bit of a scare, that's why.

WEHRHAHN. Do bargemen on the Spree frequently wear fur coats?

WULKOW. A lot of them has fur coats, sure.

WEHRHAHN. [*Pointing to* FLEISCHER.] This gentleman has seen a bargeman standing on deck in a fur coat.

WULKOW. Nothing suspicious about that, Herr Justice. There's a lot of them got real nice fur coats. I even got one myself.

WEHRHAHN. There you are! This man has a fur coat himself.

FLEISCHER. But surely not a beaver coat.

WEHRHAHN. You said yourself you didn't get close enough to see exactly what it was.

KRUEGER. What? Does this man have a beaver coat?

WULKOW. There's plenty, I tell you, that's got the finest beaver coats you ever saw. And why not? We got the money to pay for them.

WEHRHAHN. [*Filled with a sense of triumph but pretending indifference.*] So. [*Nonchalantly.*] Please continue, Herr Krueger. That was only a small digression. I just wanted to demonstrate to you the value of Herr Fleischer's "observation."—As you see, this man has a fur coat himself. [*Vehemently.*] And on the basis of that evidence we wouldn't dream of accusing him of having stolen it! That would be positively absurd!

KRUEGER. What? I didn't understand a word you said.

WEHRHAHN. In that case I'll have to talk a little louder. And while I'm at it, there's something else I'd like to tell you. Not in my capacity as an official, but simply as one human being to another, Herr Krueger. A man of honor should be a little more careful about the people in whom he places his confidence. He shouldn't call upon the testimony of those who . . .

KRUEGER. Are you talking about my friends . . . ?

WEHRHAHN. Yes, your friends!

KRUEGER. In that case you'd better be a little more careful yourself. People like that Motes you're so chummy with—I throw them out of my house!

FLEISCHER. The man who's waiting at your home right now—I've shown him the door myself!

KRUEGER. He cheated me out of my rent.

FRAU WOLFF. There's not too many around here he ain't cheated out of money—pfennigs, marks, talers, even gold pieces!

KRUEGER. That man has developed a regular system of taxation!

FLEISCHER. [*Pulls a piece of paper out of his pocket.*] And now he's ready to face the state's attorney. [*He puts the piece of paper on the table.*] Kindly do me the favor of reading this.

KRUEGER. Frau Dreier has signed that paper herself. He tried to get her to commit perjury!

FLEISCHER. She was to have testified against me!

KRUEGER. [*Taking hold of* FLEISCHER'*s arm.*] This is a reproachless man, and Motes has been trying to ruin him. And you lend an ear to that scoundrel! [*In the following,* WEHRHAHN, KRUEGER, FLEISCHER, *and* GLASENAPP *all talk at once.*]

WEHRHAHN. I'm at the end of my patience! Whatever dealings you may have with Motes don't concern me. I'm not interested. [*To* FLEISCHER.] And you be good enough to get that scrap of paper out of my sight!

KRUEGER. [*Alternately to* FRAU WOLFF *and to* GLASENAPP.] That's the man the Justice of the Peace calls his friend! That's his authority. A fine authority Motes is! A gangster, that's what I would call him.

FLEISCHER. [*To* MITTELDORF.] I don't have to account to anybody. What I do and don't do is my business! Who my friends are—that's my business, too. And so is what I think and write!

GLASENAPP. I can't hear myself think anymore, there's such a racket. Herr Justice, do you want me to call a policeman? I can run right over and get one. Mitteldorf!

WEHRHAHN. Quiet, please! [*Silence is restored. To* FLEISCHER.] Will you please remove that scrap of paper?

FLEISCHER. [*Takes the piece of paper.*] That scrap of paper, as you call it, is going straight to the state's attorney.

WEHRHAHN. You may do with it what you wish. [*He gets up and takes* FRAU WOLFF'*s package from the bookcase.*] Now let's get this thing out of the way. [*To* FRAU WOLFF.] So, where did you find this?

FRAU WOLFF. It wasn't me who found it, Herr Justice.

WEHRHAHN. Well, who did find it then?

FRAU WOLFF. My younger daughter.

WEHRHAHN. And why didn't you bring her along?

FRAU WOLFF. But she was here before, Herr Justice. I can certainly go and get her again real fast.

WEHRHAHN. No, that would only delay the matter further. Didn't the girl tell you anything?

KRUEGER. She said she found the package on the way to the train station.

WEHRHAHN. In that case the thief has probably gone to Berlin. We'll have a tough time finding him there.

KRUEGER. I don't believe that at all, Herr Justice. Herr Fleischer has the right idea, it seems to me. He thinks this whole business with the package is a trick designed to throw us off.

FRAU WOLFF. Uh-huh, that could be, too. That's really quite possible.

WEHRHAHN. Now, Frau Wolff, you're smarter than that about most things. Stolen goods go straight to Berlin from here. That fur coat was sold in Berlin before we even knew it was stolen.

FRAU WOLFF. No, Herr Justice. I can't help it but I don't quite agree with you there. If the thief's in Berlin, then what does he have to go and lose a package like this for?

WEHRHAHN. Well, one doesn't always lose things intentionally.

FRAU WOLFF. Why, just take one look at this package. Everything's wrapped up so nice: the vest, the key, the piece of paper . . .

KRUEGER. I'm convinced the thief is here in town.

FRAU WOLFF. [*Backing up* KRUEGER.] You've got it right, Herr Krueger.

KRUEGER. [*Now completely convinced.*] I'm absolutely sure of it!

WEHRHAHN. Sorry, but I don't share your opinion. I've had far too much experience . . .

KRUEGER. What? Experience? Hah!

WEHRHAHN. Certainly. And on the basis of that experience I can say that your theory deserves hardly any consideration at all.

FRAU WOLFF. Now, now, you can never be too sure, Herr Justice.

KRUEGER. [*Pointing to* FLEISCHER.] After all, he saw a bargeman . . .

WEHRHAHN. Oh, no! Not that story again! Look, if I followed your advice, I'd have twenty policemen doing nothing but searching houses every day of the week. I've have to search every single house in town!

FRAU WOLFF. Then you can start right in with mine, Herr Justice.

WEHRHAHN. Now isn't that ridiculous? No, no, gentlemen: that's not the way. We'll never get anywhere using that method. You'll just have to let me handle this on my own. I have some suspicions, but for the time being I just want to sit back and observe. There are a few shady characters around here I've had my eye on for quite a while. Early in the morning they ride into Berlin with heavy packs on their backs, and in the evening they come back—with their packs empty!

KRUEGER. That's what the vegetable women do—they carry the vegetables on their backs.

WEHRHAHN. Not only the vegetable women, Herr Krueger. Your fur coat probably took the same trip!

FRAU WOLFF. That's possible all right. There ain't nothing impossible in this world, I tell you.

WEHRHAHN. [To WULKOW.] Well, then. Now, you wanted to report . . .

WULKOW. The birth of a baby girl, Herr Justice.

WEHRHAHN. [To KRUEGER.] I'll do my best.

KRUEGER. I won't rest, Herr Superintendent, until I get my fur coat back.

WEHRHAHN. We'll do everything we can. Maybe Frau Wolff could help us by keeping her ears open a bit.

FRAU WOLFF. I'm not much good at that sort of thing. This business better get cleared up, though. Heavens, there ain't nothing safe anymore!

KRUEGER. You're absolutely right, Frau Wolff, absolutely! [To WEHRHAHN.] I must ask you to examine that package carefully. There's some handwriting on the piece of paper inside, and it may lead us to the thief. The day after tomorrow, early in the morning, I'll take the liberty of dropping by again, Herr Justice, so I can find out what you've learned. Good day! [Exits.]

FLEISCHER. Good day. [Exits.]

WEHRHAHN. [To WULKOW.] How old are you?—Good day, good day!—Those two fellows both have a screw loose. [Again to WULKOW.] What's your name?

WULKOW. August Philipp Wulkow.

WEHRHAHN. [To MITTELDORF.] Go over to my house. Motes is sitting there waiting for me. Tell him I'm sorry, but I have other things to do this morning.

MITTELDORF. Then he shouldn't wait?

WEHRHAHN. [*Short.*] No, he's not to wait! [MITTELDORF *leaves. To* FRAU WOLFF.] Do you know the writer Motes?

FRAU WOLFF. Where people like that are concerned, I'd rather not say anything. There ain't much good that I could tell you.

WEHRHAHN. [*Sarcastically.*] You could tell me lots of good things about Fleischer, though.

FRAU WOLFF. He really ain't such a bad fellow.

WEHRHAHN. Aren't you being a little cautious in your choice of words?

FRAU WOLFF. Now you know I'm no good at that. I'm always straightforward, Herr Justice. In fact, if I wasn't always coming right out and saying what I think, I'd be a lot further along in the world.

WEHRHAHN. Well, saying what you think has never done you any harm with me.

FRAU WOLFF. No, not with you, Herr Justice. You can take a little frank talk. A person don't have to hide things around you.

WEHRHAHN. So in a word, you think Fleischer is a respectable citizen.

FRAU WOLFF. Yes sir, that's what he is. That's him.

WEHRHAHN. Now don't forget that you said that.

FRAU WOLFF. Don't you forget it, either.

WEHRHAHN. Very well, we shall see. [*He stretches, gets up, and starts walking up and down to get the stiffness out of his legs. To* WULKOW.] This is none other than our hardworking washerwoman. She thinks that everybody is like her. [*To* FRAU WOLFF.] Unfortunately, though, the world is not made that way. You just look at the outside of people. Men like myself have learned to look a little deeper. [*He takes a few steps, then stops in front of her and puts his hands on her shoulders.*] And just as it's true when I say that you, Frau Wolff, are an honest soul, it's true with the same degree of absoluteness when I tell you that this Dr. Fleischer of yours is an extremely dangerous individual!

FRAU WOLFF. [*Shaking her head resignedly.*] Well, I don't know . . .

Curtain

Select Bibliography

Behl, Carl Friedrich Wilhelm. *Gerhart Hauptmann: His Life and His Work.* Translated by Helen Taubert. Würzburg: Holzner, 1956.

Garten, H. F. *Gerhart Hauptmann*. New Haven: Yale University Press, 1954.

———. "Gerhart Hauptmann." In *German Men of Letters: Twelve Literary Essays,* edited by Alex Natan, vol. 1, 237–49. London: Oswald Wolff, 1961.

Holl, Karl. *Gerhart Hauptmann: His Life and Work*. Chicago: A. C. McClurg, 1914.

Keefer, L. B. "Woman's Mission in Hauptmann's Dramas." *The Germanic Review* 9, no. 1 (January 1934): 35–53.

Klenze, Camillo von. "Hauptmann's Treatment of the Lower Classes." In Klenze, *From Goethe to Hauptmann: Studies in a Changing Culture,* 223–75. New York: Viking, 1926.

Löb, Ladislaus. *From Lessing to Hauptmann: Studies in German Drama*. London: University Tutorial Press, 1974.

Marshall, Alan. *The German Naturalists and Gerhart Hauptmann: Reception and Influence*. Frankfurt: Peter Lang, 1982.

Maurer, Warren R. *Gerhart Hauptmann*. Boston: Twayne, 1982.

McFarlane, J. W. "Hauptmann, Ibsen, and the Concept of Naturalism." In *Hauptmann Centenary Lectures,* edited by K. G. Knight and F. Norman, 31–60. London: Institute of Germanic Studies at the University of London, 1964.

McInnes, E. O. H. "The 'Active' Hero in Gerhart Hauptmann's Dramas." In *Hauptmann Centenary Lectures,* edited by K. G. Knight and F. Norman, 61–94. London: Institute of Germanic Studies at the University of London, 1964.

Osborne, John. *The Naturalist Drama in Germany*. Manchester: Manchester University Press, 1971.

Reichert, Herbert W. "Hauptmann's Frau Wolff and Brecht's Mother Courage." *German Quarterly* 34, no. 4 (November 1961): 439–48.

Reichert. W. A. "The Totality of Hauptmann's Work." *The Germanic Review* 21, no. 2 (April 1946): 143–49.

Shaw, Leroy R. *Witness of Deceit: Gerhart Hauptmann as Critic of Society*. Berkeley: University of California Press, 1958.

Sinden, Margaret. "Gerhart Hauptmann." *University of Toronto Quarterly* 19, no. 1 (October 1949): 17–34.

———. *Gerhart Hauptmann: The Prose Plays*. Toronto: University of Toronto Press, 1957.

Steinhauer, Harry. "Gerhart Hauptmann." *University of Toronto Quarterly* 32, no. 3 (April 1963): 247–65.

Stockius, A. *Naturalism in Recent German Drama, with Special Reference to Hauptmann*. New York: 1903.

Wahr, F. B. "Theory and Composition of the Hauptmann Drama." *The Germanic Review* 17, no. 3 (October 1942): 163–73.

Weigand, Hermann J. "Gerhart Hauptmann's Range as Dramatist." *Monatshefte* 44, no. 7 (November 1952): 317–32. Reprinted in Weigand, *Surveys and Soundings in European Literature,* edited by A. Leslie Willson, 223–42. Princeton: Princeton University Press, 1966.

Ziolkowski, Theodore. "Gerhart Hauptmann and the Problem of Language." *The Germanic Review* 38, no. 4 (November 1963): 295–306.